D1570781

Abortion Politics in Congress

This book examines how legislators have juggled their passions over abortion with standard congressional procedures, looking at how both external factors (such as public opinion) and internal factors (such as the ideological composition of committees and party systems) shape the development of abortion policy. Driven by both theoretical and empirical concerns, Scott H. Ainsworth and Thad E. Hall present a simple, formal model of strategic incrementalism, illustrating that legislators often have incentives to alter policy incrementally. They then examine the sponsorship of abortion-related proposals as well as their committee referral and find that a wide range of Democratic and Republican legislators repeatedly offer abortion-related proposals designed to alter abortion policy incrementally. *Abortion Politics in Congress* reveals that abortion debates have permeated a wide range of issues and that a wide range of legislators and a large number of committees address abortion.

Scott H. Ainsworth is an associate professor of political science in the School of Public and International Affairs at the University of Georgia. His work on lobbying, interest groups, and the U.S. Congress has appeared in numerous outlets, including the *American Journal of Political Science, Journal of Politics*, and *Legislative Studies Quarterly*. He is the author of *Analyzing Interest Groups*.

Thad E. Hall is an associate professor of political science and a research Fellow at the Center for Public Policy and Administration at the University of Utah. He has authored or coauthored three books – *Point, Click, and Vote: The Future of Internet Voting; Electronic Elections: The Perils and Promise of Digital Democracy*; and *Authorizing Policy* – and coedited the book *Election Fraud: Detecting and Preventing Electoral Manipulation*. He has written more than twenty articles and book chapters examining various aspects of public policy.

Abortion Politics in Congress

Strategic Incrementalism and Policy Change

SCOTT H. AINSWORTH
University of Georgia

THAD E. HALL
University of Utah

1/12/12
Lan
$ 24.99

CAMBRIDGE UNIVERSITY PRESS
Cambridge, New York, Melbourne, Madrid, Cape Town, Singapore,
São Paulo, Delhi, Dubai, Tokyo, Mexico City

Cambridge University Press
32 Avenue of the Americas, New York, NY 10013-2473, USA

www.cambridge.org
Information on this title: www.cambridge.org/9780521740043

First published 2011

Printed in the United States of America

A catalog record for this publication is available from the British Library.

Library of Congress Cataloging in Publication data
Ainsworth, Scott H.
  Abortion politics in congress : strategic incrementalism and policy
  change / Scott H. Ainsworth, Thad E. Hall.
    p. cm.
  Includes bibliographical references and index.
  ISBN 978-0-521-51581-8 (hardback) – ISBN 978-0-521-74004-3 (pbk.)
    1. Abortion – Law and legislation – United States.   2. Abortion – Government
  policy – United States.   3. Abortion – Political aspects – United States.   I. Hall,
  Thad E. (Thad Edward), 1968– II. Title.
  KF9315.A96 2011
  362.19'88800973–dc22   2010031511

ISBN 978-0-521-51581-8 Hardback
ISBN 978-0-521-74004-3 Paperback

Contents

Tables

Figures

Acknowledgments

Virtually year after year, the U.S. Congress remains the least trusted of American political institutions, and virtually year after year abortion remains one of the most complicated and volatile of issues in American politics. How does a mistrusted institution filled with electorally minded legislators handle such a volatile issue as abortion? The primary question driving our research efforts has been: "Why would legislators pursue the abortion issue given that it is so volatile?" Why isn't abortion another third rail issue that legislators avoid at all costs? Legislators presumably gain some votes by pursuing certain legislative proposals, but abortion policy carries considerable risks because of its divisiveness.

One might also reasonably ask why scholars would explore such a volatile issue. For scholars, there are many other safer issues to explore. Writing about such a divisive issue that touches on personal politics is difficult. A lack of subtlety or poor wording when exploring some well-traveled issue is not so dangerous. However, writing about abortion, war, gun control, immigration, or some other volatile issue might raise eyebrows in one's family, one's circle of friends, and even among one's professional colleagues. Why should scholars pursue topics that might make them stand out in an unpopular way? Although abortion is worthy of independent study, we strongly believe that by exploring abortion policy making we can understand the workings of Congress and the strategic reasoning of legislators better. As much as we focus on abortion and abortion policy making, we also focus on the U.S. House of Representatives and its members.

John Lapinski (2008, 235) laments that "Congress scholars have focused nearly all of their intellectual energy into studies of rules, procedures, and institutions, leaving the study of policy outputs, particularly the study of specific policy issues, to other subfields." Lapinski argues that congressional scholars need to explore policy. We would go one step further – congressional scholars need to explore the most politically charged issues of the day. Charles E. Merriam, an early president of the American Political Science Association, wrote that it was essential for the health and growth of the political science discipline that scholars study politically charged issues. Merriam (1921, 177) noted, "in many instances the counsels of professional students of politics ... would be divided ... but in many other instances they would be united." Indeed, if we continually eschew the most politically charged topics, we highlight the weaknesses within our discipline. Merriam (1921, 177) wrote, "if professional students of politics cannot come together to discuss ... the fundamentals of political [understandings] ... should not that circumstance itself cause sober reflection ... might it not suggest [the] remodeling and reorganization of ... methods." When scholars ignore the most volatile issues of the day, those issues are not ignored – they are defined and discussed by everyone and anyone save scholars. If our methods are valuable, they should be widely applicable, and we should not let lamentations about policy crowd out careful social science research.

We have spent many more years on this project than either of us imagined. Over those years, many friends and colleagues have helped us find our way. So many folks have helped us over the years that we are bound to overlook the assistance of some. For that, we apologize. We should also note that all errors in fact or interpretation are our own. Collecting data on abortion-related proposals over a three-decade period is daunting. Janna Dietz, Wendy Gross, Jessica Taverna, and Austin Clemens provided invaluable assistance with those data collection efforts. Janna Dietz, associate professor at Western Illinois University (and graduate school colleague with Thad), was also very helpful early on in helping us identify important issues associated with the abortion debate.

Numerous drafts of one chapter or another were presented at conferences or universities. Ainsworth would like to thank the Political Science Departments at the University of South Carolina and Texas Tech. In particular, comments and encouragement from Brad Gomez, Tom Hansford, Chris Kam, George Krause, and Tim Nokken were most helpful. At one or more conferences, Barry Burden, James Cox, Christine DeGregorio, Christopher Kenny, Beth Reingold, Wendy Schiller, Barbara Sinclair, and John Wilkerson provided helpful comments. We received wonderful comments from a smaller set of individuals who were willing to read sections of this book. Gary Miller noted a fundamental oversight in Chapter 2 that slipped by the authors and other reviewers. John Wilkerson read almost the entire book and provided helpful ideas for this project (and the next one). We also thank Jamie Carson, David King, John Maltese, Jeremy Pope, Itai Sened, and Tracy Sulkin for their discussions and comments on one or more chapters. Eric Crahan, our editor at Cambridge, secured very helpful reviews in a timely fashion for us. We would like to thank Eric and the Cambridge reviewers. Hall had several nonacademics, including his sister Leigh Boyce and a friend, Natalie Knowles, read the book, and their comments were very helpful in ensuring that the book was accessible to the "real" world.

There is little doubt that beyond all others, Ainsworth thanks his family for their support as well as their regular diversionary tactics. He is fortunate to have Susan, Sam, and Benjamin as his better halves. Ainsworth would like to dedicate his efforts on this book to Audrey, Jeanette, and Susan. Hall would like to thank his wife Nicole and his son Ethan for all of their support over the years that he and Scott worked on this project and dedicates the book to them.

PART I

STRATEGIC INCREMENTALISM
AND THE POLITICAL BACKDROP
FOR ABORTION POLITICS IN CONGRESS

I

Some of the Politics Surrounding Abortion Policy

[T]he abortion issue poses constitutional problems not simply for judges
but for every federal, state, or local official who must at some point address
the issue. (Tribe 1992, 77)

INTRODUCTION

When the Supreme Court upheld the congressional Partial-Birth Abortion
Ban Act in *Gonzales v. Carhart*, Robin Toner wrote in the *New York
Times* that the case represented a successful new tactic in abortion politics (2007). Both the U.S. Congress and the Supreme Court accepted a
new understanding, or framing, of the abortion issue. Abortion was, at
least for the moment, framed as being a danger to the interests of women.
Pro-life groups had sought to reframe the abortion debate along these
lines for some time. Indeed, proponents on each side of the issue have
sought to control the language used to describe a fetus – language that is
then sometimes reflected in law.

How did abortion move from an issue of choice or an issue of morality
to an issue that – judged by the Supreme Court – posed dangers for
women? The framing and reframing of the abortion issue has been ongoing for decades. Legislators, judges, the public, and those individuals most
directly affected by abortion procedures have understood and explained
the issues tied to abortion in diverse ways. The framing of the abortion debate in the 1800s maintained that the practice was wrong unless
medically necessary, which was best determined by a licensed physician.
The conflict at this time was not simply grounded on moral argument;
there was considerable tension between doctors and midwives over the

provision of medical services to women (e.g., Craig 1993). Abortion politics was enmeshed in the debates about who should be allowed to practice medicine and whether physicians should be granted market protections.[1] In the end, the doctors won the argument and, by 1910, abortions were illegal in all states except one and in all cases except when the abortion was necessary to save the life of a woman.[2]

In the 1960s, states began to debate legislation to ease restrictions on abortion that had been put into place in the latter half of the 1800s and the first decade of the twentieth century. By the 1960s, the abortion debate began to resemble the debates that most Americans living today would recognize. On one side of the debate were organizations concerned about women's rights. Abortion was fundamentally a choice emblematic of individuals living in a free society. Limits on abortion were interpreted as limits on women's freedoms. Abortion attracted greater, widespread public attention at this time in part because of the links between the sedative thalidomide and birth defects. Although few Americans were exposed to thalidomide, it was readily available in European countries – and sometimes sold over the counter. The infant mortalities and the severity of the birth defects linked to thalidomide prompted many Americans to reconsider their attitudes toward abortion. Autonomy over birth decisions, coupled with the sexual revolution and the arrival (and legal protection of access to) birth control, made abortion a prominent issue of discussion in the 1960s.

The liberalization of state-level abortion laws from 1967 to 1973, during which time the number of states allowing abortions increased from three to more than fifteen, and the concomitant rise in the number of abortions occurring nationally, led to a rise in pro-life interest group activity. The U.S. Catholic Conference and the National Committee for a Human Life Amendment spearheaded the opposition to relaxed abortion laws at the state level in the 1960s and 1970s. Most antiabortion groups were associated with churches but important antiabortion advocates emerged most directly from the antiwar movement (Risen and Thomas 1998).

With the issuance of the *Roe v. Wade* decision in 1973 by the U.S. Supreme Court, pro-life groups were energized anew to fight the

---

[1] The American Medical Association (AMA), formed in 1847 and incorporated in 1897, played a key role in the regulation of medical services. For a critique of the AMA's role in the creation of market protections for physicians, see Milton Friedman's *Capitalism and Freedom* (1962).

[2] At this juncture, we do not address the differences between de jure and de facto limits on abortion.

expansion of abortion rights. The Roman Catholic Church issued many proclamations stating their strong opposition to abortions. The Church asked members to engage in civil disobedience if asked to perform any activities related to abortion and noted that church members who were involved in abortion activities could be excommunicated. The National Conference of Catholic Bishops also mobilized against the *Roe* decision, funding many pro-life activities (Rubin 1987). In the mid and late 1970s, the National Right to Life Committee and the Moral Majority augmented the Roman Catholic mobilization against abortion. The language in *Roe* indicated that constitutional rights were central to the current under-standings of abortion. To attack *Roe*, therefore, required a constitutional counterattack. Antiabortion mobilization centered on efforts to pass a constitutional amendment to ban all abortions.

Abortion was not a prominent issue in the immediate elections after the *Roe* decision. Both President Gerald Ford and the 1976 Democratic presidential candidate, Jimmy Carter, were pro-life, albeit with differ-ent views on how the abortion decision should be handled. By 1980, abortion did become a major issue, as conservative groups linked liberal members of Congress to pro-choice positions, even when the individu-als in question were not pro-choice (Rubin 1987, 110). At this point, abortion started to become linked to ideology and party in ways that had not occurred before.

The pro-choice community had its own mobilizations during this same period of time, with organizations such as NARAL – the National Abortion Rights Action League (formerly the National Association for the Repeal of Abortion Laws) – Planned Parenthood, and the National Association of Women spearheading efforts to maintain a woman's right to choose to have (or not have) an abortion. Pro-choice groups watched with considerable concern as an increasingly conservative U.S. Supreme Court heard *Webster v. Reproductive Health Services*, *Planned Parenthood v. Casey*, and other cases challenging *Roe*. The *Carhart* decision, however, was unique because it was the first time a majority on the Supreme Court had used a framing in an abortion decision that questioned the ability of women to make rational choices related to abortion. The ability of women to make reasoned choices about abor-tion has been questioned by state legislatures at numerous times. Some state legislatures have adopted legislation that requires women to receive information and counseling about the effects of the abortion on the embryo and the mother. Ostensibly, the counseling is meant to protect women from their own poorly informed choices. Consider the language mandated by South Dakota law (Sections 1 and 7, H.B. 1166, 2005).[3] Any physician discussing abortion services with a woman must state that an abortion "will terminate the life of a whole, separate, unique living *human being*" (italics added). In some localities, women are encouraged or even required to undergo ultrasound procedures so that they can see an image of the fetus. Again, proponents of these regulations seek to protect women from their own uninformed choices. These laws are also part of a general effort to move away from the traditional debate, which pitted pro-choice groups arguing for the interests of women versus the pro-life groups arguing about the rights of fetuses, and it was this new issue framing that was cited by Justice Anthony Kennedy in his majority opinion in *Gonzales v. Carhart*. Kennedy writes that it is "unexceptionable to conclude some women come to regret their choice to abort the infant life they once created and sustained."[4]

Two points related to the Kennedy decision have received considerable attention. First, Kennedy clearly states that some women come to regret their choices about abortion. The Court decision seeks to protect women who might otherwise feel badly about their abortion choice. Critics of the decision were quick to note the paternalism; there are many decisions protected by constitutional rights that one might make only to regret them later.[5] Why was abortion treated differently? The Court would protect women from making decisions about abortion that they themselves might regret at a later date. Second, the fetus is referred to as an infant. The decision did not focus on questions about the beginning of life or fetal viability. Instead, Kennedy stated that an *infant's life* was in the balance. In a rare move, which typically signals deep dissatisfaction with the Court's reasoning and the case outcome, Justice Ruth Bader-Ginsberg read her dissent aloud to the Court. In part, she wrote that the decision "blurs the line, firmly drawn in *Casey*, between pre-viability and post-viability abortions. And, for the first time since *Roe*, the Court blesses a prohibition with no exception safeguarding a woman's health."[6] The earlier framing of the abortion issue and abortion restrictions that referred to fetuses and relied on pre- and post-viability for the fetus was swept away.

[3] House Bill 1166 amended South Dakota common law S.D.C.L. § 34–23A-10.1.
[4] This decision can be found at http://74.125.155.132/search?q=cache:M29LfndYw-cJ:www.supremecourtus.gov/opinions/06pdf/05–380.pdf+gonzalez+v.+carhart&cd=2&hl=en&ct=clnk&gl=us with the quote taken from page 29 of the decision.
[5] See Ladwein (2008).
[6] This quote can be found on page 19 of her dissent.

The *Carhart* decision is profound but its ultimate impact remains unknown. Many commentators have speculated that the Supreme Court decision will result in numerous states enacting so-called "informed consent" laws and mandatory pregnancy counseling for women seeking abortions.[7] By most accounts the *Carhart* decision portends great change, but will it prevent abortions? Informed consent and counseling requirement laws do not deny or *directly* limit the right of a woman to receive an abortion. Both sides of the abortion debate are focused more intently on the indirect effects of the policy changes. Even the Partial-Birth Abortion Ban Act, which is a ban on a specific abortion-related procedure, will directly ban only a small number of abortion procedures annually and some number of the individuals affected by the partial-birth ban will still have abortions but will do so using a different medical procedure.[8]

The data on abortion generally show that the estimated number of abortions performed annually in the United States grew from between 850,000 and 1,000,000 in 1975 to between 1.3 million and 1.5 million in the 1980s.[9] The peak year for abortions was 1990, when an estimated 1.5 million abortions were performed. Current estimates suggest there are now about 1.3 million abortions performed annually. In 2005, 60.8 percent of all abortions occurred at fewer than eight weeks after gestation and 77.6 percent occurred in the first ten weeks. The Centers for Disease Control and Prevention (CDC) reports that 1.3 percent of abortions occurred after twenty weeks of gestation; 5.0 percent of abortions occur after the fifteenth week of pregnancy.[10] The partial-birth ban focuses exclusively on the 1.3 percent of abortions that occur after twenty

---

[7] Informed consent requires that a woman seeking an abortion first be told of the risks and implications of the procedure.

[8] There are questions about the medical relevance of the ban on partial-birth abortions because "partial-birth abortion" is not a medical term. However, it is generally recognized that the ban is intended to address the use of some intact dilation and extraction procedures.

[9] There are two primary sources of data on abortions in the United States. The Centers for Disease Control and Prevention (CDC) conducts an annual abortion survey. The report has only received consistent abortion data from 46 jurisdictions since 1995 and the nonreporting jurisdictions include New York City and California. (See http://www. cdc.gov/reproductivehealth/Data_Stats/Abortion.htm.) The other primary source of abortion incidence data is the Alan Guttmacher Institute (AGI; http://www.guttmacher. org/sections/abortion.php). AGI generally reports higher incidents of abortions than does the CDC, in part because CDC obtains its data from state health departments and AGI obtains its data from abortion providers. National Right to Life reports both data on its Web site.

[10] These data come from the CDC Abortion Surveillance Report 2005, Table 6, available online at http://www.cdc.gov/mmwr/preview/mmwrhtml/ss5713a1.htm?s_cid=ss5713a1_e.

weeks of pregnancy, and even for late-term abortions, partial-birth procedures were used less than 20 percent of the time. Given that more
than one million abortions are performed annually in the United States,
the partial-birth ban will affect very few cases. Of course, the eventual
impact of informed consent and the partial-birth ban remains unknown.
Some women may continue to opt for legal abortion procedures, but
others may sense that abortion procedures are increasingly difficult to
secure and avoid seeking any information at all about abortion services.
For some pro-choice advocates, the greatest concern about *Gonzales v.
Carhart* was the court's decision not to reaffirm or retain earlier holdings
in *Planned Parenthood v. Casey* or even in *Roe v. Wade*. To be certain, the
Carhart decision was a loss for pro-choice advocates, but much of their
anxiety was focused on what might come next. Given the small number of abortions that are affected by the Partial-Birth Abortion Ban Act,
one might even ask whether the *Carhart* decision is a Pyrrhic victory for
pro-life groups. Indeed, some elements in the pro-life community remain
deeply concerned about limited measures to affect abortion policy (Davey
2006; Saletan 2009). In their view, if an "infant life" were at stake, then
why would any abortion measure be acceptable?

The *Gonzales v. Carhart* decision reflects aspects of the long-held strategies adopted by pro-life proponents. Pro-life advocates have repeatedly
sought legislative gains in the states (e.g., McFarlane and Meier 2001;
Rose 2006; Segers and Byrnes 1995) as well as in the U.S. Congress. In
this book, we explore how members of the U.S. House of Representatives
have handled abortion policy. Given the tremendous prominence of *Roe
v. Wade* and subsequent abortion decisions by the U.S. Supreme Court,
one might presume that abortion policy is largely a legal affair. However,
since the pronouncement of *Roe v. Wade* in 1973, pro-life advocates in
the U.S. House of Representatives steadily pursued a legislative strategy
of incremental change.[11] The partial-birth abortion ban, as affected by
Carhart, is simply the latest in a long series of attempts to alter abortion
policy incrementally.

Incrementalism is not typically the strategy that we think of when
we consider the abortion debate. Abortion politics is often framed as an
all or nothing debate. "Do you support the right of a woman to choose
what happens to her body?" Stark language is often employed. "Do you
support the murder of innocent children?" Although some nuance does

---

[11] See Meernik and Ignagni (1997) for a review of the conditions that lead Congress to
reverse Court findings with the passage of new legislation.

exist in this debate – pro-choice supporters do not necessarily support abortions when the fetus can be viably delivered, and pro-life supporters do not necessarily oppose a woman obtaining an abortion if the child is the product of a rape or incest or if the birth of the child could seriously harm the mother – these nuances are not stressed in the heated debates over abortion.

INCREMENTAL IMPERATIVE

In the language surrounding the public debates on abortion, there is little opportunity for subtlety or nuance. The lack of fine distinctions is evident in the terms that these abortion policy groups prefer using – "pro-choice" and "pro-life" – both of which reflect this lack of nuance in the debate. The "pro-life, under some conditions" or "pro-choice, up to a point" positions are not well-reflected in the public debate over abortion politics. Numerous scholars have cataloged the language and rhetoric of the two sides of the abortion debate (Condit 1990; Dillon 1993a; Ferree et al. 2002), evaluated media portrayals of the issues (Press and Cole 1999), or portrayed the lives of activists (Maxwell 2002; Munson 2009; Reiter 2000; Risen and Thomas 1998). The conclusions are straightforward. Activists and the movements they inspire are seldom moderate in their tone. In his assessment of the U.S. Congress in the 1980s, political scientist Eric Uslaner stated that "Moral issues such as ... abortion ... became ... political dynamite. Activists on each side rejected any type of compromise" (1993, 60). Whole books have noted an absence of "neutral ground" (O'Connor 1996) in the abortion debates. "In its simple American form, the language of rights is the language of no compromise. The winner takes all, and the loser has to get out of town" (Cook, Jelen, and Wilcox 1992, 194). "Prolife and prochoice advocates alike have overwhelmingly opted for rights talk, a choice that has forced the debate into a seemingly nonnegotiable deadlock between the fetus's 'right to life' and the pregnant woman's 'right to choose'" (Glendon 1991, 66).

In the spring of 2009, the acrimony and hostility tied to the abortion debate came into sharp focus. On May 31, 2009, Dr. George Tiller was killed in Wichita, Kansas, by Scott Roeder, a radical antiabortionist who was convicted in 2010 of first-degree murder. As one of the few U.S. physicians who openly performed late-term abortions, Tiller was a lightening rod in the midst of the abortion debate. Upon Tiller's murder, numerous antiabortion groups made public statements distancing themselves from such violent measures to prevent abortions. Rightly or not, such extremism and polarization is often blamed on interest groups or extreme media portrayals. Groups often use charged language, even when they eschew extreme actions. Interest groups are better able to mobilize their supporters when they take a strong, unequivocal position for a given policy, especially one with such a strong moral dimension as abortion. By taking a strong and unequivocal position, interest groups can keep their members energized about the issue and can portray any proposed change in abortion as either a great success or a dire threat. In such debates, and for such groups, abortion serves a symbolic purpose. It offers a way for individuals to define themselves in contrast to others and acts as a signal regarding the individual's politics, be it liberal or conservative. Symbolically, maintenance of the abortion debate can be very helpful for politicians because it serves this symbolic shorthand and definitional purpose.

If, however, one moves beyond symbolic purposes, "the increased salience of the abortion issue is not entirely welcome by politicians, who find themselves facing two opposing sets of motivated activists, each ... [of which] sees the abortion issue as one in which compromise is impossible" (Cook, Jelen, and Wilcox, 1992, 161). Both sides have pushed Congress to codify their position into law, with pro-life groups wanting a constitutional amendment banning abortion and pro-choice groups wanting the tenants of the *Roe v. Wade* decision enacted in, or protected by, statute. Few legislators may be intimately involved in the pro-life or pro-choice movements, but every legislator has been called upon to cast votes on abortion-related proposals. Did members of Congress adhere to the movements' grand goals, or did they develop and follow more traditional, incremental approaches to policy change? For die-hard adherents to a movement, a gradual, incremental approach may be an anathema, but we argue that there are clear strategic underpinnings to incremental policy change.

The incremental change strategy is predicated on several basic ideas. First, there is a recognition that overturning Supreme Court decisions is difficult, making major changes to federal laws is difficult, and making sustained change to any policy takes time. Quite simply, the structure of the American policy-making system ensures that change is difficult. Consider, for the moment, the U.S. Congress. At the most basic level, one difficulty that supporters of policy change must overcome is that legislative changes require majorities of both the House and Senate to agree on the same legislative wording. For politically sensitive issues, such as those related to abortion, advocates need at least sixty senators to guard against a filibuster. If the legislation is vetoed, two-thirds of the members in each chamber have to vote to override the president's veto. Major policy change, therefore, is something that requires large majorities in Congress before it can be enacted.

Second, legislators also have to negotiate the complexities of the legislative process within each chamber to get any policy change enacted. One of the most interesting questions members face is how to frame their proposed change in order to gain access to a legislative venue – initially, a committee – that is sympathetic to their position. Scholars of congressional committees have long-noted that committee jurisdictions are carefully guarded by members (King 1997; Shepsle 1978). A committee's jurisdiction, or turf, is important in part because it ensures the committee's agenda control and policy-framing powers. Entrepreneurial members who seek a policy change may attempt to change a committee's jurisdictional monopoly, or they may reframe their policy proposals to allow for referrals to other, more favorable committee venues. Determining when to seek out new turf, and when to stay in the old arena, is a key policy question facing entrepreneurial members of Congress who are seeking policy change (e.g., Baumgartner and Jones 1993; 2009).

Third, in addition to the institutional issues associated with incrementalism, individual members also have an interest in the political and symbolic implications of incremental policy change.[12] Members need to be able to tell a coherent story that explains the legislation at hand and that puts their vote into an easily understood context. Even the mildest reforms are often framed starkly around issues of freedom, autonomy, liberty, life, health, morality, choice, and the like (Saletan 1998; 2004). Given the starkness of the language and the framing of the abortion debate, members sometimes struggle to construct a clear story about their abortion votes that is easily understood in their home districts. One commentator lists three "fundamental axes," each with several lines of argument that can frame the issue (Saletan 1998). Abortion-related proposals might touch upon tensions including legal pragmatism versus legal moralism, traditionalism versus radicalism, equality versus motherhood, women versus fetuses, medicine and science versus morality, and families versus governmental paternalism (Saletan 1998). There may be slippery slopes in all directions. If we consider the partial-birth abortion ban, the incremental implication of the ban is noted in the legislative title – not

---

[12] Symbolism is very important in political debate. See, for example, the discussions of symbols by Deborah Stone (1997) or Murray Edelman (1985).

all abortions are banned. With incremental policy change, some of the noted tensions are sidestepped. A member who cannot tell a simple, clear story is more likely to encounter electoral difficulties with both supporters and opponents.[13] Simply put, the rationale for the vote must be clear. Incrementalism allows a member to refer back to earlier votes and decisions, noting that the new decision is not markedly different from previous votes or decisions that the legislature or member made in the past. In this regard, incrementalism may suggest consistency.

Fourth, incremental legislation has the advantage of being minor. Small or minor moves may not seem like an advantage, but small policy moves are less prone to counteractive lobbying by opposition advocates.[14] The incremental proposal will not fundamentally remake the policy landscape; it only makes a small change. The legislator who is proposing the incremental change can argue that the new policy is only a small and reasonable change to the status quo. The critics, if they react too strongly, may seem out of step – hysterical even – for criticizing the incremental change. Groups opposing incremental change have to walk a fine line between being unresponsive and alienating their own members versus reacting too strongly and causing a backlash against what many see as reasonable change. In the case of abortion politics, incremental restrictions on abortion may seem quite reasonable on their face and become difficult for pro-choice interests to oppose. Of course, enough incremental changes, combined together, can yield a large shift in public policy over time (cf. Schulman 1975, 1366).

Fifth, recent research in the area of public opinion shows that, on many important issues, a sizable segment of the public is either ambivalent about the policy debate or does not feel knowledgeable enough to state an opinion. In short, the answer "I don't know" is the honest response for many Americans to many of the questions that are being debated in the public forum (Berinsky 2004). Of course, after a policy is adopted and its full implications are felt, public opinion is aided by hindsight. *After* a legislator's vote, some of the "didn't knows" may conveniently forget their earlier ambivalence and question the legislator's judgment.

---

[13] The list of authors developing this theme continues to grow. The interested reader may start with Arnold (1990), Bianco (1994), Fenno (1978), and Kingdon (1989).

[14] Austen-Smith and Wright (1994) evaluated counteractive lobbying in the U.S. Senate in relation to Robert Bork's 1987 Supreme Court confirmation battle. In Austen-Smith and Wright, counteractive lobbying prevented fencesitters from voting the "wrong" way. Here, opportunities for counteractive lobbying are tied to the nature of the proposed policy change.

Incremental policy movements decrease the probability of misjudging the level of public acquiescence surrounding the policy area in question. Even with an issue like abortion, which has a relatively high profile in the public discourse, the public shows high levels of ambivalence. When asked their views about abortion, many Americans hold conflicting views (Alvarez and Brehm 1995). For instance, an individual might believe choice and personal liberty are paramount concerns but also approve of parental notification requirements. Such attitudes may suggest sophisticated nuance or ambivalent or conflictual beliefs. In any event, it appears that large majorities do not want abortion to be illegal, but they do not want abortions to be offered unfettered either. The public seems to want abortions to be legal but with restrictions. Incremental policy proposals can take advantage of the public's ambivalence and promote legislative actions that are within the middle range of options, the place where much of the public is relatively indifferent to change.

Of course, the benefits of strategic incrementalism can also be understood by comparing it to the failure of nonincremental efforts to change abortion policy. Following the *Roe v. Wade* decision, members of Congress faced an issue that had only been addressed in hushed tones and that had largely been a state rather than a federal matter. To be certain, some national government officials and political observers had expressed opinions about abortion before *Roe*, but the Supreme Court's decision in *Roe* thrust the issue to the forefront of the debate over social policy in America, and political figures in Washington were forced to address an issue that many had purposefully avoided.

To many supporters of reproductive rights, the *Roe* decision was a resounding victory, capturing in constitutional law a policy position that they had been fighting for state by state with limited success. For *Roe* supporters, the Constitution spoke to the born, not the unborn. For opponents of abortion, the *Roe* decision was a policy that had to be stricken completely because it denied fundamental rights to the unborn. In line with the antiabortion movement, members of Congress who opposed *Roe* sponsored numerous constitutional amendments that would directly undermine the *Roe* decision. Indeed, during the 1970s, more than 100 different constitutional amendments were introduced to ban abortions. These amendments countered the constitutional debates addressed by the Court and reflected the instinctive desire of pro-life members to respond directly to the actions taken by the Court in a way that they viewed as being proportional. If the Court were going to codify abortion rights into the Constitution, then abortion opponents would attempt to codify a ban on abortion by amending the Constitution. Each side of the movement sought grand, sweeping change. The failure of these grand, sweeping, legislative proposals is related to the costs of creating and maintaining large majorities in the House, the Senate, and the public at large. The nonincremental strategy fails to handle the intricacies of public opinion, the potential for counteractive lobbying, and the difficulties of maintaining legislative majorities. Constitutional amendments designed to define the beginning of life, alter the jurisdiction of the federal courts, or establish a new understanding of equal protection all failed.

Finally, the advocates of the nonincremental policy option often recognize that the sum of incremental decisions can yield a nonincremental outcome (Schulman 1975). If we consider nonincrementalism in the context of abortion politics, the pro-life side of the debate is especially sensitive to this last point. As long as abortions are constitutionally legal, no amount of incremental policy change will allow the pro-life position to be completely achieved. Only a nonincremental change – banning all abortions – will allow the pro-life community to be completely successful. Likewise, for true pro-choice interests, only a codification of the right to have an abortion with as few restrictions as possible, especially during the first trimester, allows pro-choice proponents to achieve their goals. The staunchest advocates on either side of the issue may long for nonincremental policy success, but, despite their protestations, we show in the following chapters that the legislators in the U.S. House of Representatives have regularly treated abortion incrementally.

WHY ABORTION?

We chose to study strategic incrementalism in the context of abortion politics for several reasons. First, abortion is a centerpiece of one of the most important political movements of our era. Political movements have played dominant roles during crucial moments in the political history of the United States. Movements pervaded each decade of the recently closed twentieth century. The progressive, suffrage, labor, and prohibition and antiprohibition movements marked the first half of the century; anticommunist crusades dominated the middle decades; and the civil rights, antiwar, consumer, environmental, women's, gay rights, and pro-choice and antiabortion movements altered many of the political currents of the last decades of the twentieth century. Abortion remains one of the linchpins of conservative politics today. "*Roe v. Wade* is undoubtedly the best-known case the Unites States Supreme Court has ever decided" (Dworkin

1993, 102). Many political observers argue that the abortion issue defines much of the "Red state-Blue state" division of America and is a core issue in the so-called culture wars (Abramowitz and Saunders 2005). Stands on abortion are used to define candidates, and attitudes toward abortion often determine citizens' vote choices (Abramowitz 1995). Abortion remains a hot-button issue in American politics, affecting citizens as well as elected and nonelected government officials.

❧ In this book, we evaluate how members of the U.S. House of Representatives handled the abortion issue. We focus on the House of Representatives for three main reasons. First, we can make a cleaner and more parsimonious argument about abortion by focusing on the House. In examining the historical narrative, we see that the House has been, for much of this period, the focal point of congressional debate over abortion. Senators have been less active in the abortion debates. Second, members of the House are from smaller constituencies and face unrelenting electoral pressures. Six-year cycles create electoral anxieties less frequently than two-year cycles. Third, the House rules enrich the study of abortion politics. In the Senate, members can introduce amendments more readily and can add nongermane issues to legislation much more easily than is the case in the House. The procedural politics of the House creates a richer backdrop for our study of how a tradition and rule bound institution handles an emotionally laden issue that is seldom addressed in polite company.

Many issues have a natural life cycle. Public attention to an issue often wanes after legislative or judicial action. The American public often considers a federal court decision on an issue as a definitive, final statement. For abortion rulings, this is most certainly not the case, as we were just reminded by *Gonzales v. Carhart*. *Roe* and its numerous predecessors have failed to quiet, let alone end, the abortion debate. Recently, scholars of the Supreme Court have suggested that judges actively *avoid* making definitive statements on delicate issues (Rosenberg 1991; Sunstein 2005, 104–105; cf. Kloppenberg 2001). University of Chicago political science and law professor Gerald Rosenberg argues that, rather than charting a new course, *Roe* was a response to changing currents and practices already well underway. Professors Lisa Kloppenberg and Cass Sunstein assess numerous federal court decisions related to abortion, but they do not view any of those decisions as definitive. For Kloppenberg and Sunstein, none of the decisions they studied settled key issues or ended any of the abortion debates. In other words, the Supreme Court has acted in such a way as to allow other political actors to address the abortion issue. Consider that, regardless of Court decisions, abortion politics has remained one of the most intractable political debates the United States has faced in the last thirty-five years. Views on the subject cut across party and class lines and affect far-ranging political debates – from states rights and federalism, to public health, to individuals' constitutional rights. Not only have the courts not settled the issue but decisions like *Carhart* have invited legislators to take a more active role in addressing abortion policy.

Although many aspects of abortion policy have been studied, abortion politics within the context of the U.S. Congress has been almost completely ignored by researchers. There are a handful of scholars who have studied roll call voting (e.g., Tatalovich and Schier 1993), trying to determine the characteristics of congressional coalitions on either side of the issue. However, we know of no works exploring the emergence of the abortion issue or the handling of abortion-related proposals in the U.S. Congress. Indeed, there is a presumption that legislators themselves have rarely addressed the issue. For instance, political scientist Karen O'Connor argues that elected officials' inability "to moderate – if not resolve [the abortion debate] – leads conservatives to argue that the political system has failed ... and liberals to argue that abortion is an individual decision properly made apart from government" (O'Connor 1996, 115–116). Such an oversight is unfortunate because adherents to political movements often think creatively about nontraditional strategies. Within a tradition-bound institution like the U.S. Congress, the use of nontraditional strategies may create a temporary strain or initiate a fundamental shift in long-held procedures and norms. Political scientist Roger Davidson, writing about abortion policy and the U.S. Congress in the 1980s, argued that "passion and procedure are often at odds; whichever prevails, the other is bound to suffer" (Davidson 1983, 46). In this book, we evaluate how members of Congress juggled passions related to abortion and the technical nuances of congressional procedures over the last few decades.

PREVIOUS WORK ON ABORTION

There is a vast literature on abortion in the context of public opinion, feminist theory, constitutional and state politics, and public health but little has been published on abortion as public policy in the U.S. Congress. Social scientists interested in the abortion question have focused extensively on understanding public attitudes toward abortion. Extensive research has been devoted to examining the demographic and ideological variables underlying individual attitudes. The major factors that affect such attitudes include religious belief and practice, race, education, political ideology, party identification, and core moral beliefs on issues such as gender roles and premarital sex (see, e.g., Alvarez and Brehm 1995; Cook, Jelen, and Wilcox 1992; 1993; Craig, Kane, and Martinez 2002; Jelen and Wilcox 2003; Legge 1983; Luker 1984; Tribe 1992). Religion is among the most widely studied variables, as researchers seek to understand what elements of religious belief and practice influence abortion attitudes (see, as a representative sample, Cochran et al. 1996; Emerson 1996; Evans 2002; Jelen 1984; Peterson 2001; Woodrum and Davison 1992).

Although abortion is among the most contentious and divisive political issues in the United States, public opinion data has revealed some striking patterns that suggest perhaps more room for compromise exists than is apparent from observing the battles between pro-life and pro-choice activists. First, examination of General Social Survey data demonstrates that, at the aggregate level, public attitudes about abortion have remained remarkably stable since 1972. Second, attitudes toward abortion policy are affected by the circumstances and rationales surrounding a *particular* abortion decision. Most Americans do not identify with the extreme pro-life or extreme pro-choice positions. Instead, between 80 and 90 percent of Americans accept abortion for traumatic or medical reasons (when the woman has been subjected to rape or incest, when the mother's health is threatened, or when there is a risk of birth defects). Comparatively, only 40 to 50 percent would allow abortion for elective or social reasons (in cases of a woman living in poverty who does not think she can afford more children or where a woman simply does not want to have a child).[15] The abortion issue has often been portrayed simplistically as pro-life versus pro-choice, but, for most Americans, attitudes toward abortion and abortion policies are much more nuanced.

Despite such results, those on the extremes – either pro-choice or pro-life – receive the greatest attention from the media, and the pro-choice

---

[15] Not surprisingly, these evaluations of abortion vary based on one's ideological position. However, even among conservatives, large majorities support access to abortion if the woman has been raped, if the child might have a serious birth defect, or if the mother's health would be seriously endangered. Even when asked about purely elective abortions, more than one-quarter of conservatives support abortions for women who cannot afford or do not want to have additional children. See the "Quick Tables" tool for examining the General Social Survey, available at http://sda.berkeley.edu/quicktables/quicksetoptions.do?reportKey=gss06:3.

versus pro-life construct defines the issue for many. Researchers have studied these extreme camps as well. Studies examine the relative strength of each position among the public, as well as the depth of commitment to the cause on each side (Scott and Schuman, 1988). Others examine the movements in the wake of seminal Court decisions, such as *Roe v. Wade, Webster v. Reproductive Health Services,* and *Planned Parenthood v. Casey* (Segers 1995; Tribe 1992; Wlezien and Goggin 1993;).

In addition to attempts to understand the foundations of abortion attitudes, other research seeks to connect attitudes with abortion rates. Some studies examine the impact of protests on the supply and demand of abortion resources, finding that extreme protests have reduced both the demand as well as the supply of abortion services (see Kahane 2000). Others look at how demographic and attitudinal variables affect not only public opinion, but also availability and utilization of abortion services (see Brazzell and Acock 1988; Trent and Powell-Griner 1990; Wetstein and Albritton 1995; Williams 1982). Some scholars examining individuals' abortion attitudes and religious beliefs move a step further by also examining the connections between abortion activism and religious groups and organizations (Nossiff 1995; Risen and Thomas 1998; Smith 2008).

Abortion has also been studied in historical terms, as scholars seek to understand the various beliefs and values underlying the changing legal status of abortion. Law professor Laurence Tribe (1992) provides an insightful overview of the history of abortion in the United States, which demonstrates that abortion politics have been framed in numerous ways throughout our history. Those opposed to abortion were not always concerned solely or even primarily with the life of the fetus, and those supporting abortion were not necessarily interested in a woman's right to control her body. Many scholars point to racial and ethnic concerns as predominant among early abortion debates (Beisel and Kay 2004).

Those scholars focusing on political institutions, as opposed to public opinion, typically concentrate their attention on either the courts (in particular, the Supreme Court and its landmark cases such as *Roe, Webster,* and *Casey*) or the states. Legal scholars often examine the idea (and, indeed, the very existence of) a constitutionally protected right to an abortion, and the ways in which restrictions on such a right have been established in various court decisions (see, e.g., Sezer 1995; Tribe 1992). Justices, academic researchers, and everyday citizens have all grappled with the questions of whether abortion decisions are primarily or secondarily the domain of the women involved, the state, a potential father, or the parents of the woman (or girl) involved. Within any of these domains, the relative standing of the fetus may vary considerably.

States are often at the center of the struggles over abortion. Both pre- and post-Roe, many of the most visible abortion policies have been made by the states (e.g., Rose 2006). Numerous researchers have examined state policies, particularly where they have pushed toward increased control over or outright restrictions on abortion, seemingly in contravention of the standards set in *Roe*. Although studies have found no substantive differences in public opinion across the states (Cook et al. 1993), there is still a wide range of approaches to abortion policy. States have been categorized by the extent to which they actively support (through progressive funding provisions and a lack of restrictions on access), clarify (through rewriting laws), or challenge (with restrictions on access and funding) the *Roe* decision (Halva-Neubauer 1990).

A few states have adopted policies amounting to nearly total abortion bans, but most have tread somewhere in the middle ground, restricting access for certain cases, requiring parental and spousal notification, mandating waiting periods and particular forms of counseling (Rose 2006). A wide array of policy mechanisms has served as compromises between the most extreme pro-life and pro-choice positions. Another tactic, utilized by both states and the federal government, has been to restrict public funding for abortions, effectively pricing abortion out of the reach of certain groups of people. The main rationale behind funding limits is straightforward: A state may recognize any number of rights without choosing to subsidize the practice of that right. At each step and with each new "compromise" policy, court challenges have forced the issue back to the judicial system for reconsideration of exactly what is the content and status of the "right" to an abortion.

The notion of an abortion right has been framed, supported, and challenged on many different grounds. For many in the pro-choice camp, abortion is deeply connected to the feminist movement, and the right to have an abortion represents the full realization of women's control over their bodies and lives, their ability to decide if, when, and under what conditions to remain pregnant and become mothers. But, as Tribe (1992) emphasizes, the dialogue of "choice" reaches beyond the feminist movement and into the fabric of American identity as shaped by our liberal heritage.[16] Supporters of abortion access also often point to the problems of "back alley" abortions obtained when abortion was illegal or access

---

[16] See Glendon (1991) for a now classic critique of the "rights talk" surrounding abortion. In Glendon's view, "poor, pregnant women ... have their constitutional right to privacy and little else" (65). "[W]e have ... a tendency to formulate important issues in terms of rights; a bent for stating rights claims in stark, simple, and absolute fashion" (107).

was restricted, regarding increased restrictions on abortion as fostering a public health crisis.

On the other side, pro-life advocates emphasize the sanctity of life and the importance of the family and traditional values. The cultural historian Christopher Lasch viewed the unceasing demands for unlimited access to abortion as indicative of a general unwholesomeness in American society. In Lasch's view (1991, 33), the unmistakable "unwholesomeness, not to put it more strongly, of our way of life" was illustrated by a litany of failings – one of which was abortion.

[O]ur obsession with sex, violence, and the pornography of "making it"; our addictive dependence on drugs, "entertainment," and the evening news; our impatience with anything that limits our sovereign freedom of choice, especially with the constraints of marital and familial ties; ... our third rate morality; our refusal to draw a distinction between right and wrong, lest we "impose" our morality on others and thus invite others to "impose" their morality on us; our reluctance to judge or be judged; our indifference to the needs of future generations, as evidenced by our willingness to saddle them with a huge national debt, an overgrown arsenal of destruction, and a deteriorating environment; our inhospitable attitude to the newcomers born into our midst; our unstated assumption, which underlies so much of the propaganda for unlimited abortion, that only those children born for success ought to be allowed to be born at all. (Lasch 1991, 33–34)

Clearly, Lasch did not mince words, and he was not at a loss for words when describing the moral and spiritual shortcomings in American society.

Lasch tied abortion and medical fine-tuning to attitudes toward progress and the acquisition of wealth and creature comforts. The unrelenting drive toward progress, however poorly defined, and the quest for human control and dominion meant that children and family life (as well as anything conceptually tied to family life or children – such as fetuses) would have to fit in as best they could. There was, in Lasch's view (1991, 490), an "impatience with biological constraints of any kind, together with a belief that modern technology had liberated humanity from those constraints and made it possible for the first time to engineer a better life for the human race as a whole." Any reluctance to embrace choice was equivalent to a refusal to embrace the future. Opposition to choice "amounted to a betrayal not only of the rights of women but of the whole modern project: the conquest of necessity and the substitution of human choice for the blind workings of nature" (Lasch 1991, 491).

Pro-choice people welcomed the medical technologies that made it possible to detect birth defects in the womb, and they could not understand why anyone would knowingly wish to bring a "damaged" child, or for that matter an "unwanted" child, into the world ... [An] unwillingness to grant such children's "right not to be born" might itself be considered evidence of unfitness for parenthood. (Lasch 1991, 490)

Lasch was not a legal scholar and he did not question the constitutionality of *Roe*, but he clearly did reject much of the reasoning and most of the attitudes underpinning the pro-choice movement. Abortion reflected one flank of an assault on a wide range of traditional moral values.

As noted previously, the majority of Americans fall somewhere between these stark pro-choice and pro-life positions. Some who are closer to the pro-choice camp may be willing to accept certain restrictions on a woman's right to choose, recognizing that individual choice in many matters is often constrained by competing concerns. Those individuals who are generally pro-life may be willing to allow abortion in cases where the mother's health is in jeopardy or where the woman has been raped, where the balance of interests between two lives – woman and fetus – tip in favor of the woman. As Jelen and Wilcox (2003, 494) note, "the basic frame ('life' versus 'choice') has been unaltered for over a generation, and many Americans (perhaps uncomfortably) seek to balance these important considerations." Although not always satisfactorily, judicial decisions and state policies attempt to reflect these subtleties and to balance competing interests. The recent *Carhart* decision suggests that some members of the Supreme Court no longer view "choice" as a concept holding down one end of the debate. The woman's choice itself is perhaps inconstant, so the concept of "choice" is no longer inviolable.

A final approach to understanding the abortion issue has been to consider its impact on voting behavior and party identification. That is, how do attitudes toward abortion affect basic political behaviors such as voting? Numerous studies examine the relationship between abortion attitudes and voter choice at all levels of government (Abramowitz 1995; Cook, Jelen, and Wilcox 1992; Howell and Sims 1993). Of course, voters' attitudes also interact with political parties. Political scientist Greg Adams (1997) provides a thorough analysis of the increasing polarization of the two parties on abortion, and the ways in which this elite-driven process has influenced party identification at the mass level. Ted Carmines and James Woods (2002) continue this line of research using National Election Survey data to illustrate the patterns of polarization among party activists, presidential nominating convention delegates, and the public at large.

For political science scholars and observers of politics, abortion has affected virtually every aspect of politics and governance of interest. As we will show, abortion politics has changed dramatically in the thirty-five years since the Supreme Court decision in *Roe v. Wade*. This evolution of politics, combined with the changes in the institution of Congress over that time, provides a highly dynamic issue, in a highly dynamic political environment, for us to study. Given that we are interested in the question of incrementalism, we necessarily are interested in pursuing a topic that has remained high on the public agenda over a long period of time, so we can view incremental or nonincremental change at different times, as attitudes and institutional contexts vary. Finally, abortion politics are not governed by any sort of short-term authorization schedule, which might facilitate regular policy reviews and incremental legislative activity over time (Adler and Wilkerson 2009; Hall 2004). Given that there is no preordained schedule for review of abortion policy, why do legislators address such a hot-button issue? There are numerous hot-button issues that legislators persistently eschew, but abortion is not one of them. Finally, given the volatility surrounding the issue, how do legislators handle abortion-related proposals? How do representatives as individuals and the House as a whole handle abortion-related legislative proposals?

SUMMARY

The political goals of movements are typically far-reaching. A movement's "purposes ... are ... framed in terms that go well beyond incremental policy shifts to urge changes in the very structures of values and institutions of society" (Salisbury 2002, 7). The standard norms and values regulating the actions of many political actors often fail to constrain the tactics of those individuals involved in a movement. When compared to the norms of the time, movement rhetoric and movement activities are often extreme. In sum, adherents to political movements think big – they are the vanguard of politics. Constitutional amendments or some other clear recognition of fundamental rights are typical goals.

Although a successful movement must, at some point, define the political vanguard, it may not be able to maintain that status. Movements are affected by the weight of their own successes. If one bars – for the sake of argument – violent revolution as a tactic, then adherents to a movement must, at some point, work within traditional political institutions. Natural, widespread support for a movement may lead more traditional political actors to co-opt movement rhetoric and policy proposals. The movement – though once a vanguard – risks becoming institutionalized and bureaucratized as interactions with more traditional political actors, such as legislators, parties, interest groups, and the media become commonplace.

Adherents to political movements also think creatively about non-traditional strategies. Whether working inside or outside of established political institutions, adherents to political movements often entertain nontraditional strategies to accomplish their goals. We should not be surprised by attempts to reform or bypass established institutional rules and procedures. If passion and procedure are at odds, as congressional scholar Roger Davidson (1983) suggests, then we are able to learn about the resilience of rules and procedures as the U.S. House faces a volatile issue such as abortion. Furthermore, we may consider how legislators pursue volatile issues. What do legislators gain when they pursue a volatile issue? To be certain, it is important to understand how the U.S. House handles typical issues; but when considering the political viability of the institution itself, it is also important to examine how legislators handle atypical and highly volatile issues – one of which is surely abortion.

Research Questions for This Book

The study of incrementalism has long been the province of policy scholars seeking to measure policy change. Despite this history in the public policy field, political scientists have made little effort to consider how the legislative process or legislators' individual strategies have been affected by the intentional pursuit of incremental policy gains. We address several key issues surrounding strategic incrementalism, including:

1. **What does the abortion political environment look like within Congress, and how has it changed from 1973 to 2006?** Although there has been a great deal of research conducted examining abortion politics, few researchers have considered the way in which abortion legislation has been developed in Congress and how the landscape in Congress has changed over time. We spend several chapters in this book examining both the way in which abortion politics have evolved in Congress and how the political landscape in the Congress has changed to facilitate this evolution.

2. **What factors lead to the use of strategic incrementalism for abortion politics in the U.S. House of Representatives?** Here, we examine the external and internal political factors that shape the use of the strategic incremental strategy in the House. We focus on external factors, such as public opinion, and internal factors, such

as the ideological composition of committees and party systems, to explain the use of this strategy.

3. **How successful have the incremental and nonincremental strategies been in the abortion fight?** There is quantitative evidence showing the success of the incremental strategy and the failure of "all or nothing" efforts. We focus on why this has been the case and how members have reacted to this political imperative.

4. **Does strategic incrementalism expand the abortion debate across the spectrum of congressional committees?** Does abortion politics revolve around just a few key committees, or does it permeate Congress? Has strategic incrementalism allowed abortion to permeate Congress? Are movement adherents changing their strategies, or are new players entering into abortion politics? We use data on bill referrals to examine how abortion politics has moved across committees and the factors that lead to this being the case.

Plan for the Book

Our analysis of incrementalism and abortion politics has three components. We start in Chapter 2 by articulating a theory of incrementalism. Incrementalism received nearly unparalleled attention in the social sciences in the 1960s and 1970s. Incrementalism was so popular and so widely applied that it came to mean virtually anything and everything. One scholar found twelve common uses of the term "incrementalism" in the budgeting context alone. Often one understanding of incrementalism conflicted sharply with other understandings. Because of the widespread use and overuse of incrementalism in an array of policy contexts, critiques of incrementalism sharpened, and today the early conceptions of incrementalism are largely moribund.

We argue that, in the public policy context, incrementalism is not a lost cause but that it requires a stronger, theoretical foundation that is sensitive to the strategic concerns of the legislators and interest groups who sponsor and promote policy solutions. Within a legislature, members face trade-offs between vote maximization for proposals and policy gains. Trade-offs also occur between policy gains and opposition members' incentives for engaging in legislative sabotage. Incremental proposals address these trade-offs and also help legislators to address informational constraints. In addition, incremental proposals often receive key interest group support because the incentives for counteractive lobbying and undue public attention are both minimized when policy gains are checked.

Our assessment of the policy-making environment within legislatures suggests that there are clear, strategic rationales for incrementalism.

In Chapter 3, we explore legislators' internal, legislative, and external environments. A legislator's internal, legislative environment is characterized by simple measures of ideology and party control. We examine whether, over the span of our study, the median House member has trended conservative or liberal, and we explore how majority party status – whether Democrats or Republicans are in control – has affected the policy-making setting for the abortion issue? Externally, policy advocates concerned about abortion issues often promote public anger (Fried and Harris 2001). How do members of Congress address abortion politics in the midst of such public anger, especially given the public distrust of Congress (Hibbing and Theiss-Morse 2001)? Public opinion surrounding abortion is sometimes highly charged. However, for a wide swath of voters, abortion creates personal tensions and ambiguity. How does public opinion and media attention given to pro-life and pro-choice activities affect abortion policy making?

We consider the nature of politics in the U.S. Congress and consider why incrementalism is effective in this environment. What characterizes a legislator's internal and external environments that encourage an incremental approach to abortion policy? When do legislators have what we sometimes call "wiggle room," the ability to maneuver and make decisions without completely angering either side in a debate? Congress is an institution in which incremental politics is much easier than supermajoritarian politics. A minority of legislators can often stymie even the simplest of legislative activity, but some congressional environments are more conducive to incrementalism than others. We also see that committees vary in their ability to navigate this landscape. Some committees are much more internally bifurcated or more distant from the House median voter compared to other committees. As we discuss in Chapter 6, this distance becomes important as House members consider which committees are best for fostering abortion-related legislation.

Chapter 4 begins with a discussion of whether legislatures are well suited to address morality issues, such as abortion. Numerous scholars have argued that courts are much better suited than legislatures for addressing abortion policy. At least one prominent scholar has also argued that the abortion issue is able to crowd the issue agenda in the U.S. Congress. In the fourth chapter, we explore whether abortion-related proposals crowd out other important legislative proposals. In the middle section of the fourth chapter, we illustrate the wide array of legislative proposals that are abortion related. Abortion-related proposals have been linked to issues or programs as diverse as the Peace Corps, personal bankruptcy laws, immigration laws, and trade status with foreign nations. In the last two sections of the fourth chapter, we discuss the possible symbolic purposes behind legislative proposals and provide an overall look at the abortion policy-making environment from the 94th to the 108th Congress.

In the second half of the book, we shift our level of analysis. Most of the empirical assessments in the earlier chapters are at the aggregate level. In the fifth and sixth chapters, we explore the individual-level dynamics associated with abortion-related proposals. In the fifth chapter, we assess the dynamics surrounding the sponsorship of abortion-related proposals. We are specifically focused on the personal characteristics of members who involve themselves in the abortion debate, and we assess which legislative environments are most conducive to abortion politics. We also consider how sensitive these members are to the political environment beyond the walls of the Capitol.

In the first half of the sixth chapter, we explore the referral of abortion-related proposals. During the earliest years of our study, most proposals were referred to the Committee on the Judiciary. As the sponsors moved away from nonincremental efforts, they developed abortion-related proposals appropriate for referral to any number of committees. We consider whether there is a movement away from the Judiciary Committee toward other committees and how such a shift was driven by changes within Congress. We also consider whether abortion created turf wars, as committees competed to protect or expand their jurisdictions.

The second half of the sixth chapter focuses on those measures that received some level of success. Most legislative proposals die in committee, and abortion-related proposals are no different. We examine what can explain the success of those few abortion proposals that make it out of their committees. We then consider how, once released from their committee, abortion-related proposals fair on the floor. Committee proposals generally fair well on the floor (see, e.g., Maltzman 1998). Is the same true for abortion-related proposals, or is abortion politics in the Congress fundamentally different from the myriad issues addressed in the U.S. House of Representatives?

2

The Strategic Foundations for Incrementalism in Legislatures

Can the pro-choice movement survive victory? (Staggenborg 1996, 170)

The anti-abortion movement has, in many ways, become part of the establishment. (Toner 2004)

INTRODUCTION

Our claim that abortion politics in the U.S. House is dominated by incremental changes in policy is founded upon our understanding of legislative politics and the larger policy-making environment. Therefore, we first want to elaborate a strategic rationale for incrementalism in legislatures and to evaluate the nonincremental alternative as well. Members may have a variety of reasons for proposing changes to alter abortion policy. On the one hand, they may merely want to make a symbolic statement to their constituents that they oppose abortion; we discuss the symbolic nature of abortion politics in greater detail in Chapter 4. For now, let us say that with symbolic abortion politics, a member may simply introduce or cosponsor a bill – any type of bill – that reflects their position on abortion, either pro-choice or pro-life. If the goal of the member is to make a real change to abortion policies, he or she has to overcome firmly established opponents. Finding the path of least resistance to achieve this goal is crucial. We argue that incrementalism is a highly effective means of achieving success in the legislative arena, especially when the policy at hand is as volatile as abortion politics.

Since the publication of Charles Lindblom's classic 1959 article, incrementalism, in one form or another, received nearly unparalleled attention in the social sciences for at least three decades. Lindblom's work received tremendous prominence partly because it dovetailed nicely with the widely influential work of the 1978 Nobel Laureate Herbert Simon (1957a; 1957b). Incrementalism affected the course of public admin- istration, public policy analysis, and especially budgeting (e.g., Davis, Dempster, and Wildavsky 1966; 1974; Gist 1977; 1982; Padgett 1980; Wildavsky 1964).[1] The emphasis on repeated (or serial) searches for local (or incremental) gains was forever linked to Lindblom's slightly pejo- rative notion of "muddling through." The emphasis on small gains and the assumed limitations in cognitive abilities created a contrast to the rational choice school of thought, which emphasized a starker model of utility maximization in which all uncertainty could be handled through simple expected utility calculations. One might argue in retrospect that the differences between satisficing and constrained maximization were hardly drastic, but two distinct camps of scholars had been set. Theoretically, satisficers and maximizers had very different cognitive qualities, which led them to practice different policy-making processes and adopt different policies.

We argue that a reconceptualization of incrementalism in the public policy context allows one to think about what policy incrementalism means in a legislative context. Here, we ask, "How do legislators them- selves evaluate incremental abortion-related proposals?" A stronger, the- oretical foundation for the concept of incrementalism can highlight the strategic concerns of the legislators and interest groups who sponsor and promote policy solutions. Within a legislature, members face trade-offs between vote maximization for proposals and policy gains. Trade-offs also occur for the sponsoring member between policy gains and opposi- tion members' incentives for engaging in legislative sabotage – intentional efforts to undermine the legislative work of rival members.[2] Incremental proposals address these trade-offs and also help legislators to address informational constraints. These incremental proposals often receive key interest group support because the incentives for counteractive lobby- ing and undue public attention are both minimized when policy gains are checked. Our assessment of the policy-making environment within legislatures suggests that there are clear, strategic rationales for incremen- talism. In this chapter, we detail the strategic rationales for incremental

---

[1] Note that Wildavsky in 1992 argued that the more recent budgetary process is less incre- mental than in the days of old. This shift is rejected by Jones, True, and Baumgartner (1998).

[2] Brehm and Gates (1999) discuss sabotage within bureaucratic agencies.

efforts and also specify the difficulties associated with nonincremental policy making, especially in the abortion context.

INCREMENTALISM AND PUBLIC POLICY

Referring to incrementalism, Jonathon Bendor, an organizational theorist well versed in traditional economics, wrote that "old theories ... rarely die; they just fade away" (1995, 819). Though vastly influential in the 1960s and 1970s, incrementalism is now largely moribund. Incrementalism was so popular that it practically died of its own weight as it came to mean virtually anything and everything. Indeed, in a review of the political science, budgeting, and public policy literatures, William Berry (1990) found twelve common uses of the term "incrementalism." Not surprisingly, he also found conflicts between those definitions. No scholarly term can be as broadly applied as incrementalism was without losing some force of meaning. In the end, for some critics, incrementalism meant virtually nothing.

Ironically, scholars' dwindling interest in incrementalism occurred concomitantly with an increase of interest in satisficing and behavioral game theory among economists. As some economists began to look beyond the canonical models of individual choice that highlighted expected utility maximization to pursue behavioral game theory, political scientists pursuing formal methods held fast to the established, canonical model of rational choice. Adaptive models were deemed too open-ended. Without a firm foundation for individual choice, equilibrium analysis was virtually impossible. The behavioral economist Colin Camerer (1997, 167) describes behavioral game theory as "a middle course between over-rational equilibrium analyses and under-rational adaptive analyses." Incremental adjustments in behavior or policy and satisficing are conceptually linked, so those scholars willing to entertain noncanonical models of strategic choice should also entertain another look at incrementalism. Of course, incrementalism may still retain some of its original weaknesses as well as its strengths but it surely deserves another careful look.

Interpretations of Incrementalism

Although incrementalism has been interpreted in numerous ways in the extant policy literature, we highlight two. First, compromise is sometimes equated to incrementalism (e.g., Hayes 1987). In this literature, a policy maker is encouraged to accept incremental change because various constraints prevent her from securing a policy that maximizes her utility. Compromising on the incremental change is simply a form of constrained utility maximization. For instance, time constraints or super majoritarian requirements for decision making may alter the division of the spoils.[3]

Second, incrementalism has also been linked to informational shortcomings. Incrementalism occurs because of the inability of policy actors to understand all of their options, forcing them to "satisfice" (March and Simon 1993) or "muddle through" (Lindblom 1959). As a decision-making process, incrementalism appears most directly linked to "low-understanding" environments. In these contexts, incrementalism is not presented as a constrained maximization. Incrementalism is simply a policy development strategy that allows for experiential learning and insures that any change is controlled and understandable. Incrementalism is simply a behavioral adaptation to uncertainties in the environment. No one wants to veer too far from the relative certainty secured by maintaining the status quo. Frank Baumgartner and Bryan Jones (1991; 1993; 2005) view incrementalism as a product of the "bounds" on the abilities of decision makers and the feedback from earlier policy decisions. In their model of punctuated equilibria, incremental policy change occurs during periods of limited feedback. The calm, normal moments in politics yield incremental policy shifts. Nonincremental change occurs in response to extraordinary circumstances and greater feedback providing more information to decision makers. When these circumstances arise, you get policy "punctuations," with rapid changes in policy occurring.

Critiques of Incrementalism

The various critiques of incrementalism have been quite sharp. Here, we highlight three such critiques. John Wanat (1974) argued that there were important distinctions between descriptive incrementalism and explanatory incrementalism. The outputs of the policy process may be described as incremental but that description does not yield any explanatory power in regard to the development of policy. Any number of rationales may support an incremental change in policy. In the end, there might be numerous issues at play that cause policy to change only incrementally.

---

[3] The classic references for bargaining with time constraints are Ariel Rubinstein's articles from the 1980s (1982; 1985). For a more direct application of the Rubinstein models see Jack Knight's *Institutions and Social Conflict* (1992).

Wanat's criticisms reinforced our own interests in exploring why legislators themselves might strategically pursue incremental policy changes.

Ira Sharkansky's criticism was more normative in nature (1967; 1968). If incrementalism was just one of any number of decision-making processes, then one could critique incrementalism on normative grounds as a process so beholden to the status quo that there is little opportunity for outside influences to affect the policy process. In a worst case scenario, incrementalism leads to automatic government where very little fresh decision making takes place.[4] Even a limited search for new information is lost. Yehezkel Dror (1968) suggests that a fixation on incrementalism leads to a failure to consider the possibility for great leaps forward in policy making. In the end, incrementalists may impute any number of rationales to a process that resembles the paragon of shirking, of not investing the resources and effort required to develop new policy solutions. If expected or forced to make a change, one simply makes the smallest of changes (cf. Baumgartner and Jones 1993). Even in the Baumgartner and Jones model of punctuated equilibria, dramatic policy change is reactive, not proactive.

There are also potential methodological problems with incremental theories. For example, suppose one simply wants to predict policy outcomes. Strict empiricism has been a hallmark of much of political science and public policy scholarship. That is, getting the right prediction, even if one abuses some of the tenets of science, is often deemed better than getting the wrong prediction while adhering to the strictest scientific procedures. Might not policy outcomes be best predicted by a model based on incrementalism? Consider a betting person trying to predict the weather for tomorrow. What is wrong with forecasting the weather for tomorrow based on a slight change in the weather today? More often than not, such a naïve forecast will be accurate.

Even this oft argued empirical justification for the incrementalism argument may be suspect according to Christopher Achen (2000). Policy today may be modeled as a function of policy yesterday and a set of other variables. Consider for a moment those other variables. Some of them may also have trends. If those other variables are serially correlated, from one day to another, then including the lagged dependent variable (i.e., policy yesterday) as an independent variable will absorb the effect of both the excluded variables and the included variables that are

---

[4] We believe R. Kent Weaver was the first to use the term "automatic government" in his book on indexation (1988).

themselves trended. That is, everything but the "policy yesterday" variable is artificially reduced to statistical insignificance, making incrementalism appear more important in naïve policy-making models than it actually is. Achen refers to policy yesterday, the lagged dependent variable, as a kleptomaniac, picking up significance from all possible sources (from both the included and excluded variables). If Achen is correct, many "long-standing claims based on apparently strong statistical evidence – that government budgets are caused primarily by last year's budget ... are shown to be probable statistical artifacts" (Achen 2000, 4).

THEORIES OF NONINCREMENTAL ACTIVITY

The study and promotion of incrementalism as the primary mode of policy making has led some scholars to examine the alternative: nonincremental policy making. One problem with studying either incremental or nonincremental policy is that defining these terms can be problematic. One critic of Lindblom notes that the Lindblom definition of incremental policy is self-defining; something is incremental (or nonincremental) if the observer says it is (e.g., Albritton 1979). The scale of change that might be nonincremental to one observer may be incremental to another. Thus, it becomes difficult to measure incrementalism. There have been efforts to use statistical means to define nonincrementalism. For example, Robert Albritton (1979) focuses on policy impact and presents a formulation of nonincremental policy change as having an impact that is a statistically distinct from a trend. When policy impact occurs outside a given range, the policy change is deemed nonincremental. Of course, this definition assumes that policy can be quantified, which is not a problem for budget politics. However, for scholars studying other policy areas, including abortion or a myriad of other issues, quantifying incrementalism is more problematic.

How the Albritton methodology could be used to determine if one law authorizing abortion was nonincremental compared to the status quo that existed previously is not clear. Relying only on policy impact alone can lead to puzzling situations. For instance, suppose a policy change dictates that all houses built in New Orleans after the devastation caused by the 2005 Hurricane Katrina be raised on twelve-foot piers. When the policy is adopted, residents and builders would likely view the policy as being nonincremental, a very large change in policy because of its impact on building costs and architecture. If, however, a sixteen-foot storm surge destroys these new homes, the change in policy mandating higher piers will appear minor, inconsequential, or incremental in retrospect. The Albritton strategy also discounts the direction of policy changes. A small shift toward the pro-choice or pro-life direction might be deemed statistically equivalent to no change at all. However, for advocates in the midst of the abortion debate, such shifts – though incremental – are very important.

Baumgartner and Jones, in a long series of works, have had considerable success evaluating the *distribution* of policy changes as opposed to any particular change.[5] Distributions of data are described by their moments. Most scholars are comfortable evaluating the first two moments of a distribution – the mean and variance. The third moment of a distribution describes the skewness of the data. Baumgartner and Jones evaluate the kurtosis – or fourth moment – of a distribution. Kurtosis is a measure of the peakedness of a distribution. As there are more incremental changes, one should see more peakedness around the mean of a distribution of policies.

Other theorists have defined nonincremental policies through a set of policy characteristics. These theories suggest that nonincremental policies have specific characteristics and require a specific legislative political dynamic in order to be successful. This is especially true when the nonincremental activity involves constitutional amendments, a procedure that has high legislative hurdles that are difficult to overcome. In 1975, Paul Schulman put forth a theory of nonincremental policy and the attributes thereof. Schulman's theory is predicated on the idea that nonincremental policies are not easily divisible. The first characteristic of nonincremental policy is stated thus: "*Non-incremental, indivisible policy pursuits are beset by organizational thresholds or 'critical mass' points closely associated with their initiation and subsequent development*" (1975, 1355, emphasis in the original). Such policies require large-scale allocations of resources – monetary, human, and political – to achieve success; the start-up costs for nonincremental policies are quite high. The focus of Schulman's study is manned space flight, which required spending sizable sums of money, staffing the program at its peak with roughly 420,000 personnel, and confirming the political commitment of the president to achieve the goal of putting a man on the moon. Much of this resource allocation went to conducting the research and development activities required to overcome uncharted barriers that existed in getting man from

---

[5] See http://policyagendas.org/publications/index.html for a complete list of the works that have come from the agendas project.

earth to the moon. Many of these research projects could be simulated, but they could not be piloted in the general sense of the term; projects were tested in real time on first use, where failure could result in mission failure and astronauts' deaths. Therefore, the path toward the moon required committing extensive resources to a goal that, at the outset, might or might not have been achievable.

Schulman further argues that nonincremental policies have the characteristic of requiring large-scale expansion if they are to expand at all. This rapid expansion is necessary to "overcome the inertia, external resistance, or internal start-up problems which act as barriers to policy expansion" (1356). In addition to the political and managerial issues associated with rapid expansion there is a psychological one: Achieving a nonincremental goal may require thinking big, and incrementalism typically encourages the opposite. In fact, incrementalism can induce failure merely by shaping the mental bounds regarding what policy makers and analysts view as being within the realm of the possible. Not only is this a vision problem, but it can also be an institutional and jurisdictional one. Incrementalism encourages small changes within existing institutional and jurisdictional shapes, but radical change may be needed to create the organizational and legal context in which success can be achieved.

The second characteristic of nonincremental policy is that "*non-incremental policy is in essence unstable – devoid of middle ground between self-generating states of growth and decay*" (Shulman 1975, 1363, emphasis in original). The problem, as Schulman describes it, is that nonincremental policies can outlive the public support needed to sustain the very high levels of resources that are required to achieve success. When this occurs, the policy resources allocated to the given policy outstrip the political resources needed to sustain them. Because of the scaling issues associated with nonincremental policies, the decline that occurs when nonincremental policies no longer have political support can be as rapid as the expansion was. Again examining the space program, Schulman notes that from 1965 to 1972, NASA staffing went from 420,000 to 108,000, and its budget declined by almost 50 percent during this same timeframe.

The third characteristic of nonincremental policy is that

Non-incremental policies are beset by an indivisibility that defies disaggregation into piecemeal decisions or additive partial advancements. This means simply that for non-incremental policies a "self-containment" demand must be observed. Policy requirements as well as outputs must be provided at high levels or they cannot be provided at all. (Schulman 1975, 1367, emphasis in original)

Here, we see that nonincremental policies are not necessarily the sum of a set of incremental decisions. In fact, Schulman explicitly notes that the sum of incremental decisions and policy moves do not equal one nonincremental policy shift. Only by committing to a nonincremental policy – with both political and policy resources – can a nonincremental outcome be achieved.

Schulman's definition of nonincrementalism is very beneficial in that it is complete and comprehensive. Other works on nonincremental policies supplement Schulman's work. David Nice (1987) suggests that it is helpful to explicate the meaning of incrementalism to appreciate its characteristics in different policy environments and to understand when nonincremental decisions may rise to the fore. One inherent positive trait associated with incrementalism is that, when the political and policy environments are stable, the incremental outcomes are relatively predictable. An incremental change will produce a policy outcome that is within a given tolerance range for policy makers and policy implementers. However, in an unstable political or policy environment, incrementalism can lose this attribute. A modest policy change may produce an outcome that is quite problematic if the environment underlying the policy domain has shifted so dramatically. More importantly for policy makers, incrementalism may be outpaced by public demand for change. In such situations, nonincremental policy solutions may be more politically astute as well as practically efficacious. In examining railroad policy in the states, David Nice (1987) found that, when a state's economy was threatened by a reduction in the size of a state's railroad system, it was more likely to move toward public ownership of railroads. The wealth or ideological predispositions in the state did not independently affect this policy outcome. The nonincremental move resulted from a perception of a crisis that was in part being precipitated by the reduction in railroad connectivity. For states with less of a crisis mentality, more incremental steps, such as stepped up tax incentives, were used to stimulate a revitalization of railroad usage in the state. For the nonincremental states, factors such as ideological predispositions did affect the choice of nonincremental policy tool. Nice's work presages Baumgartner and Jones's work on punctuated equilibria. When the feedback indicates turmoil in the political or policy environments, incremental policy shifts lose favor.

NASA projects and railway transportation policies are far afield from abortion policy, but the most helpful models of policy making are the most general. Recently, some law professors have regained an interest in "super-statutes." William Eskridge and John Ferejohn note that "most

substantive statutes adopted by Congress ... reveal little ... ambition"
(Eskridge and Ferejohn 2001, 1215), but super-statutes create an entirely
new policy framework with far-reaching implications. As examples,
Eskridge and Ferejohn refer to legislation such as the 1964 Civil Rights
Act and the 1973 Endangered Species Act. Clearly, one can address incremental and nonincremental policy making in areas well removed from
budgetary politics. Indeed, Eskridge and Ferejohn (2001, 1215) push us
to broaden our scope: "Appropriations laws perform important public
functions, but they are usually short sighted and have little effect on the
law beyond the years for which they apportion public monies."

For Schulman, Nice, Baumgartner, and Jones, and Eskridge and
Ferejohn, nonincremental policy is tied to dramatic transformations in
the political environment and clear public demands for policy change.
With abortion policy, there appears, prima facie, to be considerable feedback from citizens, interest groups, professional organizations, and the
media. In addition, for many policy advocates – especially on the far ends
of the debate – abortion decisions are not readily divisible. On face value,
abortion does not appear to be well suited for incremental policy shifts.

FORMAL MODELS OF LEGISLATIVE POLITICS

One point on which many scholars of incrementalism agree is that
explanations of incrementalism are quite varied. Bendor's (1995, 820)
assessment is direct and concise: "Something hard to describe must be
hard to formalize as well." At this juncture, we consider three possible
routes to take. First, one could give up on incrementalism, ignoring any
empirical tendencies and direct observations that suggest its importance.
Second, one could focus on events or situations that limit policy change.
One could, say, study Washington gridlock as a means to understand
minor policy movements that are akin to incrementalism (Brady and
Volden 1998). Finally, one could provide a clearer theoretical justification for incrementalism, focusing more tightly on legislators themselves.
We adopt this third route. In particular, we show that – across policy
domains – there is a strategic basis for a decision-making process that
lends itself to incremental policy change. In the area of abortion policies,
there are strategic, microfoundations that lead legislators to pursue incremental policy changes. Although legislators clearly have "ideal" policy
desires, they also must operate in a political environment that presents
stark realities about how policy can be achieved. Specifically, members
who want to change the status quo must be cognizant of the "brakes in

the system" that constrain opportunities for policy change. Given these constraints, members who propose policy change must recognize that (1) most House members are risk averse, (2) every House member needs to be able to explain his or her votes to constituents and interest groups alike, (3) legislative proposals are subject to sabotage by members and interest groups, and (4) there may be uncertainty about public opinion related to the policy change being proposed. Because of these factors, incremental policy changes can be seen as a strategic choice by legislators and be unrelated to attributes of the policy itself.

Some of the most important advances in congressional research have relied upon the application of simple spatial models to committees and the floor. Few congressional scholars remain unaware of Anthony Downs's work (1957) on two-candidate competition or Duncan Black's median voter theorem (1958). The gist of Downs's work on two-candidate electoral competitions is well known. In a one-dimensional, left/right (liberal/conservative) ideological spectrum, if voters prefer those platforms that reflect their own ideologies – or, in a spatial sense, that are closer to them – then candidates will adjust their platforms to attract votes.[6] The only platform that is invulnerable to certain defeat is at the median voter's ideal point. With both candidates at the median, the election is a toss-up, too close to call. If a candidate fails to move his platform to the median, the opposition candidate can move to the median and win the competition with a majority of votes. In reality, a candidate's movement to the median may be attenuated by any number of factors, including concern for core supporters or party activists, primary election dynamics or intraparty concerns, questions about voter turnout, concerns about one's own reputation, or the possible entrance of additional candidates.[7] Simply put, there may be "brakes on the system" that prevent candidates from moving platforms to the median.

When applied to committees or legislatures, Black's median voter theorem operates in the same basic fashion; however, there are some subtle differences. Legislators, analogous to the voters in the Downsian model, are arrayed along a one-dimensional ideological spectrum. Any legislator may make a proposal to alter the status quo, and then all legislators vote. In the electoral setting, there are two types of players – candidates and

---

[6] There are unstated assumptions. Most importantly, preferences must be symmetric and single-peaked, and abstention is not allowed.

[7] For formal models highlighting some of these points, see Aldrich (1983) on party dynamics, Banks (1990) on reputations and policy concerns, Palfrey (1984) on candidate entry, and Palfrey and Rosenthal (1985) on turnout without regard to platform placements.

voters – rather than just one, and there is no obvious status quo point.[8] Even with these differences, if legislators are arrayed from left to right along a one-dimensional ideological spectrum, simple majority rule yields a unique equilibrium at the median legislator's ideal point. A majority of legislators, including the median legislator and everyone to her right, would oppose any leftward shift in the status quo policy. By the same token, a majority of voters, including the median legislator and all legislators to her left, would oppose any rightward policy shift in the status quo. Any other point in the policy space could be defeated by the median, so the median itself remains the only equilibrium. The implied movement toward the median occurs regardless of the original position of the status quo, and any legislator who prefers the median to the status quo would reasonably propose the median. The differences in the models appear at first blush to have no impact because candidate platforms and legislative proposals both appear driven to the median.

Incrementalism appears to play no direct role in the legislative process, as each legislator seeks to secure policy gains or minimize policy losses. Legislators would seek small changes to the status quo only under one of two circumstances. In the first instance, the median legislator's ideal point may be near the status quo, in which case only small changes to the status quo would be possible. In the second instance, a legislator may pursue small changes in the status quo simply because other legislators have created some sort of hurdle or "brake on the system." What sort of "brakes on the system" might constrain legislators, preventing movement to the floor median? At this point, we are asking the same sort of questions that campaigns and elections scholars asked in the wake of the basic spatial model of candidate competition.

When congressional scholars have modified the application of Black's fundamental result, they have typically added another layer of institutional complexity. That is, Black's bare-boned spatial model is made more specific to Congress rather than more general. Some scholars have added one or more committees with gatekeeping powers (Denzau and MacKay 1983). The median legislator on the floor may not secure policy gains if a committee restricts the floor's ability to consider legislation. Restrictive rules of procedure create another potential hurdle.[9] Party structures may brake the movement to the floor median. At least ostensibly, party leaders

---

[8] One might imagine a modification of Downs's formulation and consider an incumbent running on her established record as something akin to a status quo.

[9] Relevant literature includes work by Dion and Huber (1996; 1997) and Krehbiel (1997a; 1997b). The work of Bach and Smith (1988) is also helpful.

control the flow of legislation, which has led numerous party scholars (e.g., Aldrich and Rhode 2001; Cox and McCubbins 1993; Rohde 1991) to argue that party medians are more important than the overall floor median. In other words, Black's median voter theorem may still be relevant, but it is relevant for the majority party and its leadership rather than for all of the legislators taken as a whole.

Another brake in the system is that actors beyond the U.S. House affect the ability of House members to secure a policy proposal at the median legislator's ideal point. Here, mechanisms such as conference committees (Shepsle and Weingast 1987), the Senate's cloture rule (Krehbiel 1998), or threatened presidential vetoes come into play (Cameron 2000). To the extent that these scholars (and numerous others) all describe brakes on the method of pure majority rule that would – without those brakes – yield Black's median voter theorem, they all describe a rationale for incremental policy movements. However, describing a policy result as more incremental than might have resulted is far different from describing the policy process itself as incremental. We strongly doubt any of the immediately aforementioned scholars sought to reaffirm incrementalism. Small policy movements may occur because of institutional constraints, suggesting that incrementalism is a byproduct of institutional hurdles, rather than a fundamental component of the legislative process. In contrast to the aforementioned works, we consider whether there is a logical, strategic underpinning for incrementalism itself.

WORKING ON THE INSIDE AND LOOKING OUT

When members consider their legislative affairs, they often do so with an eye on their electorates. That is, members work inside of the House with an eye always directed outward. Such a claim is hardly novel or complex. David Mayhew's *Congress: The Electoral Connection* (1974) emphasized the reelection motive and showed how internal congressional activity was often conducted with an eye looking outward. Richard Fenno (1978) discussed in considerable detail the activities of members in their home districts. Again, the legislator's focus is outward. How might such an outward gaze affect the sort of proposals made by legislators? We discuss, in turn, three strategic concerns for legislators, each of which highlights the rational basis for pursuing incremental policy change. First, legislators consider the trade-offs between vote maximization and policy gains linked to proposals. Second, incremental policy change affects members' incentives for engaging in legislative effort and legislative sabotage when they are evaluated on their relative performances. Finally, members' informational constraints affect their pursuits of incremental policy change.

Vote Maximization or Policy Gains

Sometimes everyday political observations lead to insights that can then be more carefully and rigorously explored. Let us start with an observation. Over the last thirty years many legislators were very well known simply on the basis of their staunch pro-life or pro-choice stands. The rewards from that recognition occurred regardless of the precise state of abortion policy. In other words, the ideological stands themselves yielded benefits even as abortion policy only shifted a bit this way or that. Within the House itself, legislators also seek policy benefits, but at least since the publication of Richard Fenno's *Congressmen in Committees* (1973) scholars have recognized that legislators also seek to enhance their reputations and power within the House. Suppose for a moment that legislators derive utility from both policy gains and the sheer numbers of votes for their proposals. How are desires for policy gains and vote maximization related? Generally, vote maximization requires a moderation of policy demands.

For those legislators known to be among the staunchest abortion advocates, the marginal benefits from policy gains are relatively small. Some slight policy shifts one way or the other will not change their reputations as staunch advocates on one side or the other of the issue. The marginal utility from votes may actually be much greater. Ironically, if a legislator is thought to be "soft" on the abortion issue and electorally vulnerable, he or she might value the policy gains more than legislators' votes. In contrast, a staunch, pro-life legislator may see greater utility gains from seeking other legislators' support and votes than from policy movement. In the remainder of this section, we show how one can begin to model the trade-offs between policy gains and vote maximization.

In the earliest spatial models, there has always been a tension between vote maximization and policy gains (e.g., Calvert 1985). To maximize votes, candidates moved toward the median, even if their true preferred policy platforms were to the left or right of the median. Each candidate preferred moderating his or her own platform to suffering under the platform of one's opposition. In the end, each candidate would be at the median voter's ideal point. In a legislative setting, slightly different maximization strategies can lead to very different equilibrium policy proposals. Consider floor proceedings protected by restrictive rules and an

Left	SQ	M	(2M–SQ)	Right

FIGURE 2.1. Policy gains v. vote maximization.

agenda that is one proposal deep.[10] Given the restrictions on the agenda, the only vote taken pits the proposal against the status quo.

In Figure 2.1, we have a policy space encompassing ideologies from left (liberal) to right (conservative). The status quo policy (SQ) is to the left side of the median voter (M). As labeled, in order to maximize policy gains, a proposer at or to the left of the status quo (SQ) should propose nothing.[11] Given the agenda and the placement of the median legislator, the status quo would defeat any proposal to its left. Proposers between SQ and twice the median minus the status quo (2M – SQ) should propose their ideal point. A proposer at or to the right of 2M – SQ should offer a policy just to the left of 2M – SQ. Now, suppose legislators seek to maximize votes for their policy initiative instead of policy gains. Legislators to the left of SQ would again propose nothing. However, in order to maximize votes against the status quo, proposers to the right of SQ must alter their proposal strategies and offer a policy just a tad away from the status quo toward the median. The status quo would receive all votes from Left to SQ, the proposal just to the right of the status quo (SQ) would receive all votes from that point to Right. The few votes between SQ and the proposal would be split evenly.

There is, quite simply, a direct trade-off between the maximization of policy gains along the ideological spectrum and vote maximization achieved by offering a proposal just to the right of the status quo. Even if the agenda is more than one proposal deep, an amender to the original proposal faces a trade-off between policy gains and votes for the amended proposal. If numerous proposals must compete to secure a coveted spot on the legislative calendar, party leaders acting as gatekeepers to the calendar must trade off policy gains and vote maximization. In addition to assessing possible policy gains, the gatekeeper might reasonably consider: "Which of these proposals is most likely to pass?" and "Which is least likely to undermine my influence and power in the chamber?"

The real question is "Why would legislators trade off votes for policy gains?" Two possibilities come to mind: risk aversion and vote explanation. Legislators tend to be risk averse. In formal models of

---

[10] Restrictive rules are commonplace (Bach and Smith 1988).
[11] We are assuming that legislators have single-peaked and symmetric preferences.

legislative politics, the mathematics undergirding risk neutrality is easier to model than risk aversion, but we often speak of legislators as running scared. In a risk neutral world, the expected utility of a lottery is simply the mathematical expectation of that lottery. However, work in decision theory has shown that risk aversion is not independent from the probabilities in a lottery (Montesano 1994), so mathematical expectations and perceived utilities may not align. In particular, risk aversion increases as the probability of success increases. We see this in the well-known finding that even all-powerful incumbents still run scared in their reelection bids. Even as their reelection appears more and more certain, their risk aversion increases. Whenever one is in the lead and success looks imminent, "Keep it simple, don't drop the ball" becomes the modus operandi in football and legislative politics.

If we apply this risk aversion to the legislative process, we know that the chances of legislative inaction are high. Few legislative proposals ever make it out of committee, let alone garner floor consideration or consideration by the other chamber. If a proposal does wend its way to the floor for a vote, its managers are likely to become increasingly risk averse, trading off policy gains for votes as might be necessary. As the legislative fate for the proposal improves, risk aversion increases. Indeed, work by King and Zeckhauser (2003) shows that floor leaders often gather more promises of support than are necessary. That is, floor leaders often hold a few "options" for legislators' votes that could be "called" in case they were necessary for passage. King and Zeckhauser's work nicely highlights how the trade-off between votes and policy can operate.[12] Securing an absolute promise to vote in favor of a proposal requires a leader to make greater policy concessions. However, securing an option, that is, a promise to vote for a proposal *only if* that vote becomes necessary, requires fewer policy concessions.

The second reason for legislators to trade-off votes and policy gains stems from the fact that legislators must explain their votes on policies – but not necessarily on the legislative process leading to incremental or nonincremental alternatives – to constituents and other political players.

---

[12] Important new work has hinted at similar dynamics. Penn (2009) shows that farsighted voters considering the stream of benefits accrued from a set of policies may forego proposals that yield that greatest "one shot" utility gains. For any given proposal, legislators may consider "what happens next." Jeong, Miller, and Sened (2009) find that legislators structuring civil right proposals in the late 1950s and 1960s neither pursued nor attained "first best" legislative outcomes. Legislators traded off policy gains for votes and stability within the supporting coalition.

There is a long, established scholarship in political science related to the notion that legislators must be able to explain their Washington activity to their constituents in the home district. Miller and Stokes (1963), Kingdon (1973), Fenno (1973), and most recently Bianco (1994) all have explored the importance of being able to explain a vote "to the folks back home." Clearly, explaining a vote is important to legislators, who are looking outward and always running scared. An easier explanation means that legislators need not run quite so scared. Large majorities in favor of legislation make an affirmative vote easier to explain on two grounds. First, when it comes to explaining votes, there is safety in numbers. Indeed, attempts to persuade voters about the rectitude of one's vote are often seen as a sign of weakness. A legislator can offer an explanation, but she or he will not expend much capital on efforts to persuade constituents on the matter (Bianco 1994, 49–53; Fenno 1973). It is easier to let constituents know that many legislators from both sides of the aisle supported the measure. For a recent example, one need only consider the congressional votes in October of 2002 to support the use of force in Iraq. Though in hindsight some legislators may come to regret their votes, a vote for a proposal with overwhelming support is easier to explain to constituents.

The framework for incremental policy change is also easier to present and explain than radical reforms. Providing "a fix" through incremental change is easier to explain than a radically new proposal. Kevin Esterling (2004, Chapter 3) argues that the "clarity of the interpretive framework" for a policy affects the support and opposition that the policy is likely to have. Simply put, the need to explain a vote affects the sort of policy a legislator would be willing to support. The more legislators' votes in favor of a policy, the easier it is to settle the interpretive framework question. If vote explanation is easiest when a proposal secures overwhelming support, then legislators will attenuate their demands for policy gains to minimize the costs of vote explanation. Vote maximization is traded off policy gains.

The incrementalism tied to vote maximization is neutral to party regime. For instance, in his work on divided government, Mayhew (1991) found that bipartisanship was the norm on major bills. This finding suggests that incrementalism may occur, not as a byproduct of legislative hurdles but because of legislators' concerns for vote explanation. Vote maximization insulates legislators from the vicissitudes of public opinion. Ultimately, vote maximization is a risk avoidance strategy for outward-looking legislators. Of course, many legislative proposals receive little public attention and hence require little explanation. When legislative proposals are in the public eye, the situation is different – vote explanation is important. In those instances in which vote explanation is deemed most important, legislators will trade away policy gains for legislative votes. When vote explanation is less important, policy gains will trump vote maximization.

Sabotage

David Brady and Sean Theriault (2001, 181) contend that "politicians exaggerate policy implications in the hopes of not only defeating ... policy but also humiliating the policy's proponents." Legislators have no incentives to give opposition partisans any reason to redouble such opposition efforts. This line of reasoning parallels key aspects of an argument developed by Gil Epstein and Shmuel Nitzan (2004). In their model of interest groups competing over policy change, Epstein and Nitzan show that the policy losses from restrained proposals may be outweighed by the savings elsewhere. To wit: there is less opposition to overcome when one proposes moderate policy change. Vote maximization reduces the incentives and opportunities for other legislators to undermine one's efforts. So, would legislators ever sabotage one another's efforts? Sabotage in other areas of politics is generally accepted (e.g., Brehm and Gates 1999). Congressional scholars are more used to considering institutional hurdles, rather than disruptive behaviors of individual members. Though the media may consider behaviors of legislators disruptive, scholars are perhaps afraid to use such terminology for fear that they themselves will be labeled partisan and biased. Academicians, and especially congressional scholars, are more comfortable linking obstructionist behaviors to institutional rules and structures (cf., Krehbiel 1985). That is, legislators use their institutional vantages to suit their own needs, but there is nothing inherently mean-spirited about legislators' efforts. Indeed, some legislators might fight policy on the grounds that they are simply working to preserve a well-established tradition or institution. Some people have argued that the complexities of bicameralism and separated branches and powers make policy change more difficult (e.g., Hammond and Miller 1987), but recent empirical work indicates that *intrabranch* issues are key to gridlock (Binder 1999; 2003). There is no denying the fact that legislators use their institutional vantages, but what we ask is whether there is something fundamental to legislators' incentive systems that promotes sabotage. Consider a legislator weighing the costs of legislative sabotage versus the costs of productive legislative efforts. In one instance, policy losses are minimized, and, in the other, policy gains are sought. When examining legislators' powers in Congress, scholars have typically noted that there are many negative powers and that these powers are easier to use than positive powers (e.g., Deering and Smith 1997). It is, therefore, easier to obstruct than it is to engage in productive efforts. In sum, the marginal cost of sabotage is lower than the marginal cost of productive legislative effort for members of Congress.

We proffer another, second reason for sabotage, a reason not linked to institutional hurdles. Quite simply, we argue that legislators' performances are evaluated on a relative scale, not an absolute scale. Relative performance scales provide the backdrop for the old *New Yorker* cartoon in which two dogs are seated at a bar. Roughly paraphrased, one dog says to the other, "It's not enough that we win, the cats must also lose." Democrats and Republicans are often locked in a competition where each side tries to limit the gains of the other. In these cases, relative gains often overshadow absolute gains. Elected officials are used to relative comparisons, especially given that the vast majority of them were elected under a system of plurality rule. There is no magic number for success under plurality rule, one simply needs more votes than the second place finisher, and big wins that stave off future challengers are preferred over close races. In their electoral lives, legislators are attuned to relative evaluations. Indeed, in most settings, there is no absolute scale for political success. In an organization, such as the U.S. House, relative comparisons create incentives for legislators to sabotage one another's efforts. One's utility is tied both to one's own successful efforts and to others' failures. Therefore, a legislator must consider how much to invest in productive efforts and how much to invest in the sabotage of others' efforts. Sabotage occurs across and within party lines. If the majority party can be undermined in the public's eye for maintaining a do-nothing Congress, the minority will engage in sabotage. If strong partisans are able to gain by attacking party moderates, again we should anticipate sabotage.

Economists, such as Edward Lazear (1989), George Baker (1992), and Bengt Holmstrom and Paul Milgrom (1994), have evaluated the links between incentive systems in an organization and the encouragement of sabotage within those organizations.[13] Suppose, for instance, that there is a fixed raise pool that will be distributed among the members of an organization. One is better positioned for a raise when others' projects

---

[13] See Gibbons (1998) for a general overview of the literature.

fail and one's own projects succeed. Where do workers invest their own
resources? They can hide themselves away and arduously pursue the
successful completion of their own projects, assist with others' projects,
and ignore all opportunities to promote their relative successes and others' failures. Alternatively, they can narrowly pursue their own projects,
refuse to assist with others' projects, and find time to engage in self-
promotion and sabotage of others' efforts. Although the time spent on
self-promotion or sabotage is inefficient for the organization as a whole,
it may still be individually rational for each member of the organization
to engage in both self-promotion and sabotage.[14]

Sometimes business managers produce parallel structures and competing groups within the same organization as a means to internalize
some competition. Jack Knott and Gary Miller relayed the following
about organizational structures in the Special Projects Office of the Navy.
"'Everyone had an actual or potential rival and no one was assured of a
monopoly. Thus, within the program everyone had a strong incentive to
watch for problems in the designs offered by others while working diligently to avoid any of their own'" (Knott and Miller 1987, 263). Watching
for problems in others' designs can certainly be productive, but at some
point it may approach sabotage. If one can imagine sabotage in firms and
other organizations in which everyone is "on the same team," then surely
one can imagine sabotage in the U.S. Congress, where Democrats and
Republicans are daily pitted one against the other.

Consider Figure 2.1 again. The more extreme a counter proposal is
to the status quo, the greater the policy losses are for those who favor
the status quo. Also, the more extreme a counterproposal is to the status quo, the greater the number of legislators who have an incentive to
sabotage the proposal. To minimize the incentives for sabotage by other
legislators, one has an incentive to trade policy gains for votes and to seek
smaller adjustments to the status quo. The opportunities for successful
sabotage are certainly tied to one's institutional vantage and that cannot be changed. However, one can limit the incentives for others to
use such institutional rules and procedures for obstructionist purposes.
Incrementalism, in short, can reduce the risks of, and opportunities for,
sabotage.

---

[14] A similar phenomenon occurs within a firm as it decides how much effort to invest
in production and how much effort to invest in lobbying for political protection. As
production efforts become more expensive, the relative value of a firm's investments in
political pressure increases. For a discussion of the trade-offs between production and
rent seeking, see Damania (2002).

Our formulation of incrementalism is not another look at gridlock as portrayed by Keith Krehbiel (1998), even though he notes that "[it] is tempting to reason that gridlock is much like incrementalism" (202). Krehbiel argues that gridlock is simply created by supermajority institutions, not malevolent legislators sabotaging one another. For Krehbiel, gridlock is based on the constitutional powers of vetoes and overrides and Senate filibusters, which limit the ability of legislators to move policy. However, when discussing the 1992 economic stimulus package, Krehbiel speaks of small incremental change as akin to gridlock, "while ... not a case of gridlock in the sense of complete policy stalemate, it is a case of incremental change and disillusionment ... attributable to supermajoritarian procedures" (1998, 31). That is, when incremental change is tied to disillusionment, it is a failure akin to gridlock.

Krehbiel's gridlock argument is strongest when the status quo policy position is close to the median legislator. That is, when one might be least concerned about gridlock, gridlock is most likely to occur. If relative performance evaluations affect legislators' willingness to sabotage one another's proposals, then one would see greater efforts as large policy gains are made. It is hard for us to become concerned about a little bit of gridlock when the status quo is close to the median. We are more troubled when something akin to gridlock occurs when the status quo is not so close to the median. To be fair, one must note that, in these two presentations, gridlock and sabotage are not mutually exclusive. However, it is also important to note that there are distinctions. Gridlock, as portrayed by Krehbiel, occurs when the status quo is relatively moderate vis-à-vis the median. Sabotage may occur whenever movement away from the status quo is attempted, regardless of the relative positions of the status quo and median legislator.

Nonincremental legislative politics is also encompassed in Krehbiel's theory of pivotal politics (1998). Constitutional amendment politics has similar characteristics to veto politics because both vetoes and constitutional amendments must garner support of two-thirds of the membership in each chamber. By necessity, this means that a proposed constitutional amendment must be more appealing than the status quo, not just to the median legislators in each chamber – the 51st Senator and the 218th House member – but also to the supermajoritarian members in each chamber – the 67th senator and the 290th House member.[15] Unlike with

---

[15] Due to the Senate's filibuster rule, the pivots are typically the two sixtieth members, one counted from the left and one counted from the right.

a veto, the president is not a player in the constitutional amendment process. However, the difficulties associated with such legislating remain and the ability of legislators to sabotage such legislation also remains high. Amending activity can work to sabotage any constitutional proposal. Given that such amendments only take a majority vote, it is much easier to sabotage a constitutional amendment than to pass one.

INFORMATIONAL CONSTRAINTS

One of the most difficult problems faced by members of Congress is that they operate under several types of informational constraints. There may, for instance, be uncertainty about the true impact of a proposed policy (Gilligan and Krehbiel 1990) or uncertainty about constituents' preferences. One may be uncertain about issue saliency regarding who is likely to be affected by a proposed policy. Legislators do tend to follow public opinion closely when it is clearly expressed, and David Brady and Craig Volden (1998) argue that gridlock occurs when there is a lack of public consensus. Considered in light of the previous discussion of risk aversion among legislators, incrementalism can be seen as being tied to the informational limitations associated with a lack of public consensus.

Imagine two actors, Congressman Dem(ocrat) and Congressman Rep(ublican), trying to agree upon some plan of action related to abortion, P_i, from a set of possible plans, P. Suppose the value of any course of action is simply determined by the state of nature. Suppose there are two equally likely states of nature, M (moral) and R (rights). Given our discussion at hand, we can let M and R represent different frameworks that constituents might use for interpreting a legislative proposal. Will abortion be predominantly interpreted as a morality issue? A rights issue? Congressmen Dem and Rep must jointly settle upon an action before they learn the true state of nature. Suppose they consider proposals P_1 and P_2. (See Figure 2.2.)

Ex ante, Dem and Rep face the same prospects under P_1 and P_2 because the states of nature, M and R, are equally likely and the players are therefore indifferent between the two plans of action. Of course, after the state of nature is revealed, Congressman Dem and Congressman Rep have strong preferences over P_1 and P_2. Dem prefers P_1 if R prevails and P_2 if M prevails. In stark contrast, Congressman Rep prefers P_1 whenever M is the state of nature and P_2 whenever R is the state of nature. Ex ante, Congressman Dem and Congressman Rep are indifferent between the proposals because each has insufficient information about the true state of nature.

P_1	Dem	Rep
R	1	0
M	0	1

P_2	Dem	Rep
R	0	1
M	1	0

P_3	Dem	Rep
R	0	0
M	1	1

FIGURE 2.2. Ex ante indifference under three different scenarios with three different ex post implications.

With more refined information about the true state of nature, the differences between the preferences of Congressman Dem and Congressman Rep become more apparent. If one actor, say Congressman Dem, expressed a preference for one course of action over the others, then Congressman Rep could infer that additional information about the true state of the world was somehow gathered. Congressman Dem's revealed preferences for P_1 over P_2 could only make sense if Dem believed that state R was more likely than state M. If Congressman Dem *insists* on P_1 over P_2, then Congressman Rep reasonably should insist on P_2 over P_1. That is, one player's move to adopt P_1 or P_2 might reasonably be sabotaged by the other player because, after the fact, P_1 and P_2 are unequal to Congressmen Dem and Rep. P_1 and P_2 treat each player equally beforehand and unequally after the fact.

Consider the third course of action, P_3. It too has the same ex ante prospects as P_1 and P_2. Ex ante, there is no reason to prefer any plan of action over any other because they all yield the same expected utility.

However, if the congressmen are risk averse and sensitive to relative gains, they may each strictly prefer P_3 over P_1 and P_2 because P_3 treats both Congressman Dem and Rep equally after the fact. In a setting where Dem and Rep closely watch one another's gains, P_3 may be preferred over P_1 and P_2 on two grounds. First, the congressmen may be risk averse, and, with P_3, no player suffers relative losses. Second, neither congressman has any reason to sabotage P_3. Recent empirical work by Gregory Bovitz and Jamie Carson (2006) dovetails nicely with this argument. Bovitz and Carson find that House roll call votes with greater consensus have limited electoral consequences for legislators. Although classic studies in the political science literature connect roll call voting behavior to electoral fates (e.g., Arnold 1990; Mayhew 1974; Miller and Stokes 1963), Bovitz and Carson show that legislators do not lose constituents' votes when those roll calls showed considerable consensus. Consensus in the U.S. Congress insulates legislators from electoral swings.

Incremental movements have been criticized because they appear to reinforce the fundamental elements of the status quo. Incremental change also minimizes the differences in relative gains. Legislators are more likely to have ex post equality under incrementalism than under more dramatic shifts in policy. For the winning side, not much was gained; and for the losing side, not much was lost. Consider abortion, which is often presented as an issue with especially stark policy options. Suppose P_1 is to remove completely all restrictions to access to abortion procedures and P_2 is to deny completely all access to abortion procedures. Depending on the state of nature, one side or the other can benefit from either P_1 or P_2. However, the qualifier is crucial. The state of nature in this instance is probably a function of public opinion, and it has been very difficult to nail down abortion attitudes. Suppose P_3 offers a middle route, allowing for the regulation of access to abortion in certain situations. Legislators may explain their votes for P_3 differently but no legislator suffers a relative loss or secures a relative gain. Legislators can always explain their actions if they dovetail neatly with some issue of concern that enjoys high levels of recognized public support. Incremental movements are important in other more difficult situations because they decrease the probability of misjudging the level of public acquiescence surrounding the policy change in question.

FROM THE OUTSIDE LOOKING IN

Legislative incrementalism can also be viewed strategically when we consider how groups from the outside consider the affairs within a legislature. It is widely accepted that legislators are constrained by public opinion, but public opinion also affects the viability of group strategies (Kollman 1998; Shin 2004). Is there any basis for groups viewing the legislative process from the outside to seek incremental change rather than more dramatic policy shifts? Group leaders and lobbyists consider distinct audiences as they formulate their plans (Ainsworth and Sened 1993; Baumgartner and Leech 1998, 140). Group leaders are concerned about the retention of their own members and the mobilization of opposition groups. We suggest that incrementalism is inherently a strategic response on the part of groups to these distinct environments. Groups must worry about not only their interactions with legislators (e.g., Ainsworth 1993) but also the opportunities for opposing groups to lobby counteractively (Austen-Smith and Wright 1994) and public opinion (Kollman 1998; Shin 2004). Incrementalism addresses these problems simultaneously.

Groups often rely on threats to their own policy positions to mobilize their current members and gain new members (see, e.g., Hansen 1985). An incremental proposal limits the fund-raising and counteractive lobbying opportunities for opposition groups. It is harder for opposition groups to mobilize their erstwhile supporters to oppose minor changes (Godwin 1988; Kahneman and Tversky 1979). Incremental amending behavior in the legislature is also harder for opposition groups to detect because minor amendments to bills can be attached at any point in the legislative process. Indeed, incremental change can be relatively easy to sneak in during the latest stages in the legislative process, such as in conference committees. Even if incremental proposals are detected, opposition groups may still have difficulty countering incremental changes if it appears that they are attacking what might seem to be perfectly harmless proposals. For those groups ultimately desiring greater policy gains, incrementalism is not automatically rejected or necessarily seen as a shortcoming. Incrementalism still allows for photo-ops. It highlights the difficulty of the ongoing struggle, and it undermines opposition groups' counteractive lobbying efforts. For groups, there are distinct advantages to an incremental approach to policy change.

IS ABORTION INCREMENTAL OR NONINCREMENTAL?

Now that we have discussed the theoretical rationale for incremental and nonincremental policy making, the next step is to determine if abortion is an inherently incremental or nonincremental activity. Using the same four criteria that come from our earlier description of nonincremental policy making, we can examine abortion policy to determine whether it meets the theoretical definition of an indivisible policy that requires a nonincremental policy solution, such as a constitutional amendment, in order to be achieved. Meeting these criteria suggests that abortion policy can be addressed through nonincremental means, but it does not preclude incremental efforts.

First, consider whether abortion policy has high start-up costs. In the pre-*Roe* United States, abortion rights were decided on a state-by-state basis, with different states allowing different levels of abortion-related services. Some states provided no abortion services for their citizens, but other states allowed regulated abortion services to any eligible individuals who could afford to travel there. Since the *Roe* decision, there remains a regulated and differential level of abortion-related services in the states. Some states have more complete abortion coverage than others, depending on the ability of the marketplace or the willingness of government to provide for the service (Rose 2006). In short, the variety of services at the state level suggests that the costs associated with starting or stopping abortion services are not inherently nonincremental in nature.

Second, we consider if abortion policy is subject to rapid growth and decline. Although the number of abortions provided in the United States increased after the *Roe* decision, this fact can be seen as something driven by market forces. The availability of abortions in more locations across the country created access to a service and a market that facilitated an increase in the number of abortions obtained. Currently, the number of abortions performed in the United States has decreased from the peak in the 1990s. Current demands for abortion are no doubt affected by many things, including the increased availability of contraceptive devices and the availability of abortifacients like RU-486. Finally, the possibilities for reporting abortion statistics have varied over this same time period. Fear of prosecution may have suppressed the pre-*Roe* numbers, and a sense that the use of abortifacients is somehow different from other abortion procedures may depress current numbers. Even with the vacillation in the number of abortions performed annually, it is hard to conclude that there is either rapid expansion or retrenchment.

Third, is abortion policy amenable to incremental policy gains that in sum yield a greater policy gain? The history of abortion policy, pre- and post-*Roe*, includes incremental policy steps that when considered in sum may have yielded nonincremental policy shifts. For example, prior to *Roe*, the state of New York incrementally allowed greater abortion coverage in the years preceding *Roe*, first allowing abortion for in-state residents and then for out-of-state persons. After *Roe*, states across the country have implemented an array of incremental changes to abortion policy, such as requiring parental notification, requiring a waiting period before an abortion can be performed, or limiting specific abortion procedures, such as the so-called partial-birth abortion procedure. Although the Supreme Court has placed some limits on the restrictions that states can place on abortions, these limits do not appear to hinder numerous attempts to make incremental changes to abortion policy. In addition, several scholars have noted that numerous restrictive abortion policies had little measurable impact on the total number of abortions performed (e.g., Graber 1996, 125; Meier et al. 1996).

Fourth, we can consider the way in which crises affect abortion policy. The large-scale threats that led states to privatize aspects of railroads in their states or led the United States to attempt to place a man on the moon have not existed to the same extent in abortion politics. Although there have been threats and challenges in abortion policy – primarily posed by various Supreme Court decisions that either expanded abortion rights (i.e., *Roe*) or contracted abortion access (e.g., *Carhart*) – there have not been outside environmental shocks that would approach anything like a national crisis. Examining public opinion data, for example, for the past thirty years, we see a quite stable policy environment. Likewise, the number of abortions provided has not changed dramatically year to year, although there have been changes in abortion trends during this time.

In short, abortion politics can be viewed nonincrementally, but it is not inherently nonincremental. If abortion policy outcomes are incremental, it is because legislators have consciously pursued an incremental approach. Abortion policy can be made incrementally. Abortion policy does not have high start-up costs, does not require rapid policy expansions or contractions, and can be modified both in times of stability and crisis. Abortion policy historically has proven quite amenable to incremental changes that are additive. In many if not most states today, abortion policy is in fact the culmination of a wide array of previous incremental policies that have been melded together.

Any group or legislator naturally wants to minimize the policy distance between their ideal policy goals and a final policy outcome, but groups and legislators face multiple constraints that complicate their situations. First, proposals must stay within key preferred-to-sets in the legislature. Second, proposals need some support or at least acquiescence from the public. Proposals that meet these first two constraints may still have drawbacks. Groups may want to avoid certain grand policy proposals so as to minimize counteractive mobilization from opposition groups. Nonincremental proposals increase the scope of conflict and may mobilize one's very own opposition. Some scholars view abortion politics as a series of mobilizations and countermobilizations (Staggenborg 1991). *Roe* was central to the mobilization of the right-to-life activists, and subsequent rulings were key for pro-choice countermobilizations. "Success in the abortion conflict always has 'the unintended effect of aiding the opposition organizationally' no matter how and in what forum such victories are achieved" (Graber 1996, 126). Suzanne Staggenborg asked: "Can the pro-choice movement survive [a demonstrable] victory" (1996, 170)? Legislators may want to minimize sabotage efforts and ease their task of vote explanation. Given these constraints, we argue that incremental policy outcomes can be seen as the result of strategic actions on the part of legislators, operating in a pluralistic environment.

Previous models of incrementalism are beset with assumptions of cognitive limits or policy uncertainties. Here, we stress the strategic foundation for incrementalism. As we have shown, informational constraints in spatial models of legislatures can lead to incrementalism. Although the links between informational shortcomings and incrementalism are fairly well established in models that suppose cognitive limits, here we seek to maintain the basic elements of a rational choice environment. A keystone to this strategic foundation is legislators' quest for vote maximization, which is balanced against policy gains. Finally, it is important to stress that there is a rationale for advocates for policy change who are outside of the Congress to seek incremental change for reasons that have nothing to do with the internal dynamics of the House. All-or-nothing claims on government do not lend themselves well to the institutional structures that act as hurdles in the legislative process.

Finally, although definitions of and theories related to incrementalism are quite diverse, theories of nonincrementalism have a more narrow scope. Specifically, a nonincremental policy should have the following four attributes. First, it has high organizational thresholds that are closely associated with their initiation and subsequent development. Second, it is unstable and subject to rapid emergence and growth as well as rapid decline. Third, it is indivisible and not amenable to incremental or additive solutions. Fourth, it is most politically viable as well as practically efficacious during a time of crisis or rapid change. In the next chapter, we evaluate the two environments that legislators are most sensitive to: the immediate, internal House environment and the larger, external environment beyond the House and the Washington, D.C., beltway. Whenever crafting legislative proposals, members must consider the ideological divisions within the House itself as well as divisions in the larger society.

3

The Nature of Congress and Incrementalism in Abortion Politics

Views from the Inside and Views from the Outside

A polarized political class makes the citizenry appear polarized. (Fiorina, Abrams, and Pope 2005, 5)

INTRODUCTION

The discussion in the previous chapter regarding the legislative dynamics of incremental and nonincremental politics provides a theoretical basis for understanding the foundations of strategic incrementalism. Legislators experience diverse electoral and policy-making environments, but, for many legislators, abortion politics in both the electoral and legislative settings are particularly highly charged. In this chapter, we examine how the environments surrounding abortion politics, both in the U.S. House and in the public at large, have changed over our period of study. Specifically, we examine factors internal to the U.S. House of Representatives, such as the ideology of the chamber as a whole, the party composition of the chamber, and the ideology of specific committees in the chamber. Changes in ideology since the *Roe* decision may make the policy-making environment more conducive for either pro-choice or antiabortion advocates in either an incremental or nonincremental fashion.

Profound ideological shifts occurred during the period covered in our work, but ideological shifts do not necessarily alter key aspects of the policy-making environment. For instance, the historic shift in the House after the 1994 midterm elections overturned over four decades of Democratic control. However, even after the shift in partisan control at the beginning of the 104th Congress, the dynamics of supermajoritarian politics remained largely unchanged during this time while the dynamics associated with standard majoritarian politics – the politics that are most amenable to incremental strategies – changed dramatically. By standard measures, after the 1994 elections, conservative majorities were easier to muster, but mustering conservative supermajorities actually became harder, especially when contrasted to the 1980s.

Over the past thirty years, members of Congress have adjusted their strategies for addressing abortion and abortion-related issues. When examining bill introductions, we see abortion-related proposals falling into one of three broad categories. The earliest proposals in our dataset called for special commissions or panels to study the impact of *Roe*. A second set of proposals includes constitutional amendments. Some of those proposed amendments would have defined the beginning of life, and these sorts of amendments were typically referred to as human life amendments. Other amendments would have altered the U.S. Supreme Court's jurisdiction or returned the question of abortion to the states. Some, but not all political observers grouped these latter amendments with the human life amendments. At the time, the politics of the U.S. Supreme Court and the politics of abortion within the states undoubtedly meant that the proposals were pro-life. Not surprisingly, almost all of this activity occurred on the pro-life side of the debate, but pro-choice advocates have also attempted broad, sweeping changes. For instance, by most measures, the Freedom of Choice Act, first introduced in 1993, would satisfy the criteria for superstature status as established by William Eskridge and John Ferejohn (2001).

In addition to the proposals calling for studies and commissions and the proposals that would fundamentally alter legal views of choice and privacy or life and citizenship, there were literally hundreds of abortion-related proposals that sought to make much smaller, incremental changes. These smaller, incremental proposals sought to make an array of changes to abortion policy, including limiting abortion funding, determining whether medical programs had to provide abortion-related education in their curriculum, and implementing various "conscience" issues for doctors and other medical personnel.

Over our period of analysis, legislators have recommended studies and commissions, offered constitutional amendments, and also sought more narrow legislative gains. Although there have been distinct changes in legislators' strategies, there has been little variation in public opinion at the aggregate level about abortion. Even the tumult surrounding the

1994 election fails to correspond with a significant shift in public attitudes regarding abortion at the aggregate level.[1] Indeed, the Contract with America, a broad, ten-point Republican Party campaign pledge developed for the 1994 elections and largely designed by then Minority Leader Newt Gingrich (R-GA), was entirely silent on the issue of abortion. Gingrich focused on "60% issues" – issues that at least 60 percent of Americans supported – to ensure a more united GOP front. Even as the Republicans took charge of the House after more than four decades of Democratic control, a majority of the public remained conflicted about abortion, wanting it to be legal but also wanting certain restrictions. The decision of Republicans not to include abortion in the Contract with America illustrates how difficult policy making can be when the public remains ambivalent or torn.

In Table 3.1, we see that certain members of Congress have been dominant players in the abortion debate over the past thirty-five years. However, as we discuss in the next section of this chapter and later in Chapter 5, the key players in the abortion debate have included both Democrats and Republicans. James Oberstar, a staunch Catholic Democrat, has introduced more constitutional amendments to ban abortion than any other member of Congress. Many Democrats who served on Appropriations Committees were lead sponsors of bills that included the Hyde amendment provisions that ban federal funds being used for abortion. And, as we discuss later in more detail, several members, like Henry Hyde and Christopher Smith, have been strong policy entrepreneurs and have shaped the abortion debate through the force of their legislative skill (e.g., Wawro 2000).

In the Appendix to this chapter, we list the members who have introduced three or more abortion proposals in the 94th through 108th Congresses. The table lists the member, the number of bills the member sponsored, the number of legislative amendments offered, the number of constitutional amendments offered, the number of bills that were incremental, and the number that were pro-choice (pro-life). What is interesting to note here is that, for the first 93rd through 95th Congresses, there were many members who were highly active introducing constitutional amendments to ban abortion. In the 94th Congress, for example, Democrat James Oberstar sponsored twelve different constitutional amendments to ban abortion. By contrast, in the latter Congresses almost all of the efforts are incremental. In addition, we also see that the most active members are almost always pro-life members. With the exception of members

---

[1] At the individual level, abortion attitudes are important in shaping a person's vote choice. See Abramowitz (1995) for a discussion of this issue.

TABLE 3.1. *Top Sponsors of Abortion Legislation, 94th–108th Congresses*

Member	Party	Year First Elected	Total Sponsorships	Number of Constitutional Amendments Sponsored	Incremental Legislation Sponsored
Robert Dornan	Republican	1977	36	9	21
James Oberstar	Democrat	1975	35	30	7
Christopher Smith	Republican	1981	29	1	28
William Whitehurst	Republican	1969	18	17	0
Henry Hyde	Republican	1975	18	9	6
Julian Dixon	Democrat	1979	18	0	18
Henry Waxman	Democrat	1975	18	0	16
William Natcher	Democrat	1953	16	0	16
Philip Crane	Republican	1969	14	0	8
William Emerson	Republican	1981	14	10	5
Ron Dellums	Democrat	1971	13	0	13
Ron Paul	Republican	1976	13	1	8
David Obey	Democrat	1969	12	0	12
James Whitten	Democrat	1941	12	0	12
Dante Fascell	Democrat	1955	12	0	12
Joseph Gaydos	Democrat	1969	11	11	0
Martin Russo	Democrat	1975	11	11	0
Edward Roybal	Democrat	1963	11	0	11
Jim Kolbe	Republican	1985	11	0	11
Romano Mazzoli	Democrat	1971	10	7	2
Harold Volkmer	Democrat	1977	10	9	2
John Porter	Republican	1980	10	0	10
Neal Smith	Democrat	1959	10	0	10
Nita Lowey	Democrat	1989	10	0	10
James Istook	Republican	1993	10	0	9

like Nina Lowey, Loretta Sanchez, and Henry Waxman, multiple sponsors on the pro-choice side have been rarities. Table 3.1 lists the most active sponsors of abortion-related legislation.

PARTY CONNECTION

Abortion today is commonly thought of as a partisan issue, with Democrats being the pro-choice party and Republicans the pro-life party. The health care debates of 2009 and 2010 suggest that a refinement of the standard partisan views on abortion might be warranted. Some versions of the Patient Protection and Affordable Care Act (the official name of the comprehensive health insurance reform legislation passed by Congress in 2010) allowed for public funds to be used to cover abortions. House Democrat Bart Stupak (MI) led the charge to ensure that federal funding could not cover abortions.

The notion that abortion was a partisan issue emerged in the 1980s and 1990s. Since 1980, the Republican presidential platform has spoken strongly against abortion. Clyde Wilcox (1995, 67–71) argued that each party's platform was actually much more extreme than the ideal point of each parties' median member. On abortion, the party hierarchies appeared to guide the development of policy without much regard for rank and file members. "Since 1980 the Republican platform has contained a plank that has the support of perhaps 10% of the American public, and the Democratic [presidential] nominee has taken a position that also represents a minority position" (Wilcox 1995, 68). Wilcox notes that such extreme platform positions appear to contradict the Downsian model (Downs 1957) of two candidate electoral competition in which party platforms converge to the median voter's ideal policy position.

Of course, any comprehensive policy history is much more complicated than any narrow slice of a policy debate. That said, a couple of admittedly narrow slices might help illustrate our point. Consider that the honorary co-chairs of Planned Parenthood/World Population in 1965 were former Presidents Harry Truman and Dwight Eisenhower (Tribe 1992, 41). The first antiabortion activist on a presidential ticket was Sargent Shriver, George McGovern's 1972 vice presidential running mate. Regardless of Shriver's stand on abortion, the McGovern-Shriver ticket was considered one of the most liberal the Democratic Party had ever produced.[2]

---

[2] Political junkies might recall that Shriver was McGovern's second choice as running mate. The first choice, Thomas Eagleton, was asked to step down just a few months before the general election. McGovern's campaign was worried about the negative publicity tied to

Beyond the elite levels, Adams (1997) and Ted Carmines and James Woods (2002) uncover similar shifts in attitudes and partisan alignments. Among the public, according to General Social Survey (GSS) data, until roughly 1987 Republican partisans were more pro-choice than were Democratic partisans (Adams 1997). Similarly, examination of American National Election Study data shows that, through 1980, Republican campaign activists were more pro-choice than Democrats (Carmines and Woods 2002). Although Democratic convention delegates have been more strongly pro-choice since 1972, the gap between them and Republicans remained small until 1984 (Carmines and Woods 2002). Using congressional roll call data, Adams (1997) found a similar pattern of increasingly divergent attitudes among Democratic and Republican legislators. Both Adams (1997) and Carmines and Woods (2002) contend that the increasingly partisan nature of abortion politics represents a case of issue evolution driven by party elites and filtering down to the masses. Many scholars and popular commentators have connected the ascendance of the Republicans during the George W. Bush era to values issues – like abortion (e.g., Frank 2005). In more recent work, Larry Bartels (2008) argues that the values issues – like abortion – have not necessarily been a boon to the Republican Party. For Bartels, the *timing* of short-term economic gains by Republican presidents propels the Republican supporters, and value issues – like abortion – are window dressing.

THE IDEOLOGICAL COMPOSITION OF CONGRESS AND ABORTION POLITICS

Suppose a member of the U.S. House wanted to pursue nonincremental policy making. For nonincremental policy making – either a constitutional amendment to ban abortions or a sweeping piece of legislation sure to be filibustered or vetoed – the proposal must secure supermajoritarian support. Successful veto overrides and constitutional amendments require support of two-thirds of the membership in each chamber, so we can refer to the 290th House member and the 67th senator as veto points for nonincremental policy making.[3] Proposed amendments to the

Eagleton's regular mental health treatments. Was Shriver's antiabortion stand overlooked given the extraordinary circumstances? As it happens, throughout his Senate career, Thomas Eagleton was staunchly pro-life. McGovern chose not one but two staunchly pro-life running mates.

[3] The pivot on the right side of a chamber is found by counting from the leftmost legislator toward the right. The pivot on the left side of the chamber is found by counting from the rightmost legislator toward the left. In the Senate, the pivots are usually determined by

Constitution certainly face a herculean battle, but they do not involve the president, so by some accounts their battles are less severe than the battles surrounding other types of supermajoritarian proposals. However, the supermajoritarian nature of constitutional amendments also means that sabotage is much easier, effectively peeling off supporters and making the passage of the amendment that much more difficult.

One way to think about legislating in the House of Representatives is to think about the difficulty of finding 218 like-minded members who will vote for a given initiative. As we showed in Chapter 2, the difficulty of creating such a coalition varies based on many of factors, including the position of the status quo and the placement of the new proposal on the ideological spectrum. The majority vote standard for most legislative proposals presumes that the sponsor is attempting to garner only 218 votes for the proposal. When the proposal is a nonincremental constitutional amendment, the standard is very different. Proposals to amend the Constitution require the support of 290 members in order to overcome the supermajoritarian, constitutional veto point.

The need for votes is obvious, but the ease of securing support for legislative proposals also depends on the ideological distributions of legislators. Using the NOMINATE data developed by Keith Poole and Howard Rosenthal, we can examine ideological distances for majoritarian and supermajoritarian politics as a percentage of the total ideological space in a given Congress.[4] The NOMINATE scores developed by Poole and Rosenthal run from −1.0 to +1.0, and we determine the ideological space in a given Congress by measuring the distance between the most liberal and most conservative members. Within that ideological space, we can locate the 218th and 290th members and relate their positions to the positions of other key figures in Congress.

Partisan polarization is often linked to gridlock – both theoretically and empirically (e.g., Brady and Volden 1998; Chiou and Rothenberg 2003; 2006; Eilperin 2007; Krehbiel 1998; Lapinski 2008). In Table 3.2, we use NOMINATE scores to examine several attributes associated with the practicalities of both incremental and nonincremental legislating. During our period of study, the overall distance between the extremes from the most conservative member to the most liberal member has remained quite stable. In the ideological space spanning from −1.0 to +1.0,

---

the chamber's filibuster rule. The filibuster creates two pivots, one at the 60th member counted from the left and one at the 60th member counted from the right.

[4] A discussion of NOMINATE data can be found in Poole and Rosenthal (1997).

TABLE 3.2. *NOMINATE Ideological Scores for Key House Positions, 94th–108th Congresses*

Congress	Most Conservative	Median Legislator	Supermajority Legislator	Most Liberal	Most Conservative – Median Distance	Most Conservative – Supermajority Distance	Most Liberal – Most Conservative Distance	Median to Supermajority Distance	Supermajority as Percent of Used Ideological Space[a]	Median as Percent of Used Ideological Space[a]
94	0.885	-0.161	-0.296	-0.687	1.046	1.181	1.572	0.135	0.75	0.67
95	0.874	-0.148	-0.292	-0.687	1.022	1.166	1.561	0.144	0.75	0.65
96	0.885	-0.119	-0.283	-0.687	1.004	1.168	1.572	0.164	0.74	0.64
97	0.885	-0.024	-0.242	-0.687	0.909	1.127	1.572	0.218	0.72	0.58
98	0.885	-0.101	-0.273	-0.643	0.986	1.158	1.528	0.172	0.76	0.65
99	0.680	-0.074	-0.264	-0.687	0.754	0.944	1.367	0.190	0.69	0.55
100	0.680	-0.088	-0.261	-0.687	0.768	0.941	1.367	0.173	0.69	0.56
101	0.712	-0.090	-0.264	-0.687	0.802	0.976	1.399	0.174	0.70	0.57
102	0.712	-0.108	-0.268	-0.722	0.820	0.980	1.434	0.160	0.68	0.57
103	0.712	-0.111	-0.254	-0.722	0.823	0.966	1.434	0.143	0.67	0.57
104	0.826	0.192	-0.213	-0.687	0.634	1.039	1.513	0.405	0.69	0.42
105	0.885	0.192	-0.248	-0.687	0.693	1.133	1.572	0.440	0.72	0.44
106	0.885	0.166	-0.260	-0.687	0.719	1.145	1.572	0.426	0.73	0.46
107	0.885	0.176	-0.257	-0.687	0.709	1.142	1.572	0.433	0.73	0.45
108	0.885	0.221	-0.249	-0.687	0.664	1.134	1.572	0.470	0.72	0.42
Average	0.818	-0.005	-0.262	-0.689	0.824	1.080	1.507	0.256	0.716	0.547
94–103 Average	0.791	-0.102	-0.270	-0.690	0.893	1.061	1.481	0.167	0.715	0.601
104–108 Average	0.873	0.189	-0.245	-0.687	0.684	1.119	1.560	0.435	0.717	0.438

[a] This percentage is the distance measured from the most conservative position to the given point (median legislator, supermajoritarian legislator) as a percentage of the total most-liberal, most-conservative distance.

the most conservative member has remained near to 0.82 and the most liberal member has remained near to −0.70. On average, during the period of our analysis, there has been a NOMINATE distance of 1.52 between the most liberal and most conservative members.

A key player in many spatial models of Congress is the chamber's median voter, whose vote tips the balance to one majority or another. Given 435 members in the House, the 218th member occupies the median position. The median legislator can vote with everyone to her left or with everyone to her right. In either event, she tips the balance, determining who wins and who loses. Having the ideological ends joining forces against the middle occurs from time to time but is much less common.[5] From the third column in Table 3.2, we see that the median voter has moved during our timeframe, from an average of −0.102 in the Democratic-controlled Congresses (94th–103rd) to 0.189 in Republican-controlled Congresses (104th–108th). This switch in the median voter position has reduced the distance from the most conservative member to the median by 0.210, with the median voter moving from an average distance of 0.893 from the most conservative member under Democratic control of the House to an average distance of 0.684 under Republican control. As seen in the sixth column of Table 3.2, for a conservative member of the House, the legislative landscape has improved. Conservative members do not need to span as much ideological distance to reach the median legislator. Shifting abortion policy to a more conservative position has become easier, *as long as such a move can be accomplished through majoritarian means tied to the median voter.*

If a supermajority is required for policy change, the legislative environment is little changed during our period of study. In a nonincremental environment, the median legislator is no longer the pivotal voter. Assuming members of the House could overcome the strong assertion of control by the leadership of the majority party, the vote of the supermajoritarian member – the 290th member – would determine whether nonincremental legislation could be enacted. Table 3.2 shows this gap for each Congress since the *Roe* decision. Examining scores in the seventh column, from the 94th to the 108th Congresses, we see that the distance from the most conservative member to the supermajoritarian member has remained relatively stable. From the 99th to the 103rd Congresses, this distance was slightly less than 1.0. However, the average for the entire timeframe studied is 1.080, and from the 104th to 108th

[5] For a discussion of the "ends against the middle" scenario, see Nokken (2003).

Congresses, the average distance from the most conservative to the 290th member is 1.119. Surely, Republican control made the passage of conservative, Republican Party supported proposals easier, but the environment during the most recent congresses has become more problematic for those proposals that require a supermajority because there is now a greater ideological gulf between the most conservative member and the 290th member.

Using the data in Table 3.2, we ran some simple Pearson correlations to measure relationships between variables. The variables in the third and fourth columns are highly correlated (.83, p < .0001). As the median legislator shifts to the left or the right (third column), the supermajority legislator shifts in a similar fashion (fifth column). The electoral tides that shift the median in a conservative (liberal) direction also shift the supermajority legislator in the same fashion. However, the correlation between the variables in the sixth and ninth columns is negative (–.85, p < .0001). As the ideological distance covered to reach the median legislator is reduced (in the sixth column), the distance between the median and the supermajority legislator is demonstrably increased (ninth column). Together, these two sets of correlations indicate that general electoral trends that yield more conservative median and supermajority legislators may also yield greater divisions between the median legislator and the supermajority legislator. To date, many scholars have highlighted the growing polarization in the U.S. House of Representatives. The presence of the polarization is clear, but the strong correlation between the ideologies of the median and supermajority legislators highlights the fact that polarization may increase even when general shifts to the left or the right are reflected in many legislators' positions.

One final point about the difficulty of supermajoritarian politics – especially as compared to incremental politics – can be seen in the two far right columns of Table 3.2 as well as in Figure 3.1. The dashed line in Figure 3.1 graphs the percentage of policy space covered by a coalition consisting of the most conservative legislator to the median legislator, as a percentage of the total distance between the most conservative and most liberal members. For the 94th through the 103rd Congresses, this distance averaged 60 percent of the total policy distance. Securing the median legislator's vote required moving across 60 percent of the distance from the most conservative member to the most liberal member. By contrast, for the 104th through 108th Congresses, the ideological distance from the most conservative legislator to the median legislator diminishes to 43.8 percent of the total ideological space. Incremental

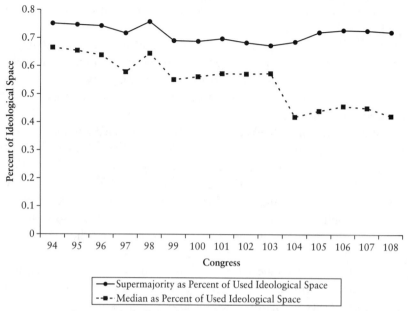

FIGURE 3.1. Percent of ideological space from the most conservative member to median and supermajority members.

politics for the most conservative member becomes easier after the 103rd Congress, as the median is much closer to the most conservative member compared to the most liberal.

The solid line in Figure 3.1 indicates the space between the most conservative member and the supermajoritarian member of Congress. For every Congress from the 94th through the 108th, the distance from the most conservative member to the supermajoritarian member, as a percentage of the total ideological space, remains relatively static. Supermajoritarian politics for the most conservative member requires moving across 71 percent of the total ideological distance in the House. This result suggests that, during this timeframe, supermajoritarian politics in the House was more difficult for the most-conservative member than the rules of the House would suggest. Because of the dispersion of member ideologies in the chamber, supermajoritarian politics requires spanning over 70 percent of the total ideological space to secure 290 votes.

Ideological Space and Committees

Just as there are variations across time in the relative position of the median voter and the supermajoritarian voter, there are also variations in the ideological position of committees and the position of each committee over time. The ideological composition of some committees more closely reflects the composition of the House chamber as a whole than do others (cf. Krehbiel 1991). Here, we focus on four committees – Appropriations, Armed Services, International Relations, and Judiciary – for the 94th Congress through the 108th Congress. Each of these committees has an interest in abortion politics and has been involved in abortion-related legislation during this period. For a strategic legislator, the ideological composition of these committees is important; members may want to focus their efforts on those committees where their proposals have the greatest potential for success. There could be several measures that a member might use to determine this. First, they might consider the over-all level of bifurcation or polarization in the committee; committees with greatly divided ideological positions may have a more difficult time selling their legislation on the floor of the House. Second, a committee with a median far removed from the House median may have difficulty getting its legislation passed on the floor. A member might also be sensitive to the relations on the committee among panel members and want to work with committees where there is ideological congruence among the members.

Intracommittee Bifurcation

The Judiciary Committee, which is the most commonly used committee for the consideration of abortion-related legislation, is the most bifurcated of the four committees we evaluate. As Figure 3.2 shows, the absolute distance from the median Democrat to the median Republican on the Judiciary Committee is between 0.60 and 1.10 during this time. For a sense of perspective, the distance between the median Democrat and median Republican on the House Judiciary Committee is similar to the distance between the most conservative member of the House and the 290th member, who would be needed to pass a supermajoritarian piece of legislation. The House Judiciary Committee is a "house divided." Proposals coming from the Judiciary Committee are unlikely to have broad bipartisan support. The House Armed Services Committee is consistently the committee where the distance between the median members of the parties is the smallest. Armed Services proposals are more likely to have bipartisan support from the committee simply because there is little ideological separation between Democrats and Republicans serving on the panel. The bifurcation measures for the Appropriations and International Relations Committees lie between those for the Judiciary and Armed Services Committees. For each committee, the distance between partisans grows from the 94th to the 108th Congresses, as there are fewer

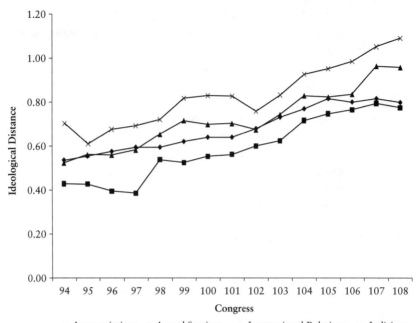

FIGURE 3.2. Absolute distance between the median Democrat and median Republican on four committees.

moderate members and more homogenous memberships in each party. The growing ideological divisions or polarization in American politics, so often written about by numerous scholars (e.g., Hunter 1991; McCarty, Poole, and Rosenthal 2006; cf. Fiorina, Abrams, and Pope 2004), are at first blush reflected in the four committees that are most involved in abortion-related issues.

Committee Median–Floor Median Congruence

In Figure 3.3, we examine the distance between each committee's median legislator and the floor median legislator for the same four committees. Here, we see that the difference between the committee median and the median on the floor often move from congress to congress. In Figure 3.3, positive numbers mean that the committee median is more conservative than the floor median; negative numbers show a committee median that is more liberal than the floor median. The data show that the median member of the Armed Services Committee is consistently more conservative

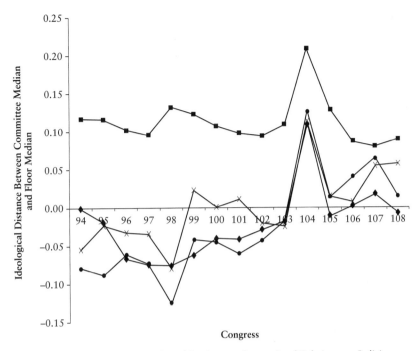

FIGURE 3.3. Ideological distance between committee median and floor median.

than the median member of the House. The median Appropriations Committee member is typically more liberal than the median member of the House, including during two of the five congresses in the Republican era of control. The location of the median member of the International Relations Committee is relatively volatile, as is the location of the median member of the Judiciary Committee, although the congruence between the Judiciary Committee median member and the floor median member is often closer than is the case for some other committees during this period.

Majority Party Committee Median–Floor Median Congruence

Figure 3.3 tracks the congruence between the median member of a given committee and the median member of the House chamber. The interplay between majoritarian politics and party politics has been at the root of

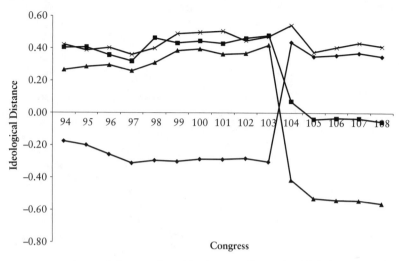

FIGURE 3.4. Ideological distance between the majority party committee median and the floor median.

persistent debates in congressional politics literature.[6] We do not mean to address these debates head on, but we do note the competing dynamics. For instance, the combination of majoritarian politics and party politics at the committee level may make the median member of the majority party on a panel the key member for getting legislation passed out of committee. However, under an open rule in the House – a rule where, generally speaking, amendments can be offered by anyone – the party dynamic may be less important on the House floor, where the median legislator again has great sway. Therefore, examining the congruence between the median member of the majority party on a given committee and the median member in the House may be important as well. When we do this in Figure 3.4, we see that the Appropriations Committee has the highest level of congruence, at least during the period of Democratic control of Congress. Under Republican control of the House, the Armed Services Committee has the highest level of congruence. Note that the Judiciary Committee is almost always the most distant committee under Democratic control of Congress and was similarly distant under the

[6] Some of the authors at the forefront of this debate include Aldrich, Binder, Cox, Krehbiel, Maltzman, McCubbins, Rohde, and many others who have trained with the aforementioned scholars.

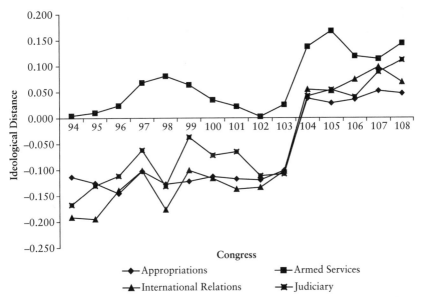

FIGURE 3.5. Ideological distance between the majority party committee median and the majority party caucus median.

Republicans, although the International Relations Committee became even more of an outlier than the Judiciary Committee starting in the 105th Congress. If the party-floor dynamics affect the flow of legislation, then legislators would be wise to direct legislative proposals to some committees and avoid others.

Majority Party Committee Median–Majority Party Floor Median Congruence

Finally, we consider a situation where the U.S. Congress is run like a majority party cartel and where the cartel controls the flow of legislation (e.g., Cox and McCubbins 1993). Under these assumptions, the congruence between the median member of the majority party on a given committee and the majority party's floor median member in the chamber is most important. In Figure 3.5, we examine the gap between these party-committee and party-floor median ideological positions. Here, we see that two committees – Judiciary and Appropriations – closely track the majority party committee median member and the majority party caucus median member. In contrast, the Armed Services Committee and International Relations Committees have a lower level of congruence when we consider the ideology of the majority party median member on the committee and majority party member on the floor.

Abortion is generally considered to be among those issues for which no acceptable political solution can be found. For many people, abortion exemplifies an issue for which fundamental moral disagreements prevent political compromises. Among the most widely cited works on abortion politics is Laurence Tribe's *Abortion: The Clash of Absolutes*, in which the "life versus liberty" paradigm is explored (1992). A "clash of absolutes" between activists hardly portends the give and take of compromise. Amy Fried (1988) calls the abortion issue a "condensational symbol" that represents or stands in for a number of deeply held core beliefs concerning life, freedom, and morality. The title of Karen O'Connor's work on abortion politics (1996) states her view that there is quite simply "no neutral ground" when it comes to abortion politics. These scholars as well as many others give the impression that abortion politics is only practiced at the barricades. For a democratic society struggling with the issue, a more complete understanding of public opinion on abortion is essential if government and society are to move beyond intractable disagreement, let alone open conflict.

Is public opinion on abortion as stark as some suggest? A wide body of research exists on this topic, from which five important findings emerge. First, at the *aggregate* level, public opinion on abortion has remained remarkably stable over the past thirty years, as seen in Figure 3.6. Second, the American public regards traumatic abortion far more favorably than elective abortion. Third, the core beliefs underlying attitudes toward abortion involve views on freedom of choice, the role of women in society, respect for life, and sexual morality. Fourth, key demographic variables correlated with abortion attitudes are religion, race, and education level. Fifth, party identification is also strongly correlated with abortion attitudes.

Stability of Attitudes

Since its inception in 1972, the General Social Survey has included a battery of questions on abortion. Respondents are asked whether they support a women's right to a legal abortion in six circumstances: (1) if the

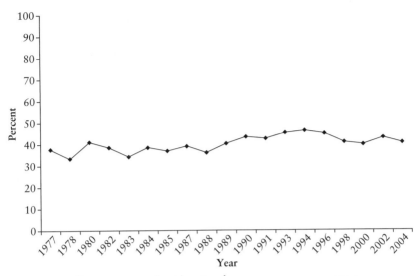

FIGURE 3.6. Percent supporting abortion for any reason, 1977–2004.

woman had been raped, (2) if her health is endangered by the pregnancy, (3) if there is a risk of birth defects, (4) if the family cannot afford the child, (5) if the woman is unmarried and does not want a child, and (6) if the woman is married but does not want a child. Responses are displayed in Figure 3.7. Since 1977, the GSS has also asked whether respondents would support abortion "for any reason." Various researchers have noted the remarkable stability of responses over time (Adams 1997; Cook, Jelen, and Wilcox 1992; Wlezien and Goggin 1993). Support for abortion in the first three cases – often termed therapeutic, traumatic, or medical – has consistently been between 80 and 90 percent. Support for abortion in the last three circumstances – usually termed social or elective – falls into the 40 to 50 percent range. Overall, from 1977 to 2004, average support for abortion for any reason hovered around 40 percent, as seen in Figure 3.6.

Attempts to understand this stability in aggregate public opinion – which stands in contrast to public opinion on most other pressing issues – often highlight the moral nature of the abortion issue. As public opinion scholar Greg Adams (1997, 729) notes, "opinions on abortion are not particularly sensitive to new information or testimony from experts. The issue is moral, not technical." Generally, respondents are less likely to let elite attitudes sway their thoughts on issues related to morality. Other researchers point to small fluctuations in attitudes that may be influenced

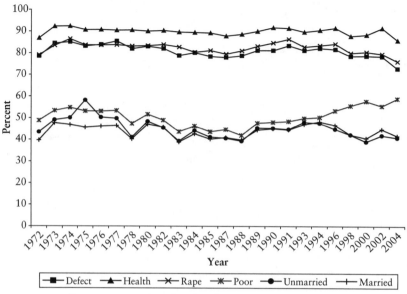

FIGURE 3.7. Percent supporting abortion for certain reasons, 1972–2004.

by court decisions, most importantly *Roe*, *Webster*, and *Casey* (Cook, Jelen, and Wilcox 1992). Often the public rallies around a court decision, especially at the Supreme Court level. The Supreme Court thus becomes a unifying force in the polity. Charles Franklin and Liane Kosaki (1989), however, noted that the public failed to rally around the Court's *Roe* decision. The ruling of the most trusted branch of the federal government failed to sway attitudes. Indeed, the decision may have made diverse preferences even more polarized and more firmly set.[7]

A Split in Attitudes: Traumatic v. Elective Abortion

As shown in Figure 3.7, GSS data indicate public support for abortion to be highly dependent on the reasons for the abortion (see Adams 1997; Alvarez and Brehm 1995; Cook, Jelen, and Wilcox 1992; Craig, Kane, and Martinez 2002; Halva-Neubauer 1990; Huckfeldt and Sprague 2000; Legge 1983; Tribe 1992; Wlezien and Goggin 1993). The American public is overwhelmingly more supportive of a woman's right to choose

---

[7] Johnson and Martin (1998) find that the Court's influence on public opinion dissipates as the Court hears more cases of a similar nature.

in so-called traumatic cases, including rape and medical threats to the mother or fetus. On the other hand, support for abortion under any of the three elective instances has rarely climbed above 50 percent. In researching potential differences in abortion attitudes at the state level, Cook, Jelen, and Wilcox (1993a) arrived at similar results.

These findings are important for various reasons, but, perhaps most significantly, they illustrate that, away from the world of activist politics, the abortion question is not an "all or nothing" matter. Majority public opinion falls somewhere between the total choice and the complete prohibition camps. However, to say simply that opinion falls somewhere between the two extremes belies the underlying complexities of abortion attitudes. Robert Huckfeldt and John Sprague (2000) explore some of the pitfalls associated with casual interpretations of survey response data. Huckfeldt and Sprague state that the "same issue position may mean different things and hold different consequences for different people" (2000, 57). A middle ground attitude on abortion may be (1) the product of a carefully articulated body of legal and moral reasoning, (2) akin to a shrug of the shoulders indicative of indifference and inattention, or (3) the product of competing or contradictory concerns. In the first situation, we might expect considerable stability in the respondent's attitudes. In the second and third instances, a respondent's attitudes may be affected by any number of contextual factors.

What do the numbers regarding American's attitudes about abortion look like? On the one hand, few Americans are willing to force a woman to continue with a pregnancy resulting from rape or incest. From 1972 through 2004, an average of only 7 percent opposed abortion in all three traumatic cases. On the other hand, 45 percent are unwilling to allow abortion in those elective cases in which a married woman simply does not want to have a child. Support for abortion "for any reason" averaged 40 percent from 1972 to 2004, according to GSS data. Although the strong pro-choice position has enjoyed more support than the strong pro-life position, as Michael Alvarez and John Brehm (1995) note, "neither the pro-life (e.g., Operation Rescue and National Right to Life Committee) nor the pro-choice (e.g., National Abortion Rights Action League) activists represent the policy preferences of the majority of respondents" to their survey. Alvarez and Brehm note that "the policy positions of the activists are unequivocal and one-sided in support for or opposition to abortion. What we have demonstrated is that ambivalence and internal conflict reign" for everyone else (1995, 1077). Stephen

Craig, James Kane, and Michael Martinez (2002) find similar results in their study of individual ambivalence.[8]

Ambivalence is not akin to uncertainty. We have frequently noted that legislators may have uncertainty about the nature of public opinion but the Alvarez and Brehm discussion of ambivalence is very different. Ambivalence occurs when an individual holds strongly to two or more somewhat contradictory notions. What might those contradictory notions be? They are different for each individual, but they might be something along the lines that abortion is wrong and governments should not tell people what to do. Or, access to safe abortion procedures is very important for women, but the government should limit the ability of my own daughter to have an abortion without letting me know. Whenever someone thinks "it was wrong, but it was the best wrong decision I have ever made," they are dealing with ambivalence.

With uncertainty, more information is always a good thing because new information reduces uncertainty and allows us to fine-tune our predictions. For that very reason, rational choice theorists often state that more information is better than less (Downs 1957, 77). The presence of ambivalence makes decision making and predictions about that decision making more difficult. A voter's decision is made more difficult by ambivalence. A legislator's attempt to predict a voter's reaction to abortion-related legislation is more difficult because of the voter's ambivalence. Does adding more information help? With ambivalence, more information may *amplify* the existing ambivalence by leading individuals to consider new and fundamentally different dimensions of issues tied to abortion policies. New information may entangle attitudes toward abortion with new contradictory considerations. If information increases a voter's ambivalence, then that information may indirectly increase a legislator's uncertainty in regard to predicting constituent reactions. One person's ambivalence (say, a constituent's) creates uncertainty for others (say, legislators). Constituents' ambivalence creates uncertainty for legislators, and more information may hurt more than it helps.

Some public opinion scholars argue that people hold "inconsistent considerations" and "unfocused and contradictory" notions (Zaller 1992, 54, 95). Ambivalence may indicate mercurial, unreasoned attitudes, or ambivalence may reflect the complexity and multidimensionality of

---

[8] Mooney and Lee (1995; 2000) offer a very different interpretation of the nature of public opinion. "Morality policy simply provides a good example of the ... *clarity* in the public's messages to policy makers" (Mooney and Lee 2000, 235, emphasis added).

the issue being considered (Sniderman and Theriault 2004). Though we are less comfortable with the notion that ambivalence is a failure of citizens to be consistent than with the notion that ambivalence is a product of issue complexity, the mere presence of ambivalence is all that we need to continue with our discussion of abortion policy making. Indeed, Glen Halva-Neubauer (1990, 43) suggests that the ambiguities in public opinion related to abortion lead policy makers to adopt "middle ground" positions rather than attempting to ban abortion outright. Tribe's (1992) examination of the pro-life and pro-choice positions echoes this assessment, and he notes that even many "pro-life" supporters are ambivalent about the tough cases such as rape or incest. He discusses a number of potential "compromise" positions including consent and notification requirements, waiting periods, restrictions on funding, and earlier cutoff dates.

Underlying Core Beliefs

The discussion thus far illustrates the broad outlines of public attitudes on abortion. With these general results as a starting point, researchers often seek to understand the driving factors behind abortion attitudes by examining two sets of potential contributing factors: underlying core beliefs (addressed here) and demographic variables (addressed in the following section). One's position on abortion is typically tied to more general beliefs (see Alvarez and Brehm 1995; Cook, Jelen, and Wilcox 1992; Craig, Kane, and Martinez 2002; Fried 1988; Luker 1984). Researchers addressing this question have looked to individual ideology, partisanship, views on gender roles, respect for life, and beliefs about "traditional" or sexual morality.

Cook, Jelen, and Wilcox (1992) find each of these variables to be related to abortion attitudes. Thus, individuals with conservative ideologies – a traditional view of women's role as wife and mother, an overall respect for life stance (measured by Cook, Jelen, and Wilcox by a question relating to euthanasia), or opposition to premarital sex – are more likely to oppose abortion. However, it is interesting to note that for each of these variables, the middle ground response – what Cook, Jelen, and Wilcox term the "situationalist" stance on abortion – forms the largest group. These findings reinforce the overall view that, for most Americans, abortion is not an all-or-nothing issue. The staunchest advocates may appear unwilling to compromise, but the typical citizen is more willing to consider some regulations related to abortion access.

Alvarez and Brehm (1995) explicitly characterize the abortion issue as a "conflict between core beliefs." Measuring ambivalence in abortion attitudes, they examine conflict in one's core beliefs as a key variable. They use awareness of and support for the Equal Rights Amendment (ERA) as a proxy for gender role beliefs, and find that support for the ERA is a "powerful predictor" of support for abortion rights. Craig, Kane, and Martinez (2002) find that ambivalent or conflicting views on moral traditionalism and marriage roles are indicative of greater ambivalence in abortion attitudes.

Demographic Variables

In addition to underlying belief systems, various demographic variables have been examined for their potential effect on abortion attitudes. Among those considered are race, gender, education level, socioeconomic status, geographical location, generation, and religion and religious practice. Early findings by Jerome Legge (1983; 1987) indicate that age, income, education, and religion are significant factors in understanding abortion attitudes. Recent findings by Martin Gilens (2009) indicate the continued link between abortion attitudes and income and education levels. Cook at al. (1992) found that all variables except gender were related to abortion attitudes, though none except religion was as strongly related as the attitudinal variables discussed previously. Of all the demographic variables, education was the most significant, with higher education levels connected to greater support for ready access to abortion services. Geographically, those in the South and in more rural areas were less likely to support access to abortion, as were those of lower socioeconomic status. Although race appeared significant, with blacks less likely to support abortion access (see, e.g., Alvarez and Brehm 1995), this relationship disappeared when other demographic and attitudinal factors – including religiosity – were controlled (see, e.g., Combs and Welch 1982; Hall and Ferree 1986; Sawyer 1982). As with the attitudinal variables discussed previously, in nearly all cases, the situationalist response was the most common. Cook, Jelen, and Wilcox (1993a) again use these demographic variables in their assessment of potential state level differences in abortion attitudes, and they find that controlling for these variables eliminates any perceived difference between states.

Perhaps the most significant and most commonly researched variable is religion and religious practice. Cook, Jelen, and Wilcox (1992) find that Catholics and evangelical Protestants are more likely to be pro-life than "mainline" Protestants, although in no category do those holding pro-life attitudes make up the majority. Cook, Jelen, and Wilcox also find that, beyond basic religious affiliation, religious involvement (measured as low, medium, and high, based on church attendance, personal prayer, and subjective religious intensity) is important. Those with higher levels of religious involvement across all three types of denominations are more likely to be pro-life. Kenneth Mulligan (2006) found that Catholics who held the late Pope John Paul II in high esteem held more negative views of abortion (and the death penalty) as compared to less devout Catholics. Alvarez and Brehm (1995) similarly found religion to be significantly related to abortion attitudes, with religious intensity being even more important. Morris Fiorina, Samuel Abrams, and Jeremy Pope (2005), looking at some of the same public opinion data suggest that the commonalities across faiths and practices are stronger than the differences.

TARGETING PUBLIC OPINION: A LEGISLATIVE VIEW OF ABORTION ATTITUDES

The previous sections in this chapter describe the space within which abortion policy is made. As legislators consider abortion policy, they are focused on their two most important environments: the chamber and the district. The space in the internal, legislative environment is defined by the ideological characteristics of committees, parties, and the chamber as a whole. The space in the external environment is defined by public opinion, and it should not be surprising that legislators are concerned about public opinion related to abortion. For legislators seeking to change abortion policy, these external and internal spaces determine the boundaries within which they must operate.

In this section, we ask why legislators would address abortion at all (Graber 1996, 148). There are numerous important issues that legislators prefer to avoid for one reason or another. Budget and tax issues are only considered after considerable foot dragging. The use of stopgap spending measures suggests an unwillingness to act unless it is absolutely necessary. Social Security and health care issues are seldom addressed in a meaningful way during periods of political normalcy. For many years, the federal government virtually ignored primary and secondary education issues, preferring to let the states retain control of education issues. Some might argue that energy policies and global environmental issues are seldom addressed in a timely fashion. Historic water shortages across vast regions of the United States have not been addressed at the federal level.

Simply waiting for improved rainfall is easier than adjudicating water rights disputes between states. Clearly, there are numerous "third rail" issues but abortion is certainly one of the most volatile. Some abortion opponents might argue that the moral imperative for legislative action is greatest for abortion. Although not denying the moral dimension to abortion, other issues have great moral implications as well. Abortion is an important issue, but it is also an issue that could hold many hazards for legislators who choose to address it. Given that polite company avoids discussion of sex, religion, and politics, why do legislators go anywhere near an issue that intertwines attitudes on religion and politics, as well as sex?

We contend that the ambivalence that many citizens feel in regard to abortion creates an opportunity for legislators to address the abortion issue. Ambivalence creates some wiggle room for legislators. This wiggle room allows pro-choice or pro-life members of Congress to introduce and coordinate legislative proposals designed to achieve important policy outcomes that also have important political implications for these members. Thus, members can be entrepreneurial and win gains for all members of the pro-choice or pro-life position. Wawro (2000, 142) discusses how Henry Hyde (R-IL) was known for his successful entrepreneurial activities related to abortion. This wiggle room allows members to secure majority coalitions for their positions more readily.

Here, we discuss how a legislator could evaluate an abortion-related proposal. (The Appendix provides a more formal sketch of the argument in this section.) The legislator considers his own (perhaps induced) ideal policy preference on abortion and evaluates the distance between his own most preferred policy and any proposed policy. The distance between the legislator's most preferred policy and the proposed policy represents a utility loss to the legislator. Policy proposals that move policy toward the legislator's ideal point are evaluated favorably, but for a vote on any sort of salient issue like abortion, the legislator must also consider how he is going to explain his vote to his constituents. If the legislator cannot explain a vote, even if it is a vote that moves a salient policy toward the member's most preferred policy position, the legislator has to consider whether he can afford to vote in favor of the proposal.

There is a long list of scholars, starting with Warren Miller and Donald Stokes (1963), who have looked at the importance of explaining votes.[9]

---

[9] Other important work in the area includes Bianco (1994), Wilkerson (1990), Denzau, Riker, and Shepsle (1985), and Fenno (1978).

Denzau, Riker, and Shepsle (1985; DRS hereafter) make it clear that legislators have incentives to balance policy goals and the political consequences related to votes and vote explanation. For DRS, the question was why Democratic legislators had voted against a bill in the mid 1950s that would have extended federal aid for public school construction. The DRS answer is that some legislators felt that they would not be able to explain their votes, which would lead their constituents to penalize them.

Legislators also have to be sensitive to the concerns of constituent groups and their attitudes related to abortion policy. Sometimes the attitudes of these groups regarding abortion attitudes will look like an unorganized mess of signals. Arthur Bentley (1908), one of the earliest group scholars in the social sciences, suggested that unorganized interests can cry themselves into oblivion, but more recent interest group scholars, starting with David Truman, have understood the importance of both extant and potential groups. For Truman (1971), Lester Milbrath (1963), and a host of other scholars, interest groups aggregate and articulate individuals' concerns. Given this division in views about the roles of groups in aggregating and articulating individual preferences, two points deserve attention. First, the sum effect of communication across all groups may not sound articulate. Congressional districts are simply not comprised of individuals with homogeneous policy preferences for all issues, so the average cry across constituents' groups may mask a terribly discordant cacophony. Second, at the individual level, abortion attitudes are particularly noisy. There is poor articulation at the individual level in part because of the nuances inherent in the abortion debate and because of individual level ambivalence. Even individuals who identify themselves as being pro-choice or pro-life may not hold pure views of either position. Given these and other factors, there is often poor articulation of abortion positions at the group level, as evidenced by party shifts and other group shifts.

Legislators are aware of the average attitudes related to abortion policy among constituent groups as well as the homogeneity of their district. However, they are also aware of the cross pressures that individuals feel when they consider abortion issues. Legislators have a sense of the variance in constituent groups' attitudes. If the variance of those attitudes is near to zero, the legislator has to line up policies and votes in accord with those homogeneous group attitudes. Legislators who fail in this regard cannot explain their votes because there is no group within the district that would understand or accept any deviation from the widely held position. No group provides any political cover. Legislators who fail to line up their votes with widely held attitudes in their district will certainly invite electoral challenges, and some of these challenges may even be encouraged by the groups who felt slighted.

Suppose, however, that district attitudes about abortion policy are heterogeneous – that there is a large variance in group attitudes. When the variance is large, legislators have a greater opportunity to explain their votes. If we consider how the legislator may calculate utility loss more expansively, we could imagine legislators considering both their own policy preferences as well as the reactions of the groups in their districts. As was the case before, if the variance of group attitudes is zero, the only way to minimize utility loss is to line up legislative positions with the position of the interest groups in the district. However, if the variance in group attitudes is positive, legislators have greater leeway because increased group variance eases vote explanation. Legislators can both play groups off one another and play explanations and rationales off one another. Considered narrowly, policies further from the average position of the member's constituent groups may appear problematic. However, as we envision legislators' decision making, they can trade off the utility gains (losses) tied to their own policy goals with losses (gains) tied to reactions from groups in the district. In short, legislators consider their own policy goals and the ease of vote explanation for their stated policy positions. When the variance of constituents' group signals is positive, legislators have more leeway, and the trade-offs between policy gains and vote explanation become explicit.[10]

Some have argued that the "Gallup poll continues to underscore how difficult it would be for policymakers to reach any compromise about the abortion decision" (O'Connor 1996, 133). We interpret the same Gallup information and see room to legislate because there is considerable variance in constituents' groups' signals. This variance operates both across the group levels and within particular groups because, as Huckfeldt and Sprague (2000) and Alvarez and Brehm (1995) argue, the same attitude toward abortion may be held by several different people for several different reasons. Variance in constituent signals can work at the group level or at the individual level, and that variance provides legislators with leeway. Bianco's (1994, 33) interpretation of DRS is informative:

DRS argue that formal models cannot assume that legislators are motivated solely by preferences across outcomes. Rather, they say, scholars must assume

---

[10] Weighting the groups by their sizes would not affect the general operation of this frame-work, though the mathematical representation would be more complicated.

that legislators hold preferences across actions that take into account both the political and the policy consequences of their behavior.

For legislators, policy consequences and district-based political consequences are both important.[11]

Concerns about policy impact and symbolism is increasingly complicated by the fact that the incidence of abortion rates varies considerably by demographic group (Stein 2008), and there is little reason to think that legislators view all demographic groups equally. It has been long accepted that some constituents receive greater attention than others (e.g., Fenno 1978), some demographic groups vote and participate more than others, and some are more conservative (liberal) than others (e.g., Leighley 2001). Although abortion rates in 2004 were at their lowest level since *Roe*, the rates across various demographic groups varied considerably. For women between fifteen and forty-four years old, approximately twenty women per thousand secure abortion services, but the rates for those under twenty are much lower than for those in their twenties.[12] Fifty-seven percent of all abortions in 2004 were obtained by women in their twenties. For those younger than 20 years old, the proportion of abortions performed dropped from 33 percent in 1974 to 17 percent in 2004. Clearly, the impact of any abortion policy is partly determined by who is securing abortions, and the demographics of the groups securing abortions are shifting. Changes are also apparent across racial groups. Women of color are three to five times as likely to secure an abortion as their white counterparts, and the rate of repeat abortions has increased (Zernike 2003). Although poverty remains a common denominator, abortion policy and its symbolic impact remain moving targets, affecting different ages and races in very distinct ways.

CONCLUSION

How does this all play out for legislators? If legislators can explain their abortion votes to the constituents who matter the most for electoral successes, then legislators will contemplate policy change. The ease of

---

[11] Jonathon Woon's work (2008) explores the willingness of bill sponsors to moderate their proposals when they have positions within the chamber that might actually allow them to see the proposal adopted. That is, as the opportunities to pass legislation increase, legislators recalibrate their policy versus electoral considerations district scale.

[12] For example, see the Centers for Disease Control and Prevention (CDC) data: http://www.cdc.gov/mmwr/preview/mmwrhtml/ss5713a1.htm?s_cid=ss5713a1_e.

vote explanation distinguishes abortion from other third rail issues. The great American poet Robert Frost said that home is where, if you have to go, they have to take you in.[13] For legislators, it is a little different. Your home district is where you have to go, but they don't have to take you in, and they don't have to send you back to Washington, D.C. For legislators in their home districts, it is best to have a vote explanation at hand.

Understanding the abortion issue and abortion politics requires moving beyond the media-hyped images of staunchly pro-life protesters blocking entrances to abortion clinics while being countered and assailed by firmly pro-choice rebuttals. For some, the abortion issue is indeed a rather simple one. Maybe the authors of the book you are reading are complicating something simple rather than simplifying something complicated. Indeed, political scientist Elizabeth Oldmixon states that "constituents know what they want, and they know what they are getting in a legislator ... This should be particularly true with regard to abortion, which has been a component of the annual rhythm of the legislative process for decades" (Oldmixon 2005, 26).

We are less steadfast than Oldmixon, and we do not think we are alone. Public opinion data belies the argument that anything related to abortion is simple and straightforward. Public opinion research clearly demonstrates that the majority of Americans situate themselves in neither of these extreme camps. To the extent that policy is driven by or reflective of public opinion, then, it should come as no surprise that abortion-related policies have often traversed a middle ground of compromise positions on abortion rights. The middle ground, however, is itself shifting when one considers the individual level attitudes. The ambivalence at the individual level creates opportunity for greater legislative involvement in an issue area that has many of the hallmarks of an issue to be avoided. In many ways, we may not know what we want, and that very ambivalence creates leeway for legislative action. In addition, the existing research demonstrates that, to understand abortion as a moral and political issue, it is necessary to acknowledge the underlying core beliefs that influence many people's views on abortion. These beliefs serve to connect the abortion topic to many other controversial and challenging issues – including gay rights, stem cell research, gender equality, and religious freedom – each of which can affect the politics of abortion.

[13] Interested readers can find "The Death of the Hired Man" by Robert Frost.

APPENDIX 3.1

For some readers familiar with spatial models, the discussion in the "Targeting Public Opinion" section of this chapter can be clarified with a slightly more rigorous framework. For those readers new to spatial modeling, there may still be value in the discussion presented here.

Consider a one-dimensional policy space along the x-axis of an x-y coordinate system. Legislators have preferences over the policy space. Utility is represented along the y-axis. Any given legislator considers his own (perhaps induced) ideal point, represented as x_i, and evaluates the distance between x_i and a policy proposal represented as x_p. We use a quadratic loss function, such as $-(x_i - x_p)^2$, to represent a legislator's utility function. The legislator's utility function allows her to evaluate the utility derived from various policy proposals. The legislator simply wants to minimize policy losses. Those proposals that are close to her ideal point yield greater utility than those policy proposals further from her ideal point.

Of course, we have argued that legislators are also sensitive to group reactions in their home districts. For a vote on any sort of salient issue, the legislator must consider how she is going to explain her vote to her constituents. If a legislator cannot explain a vote on a policy proposal, even if the proposal is close to her ideal point, then she has to consider whether she can afford to vote in favor of the proposal. To represent constituent groups' concerns about policy, we use x_G to indicate the *average* of groups' concerns or attitudes related to abortion policy. What do legislators know about x_G? Sometimes abortion attitudes look like an unorganized mess of signals. Sometimes abortion attitudes send a much clearer signal. Interest groups aggregate and articulate individuals' concerns, but these processes are imperfect and average opinion may not represent any particular group well (Ainsworth 2002).

Legislators are aware of x_G, and they also have a sense the variance in x_G. If the variance of x_G is near to zero, the legislator has to line up policies and votes with x_G because there is tremendous clarity in group signals. Legislators who fail in this regard cannot explain their votes because there is no group that would understand or accept deviation from x_G. Suppose, however, that x_G has a large variance. Are legislators any better off if they line up votes and policies with x_G when the variance of x_G is large? When the variance is large, legislators have a greater opportunity to explain their votes. Consider an extension of our original quadratic loss function $-(x_i - x_p)^2$. Legislators now consider their own ideal point as well as group demands in their districts. The new utility function becomes $-(x_i - x_p)^2 + k(\sigma^2 - (x_G - x_p)^2)$, where k is a positive scaling factor and σ^2 represents the variance of x_G. Suppose the variance of x_G is zero; the only way to minimize the second term is to line x_p up with x_G. If the variance of x_G is positive, legislators have greater leeway because increased group variance eases vote explanation. When there is greater variance in x_G, legislators' votes are less likely to be viewed as beyond the pale. The only reasons for a legislator not to line up x_i and x_p are tied to group reactions in the home district. Can the legislator explain the vote? The only reasons for a legislator not to line up x_G and x_p are tied to her own personal preferences reflected in x_i. Can the legislator live with a vote for x_p? Considered narrowly, policies further from x_G may appear problematic, but as we envision legislators' decision making, legislators can trade off gains (losses) from the first term with losses (gains) from the second. The first term represents policy goals and the second term represents the ease of vote explanation for policy x_p given groups' responses to x_p as represented by x_G. When the variance of constituents' group signals is positive, legislators have more leeway and the trade-offs between policy gains and vote explanation become explicit.

TABLE A3.2. *Multiple Sponsors of Abortion Legislation, 93rd–108th Congresses*

Congress	Member Name	Party	Bills Sponsored	Bill Amendments Sponsored	Constitutional Amendments Sponsored	Incremental Legislation	Pro-Life	Pro-Choice
93	William Whitehurst	Rep	11	0	8	3	11	0
93	Harold Froehlich	Rep	11	0	0	11	11	0
93	Margaret Heckler	Rep	8	0	0	8	8	0
93	Angelo Roncallo	Rep	14	0	3	11	14	0
94	James Oberstar	Dem	12	0	12	0	12	0
94	William Whitehurst	Rep	6	0	5	1	6	0
94	Romano Mazzoli	Dem	4	0	4	0	4	0
95	James Oberstar	Dem	10	0	6	4	10	0
95	Henry Hyde	Rep	6	0	6	0	6	0
95	William Whitehurst	Rep	4	0	4	0	4	0
95	Clement Zablocki	Dem	3	0	1	2	3	0
96	Jamie Witten	Dem	7	0	0	7	7	0
96	Romano Mazzoli	Dem	3	0	3	0	3	0
97	John Ashbrook	Rep	3	2	2	3	5	0
97	Philip Crane	Rep	3	0	0	3	3	0
97	Romano Mazzoli	Dem	3	0	2	1	3	0
97	Henry Waxman	Dem	3	0	0	3	0	3
97	Jamie Witten	Dem	3	0	0	3	3	0

(continued)

TABLE A3.2 *(continued)*

Congress	Member Name	Party	Bills Sponsored	Bill Amendments Sponsored	Constitutional Amendments Sponsored	Incremental Legislation	Pro-Life	Pro-Choice
98	Christopher Smith	Rep	1	3	1	3	3	1
98	Dante Fascell	Dem	3	0	0	3	0	3
98	Philip Crane	Rep	3	0	0	3	3	0
99	Robert Dornan	Rep	3	1	0	2	3	0
100	Robert Dornan	Rep	9	0	2	7	9	0
101	Robert Dornan	Rep	10	1	2	9	11	0
101	Julian Dixon	Dem	3	0	0	3	3	0
101	Dante Fascell	Dem	3	0	0	3	3	0
101	William Natcher	Dem	3	0	0	3	3	0
102	Henry Waxman	Dem	6	0	0	6	0	6
102	Julian Dixon	Dem	4	0	0	4	4	0
102	Ron Wyden	Dem	3	0	0	3	0	3
102	Robert Dornan	Rep	3	0	1	2	3	0
102	William Natcher	Dem	3	0	0	3	3	0
102	Christopher Smith	Rep	2	1	0	3	3	0
103	Ron Dellums	Dem	3	0	0	3	2	1
103	Robert Dornan	Rep	3	0	2	1	3	0
103	David Obey	Dem	3	0	0	3	2	1
104	Robert Dornan	Rep	6	0	2	4	6	0
104	James Walsh	Rep	4	0	0	4	4	0
104	Sonny Callahan	Rep	3	0	0	3	3	0
104	Steny Hoyer	Dem	1	2	0	3	1	2
104	John Kasich	Rep	3	0	0	3	3	0

104	Patricia Schroeder	Dem	3	0	2	1	0	3
104	Christopher Smith	Rep	4	0	0	4	4	0
105	Christopher Smith	Rep	3	2	0	5	5	0
105	Benjamin Gilman	Rep	3	1	0	3	3	0
105	Sue Myrick	Rep	3	0	0	3	3	0
105	Nina Lowey	Dem	2	1	0	3	0	3
106	Ernest Istook	Rep	6	0	0	6	6	0
106	Tom Coburn	Rep	3	2	0	5	5	0
106	Christopher Smith	Rep	4	1	0	5	5	0
106	Sonny Callahan	Rep	4	0	0	4	4	0
106	Jim Kolbe	Rep	4	0	0	4	4	0
106	Ron Paul	Rep	2	2	0	4	4	0
106	Bill Young	Rep	3	0	0	3	3	0
106	Charles Canady	Rep	2	1	0	3	3	0
106	John Edward Porter	Rep	3	0	0	3	3	0
106	Harold Rogers	Rep	3	0	0	3	3	0
107	Loretta Sanchez	Dem	2	2	0	4	0	4
107	Sue Myrick	Rep	3	0	2	3	3	0
108	Duncan Hunter	Rep	3	0	0	3	3	0
108	Ron Paul	Rep	3	0	0	3	3	0
108	Ralph Regula	Rep	3	0	0	3	3	0
108	Frank Wolf	Rep	3	0	0	3	3	0

4

A Short Legislative History of Abortion

> The "very purpose of a Bill of Rights was to withdraw certain subjects from the vicissitudes of political controversy, to place them beyond the reach of majorities and officials and to establish them as legal principles ... One's right to life, liberty, and property, to free speech, a free press, freedom of worship and assembly, and other fundamental rights may not be submitted to vote; they depend on the outcome of no elections." (Justice Robert Jackson, West Virginia State Board of Education v. Barnette, 319 U.S. 624, 638 (1943))

COURTS AND THE IDEA OF LEGISLATING ABORTION POLICY

It has long been argued that the courts are best suited to handle issues revolving around values – certainly better suited than legislatures. The prominent legal scholar John Hart Ely quotes Harry Wellington at length. "'If a society were to design an institution which had the job of finding the society's set of moral principles and determining how they bear in concrete situations, that institution would be sharply different from one charged with proposing policies ... It would provide an environment conducive to rumination, reflection, and analysis'" (Ely 1980, 56).

Ely himself is much less sanguine about the ability of judges and courts to discover or protect key guiding principles. The notion that the "judiciary has done a better job of speaking for our moral selves" rests upon "historically shaky" grounds (Ely 1980, 57). For Ely, preserving and reinforcing "representation functions" in the polity are fundamental court obligations (see, e.g., 1980, Chapter 4), but values or moral judgments

Jessica Taverna served as a co-author for this chapter.

are better left to legislative bodies (cf. Perry 1982). As long as courts ensure a wide array of free and fair election procedures, Ely feels that legislators are best capable of making policy – even those policies heavily weighted with moral judgments.

Advocates on each side of the abortion issue have used both courts and legislatures at the state and national levels to pursue their goals. In 1963, every state forbade abortion under most circumstances. By 1973 *legislatures* in Hawaii, New York, Alaska, and Washington had passed legislation creating greater access to abortion services (Graber 1996, 64). At about the same time, *courts* in California, Georgia, Texas, Florida, Connecticut, Vermont, New Jersey, Illinois, Wisconsin, Kansas, and the District of Columbia took steps to ensure greater access to abortion services. In his study of the U.S. Supreme Court, Gerald Rosenberg (1991) argued that the Court follows trends that are already clearly established within the society writ large. In Rosenberg's view, in its *Roe* decision, the Supreme Court simply affirmed a trend already underway at the state level. Mark Graber (1996), viewing the same state trends, argued that capricious enforcement of abortion laws across the states and even within the states forced the Supreme Court to strike state laws with its *Roe* decision because of equal protection issues. That is, abortion laws at the state level were never fairly administered and at times were unmanageable. The law on the books – "[b]lackletter law" – versus the law as enforced looked very different (Graber 1996, 18). Simply viewing the wording of a statute may or may not belie actual practices, especially at the state level. Graber argued that substantive due process demanded a clarification of rights and a clearer means of administration from the federal level.

Early in the abortion battles, pro-choice advocates relied heavily on the courts to preserve access. The "commitment to litigation, at bottom, is probably best explained by the widely held belief … that persons with just causes eventually triumph in the judiciary" (Graber 1996, 122–123). By the late 1980s and 1990s, pro-choice advocates were less enamored of the litigious approach to protecting abortion access. Courts might strike down various laws, but they proved to be less willing (and less able) to mandate actions to ensure access. In addition, the U.S. Supreme Court was becoming decidedly more conservative, with more and more judges questioning the reasonableness of *Roe* and welcoming limitations on *Roe*. Whether one feels that "fundamental human liberties" should not be subject "to the vagaries of electoral or legislative processes" (Graber 1996, 123) likely depends on the composition of the courts and legislatures at the time. Perhaps sound reasoning and the application of moral principles on the courts would trump mercurial electoral attitudes and poorly designed legislative attempts to broaden access to abortion services. Conversely, sound reasoning and the application of moral principles on the courts might trump mercurial electoral attitudes and poorly designed legislative attempts to limit access to abortion services.

Presuming that the courts' role and position somehow trump the legislatures' stems from two lines of faulty reasoning (cf. Graber 1996). The first "fundamental error" detailed by Ely (1980, 57) is assuming that "there is something called 'the law' whose shape good lawyers will describe identically." With apologies to Ernest Hemingway, "it is pretty to think so," but there may be no thing recognized as "the law." The behaviors of some activists in the abortion debate suggest that they too are apprehensive of some courts' interpretations of "the law." Any incidence of venue shopping indicates that some advocates do not view all courts equally. In its attempt to undo Oklahoma regulations requiring women to receive an ultrasound and for a physician or technician to "'provide a simultaneous explanation of what the ultrasound is depicting,'" the Center for Reproductive Rights opted to remain in Oklahoma's state courts and bypass the federal U.S. Court of Appeals for the 8th Circuit (Bazelon 2008). The Center for Reproductive Rights felt that the Oklahoma state courts offered greater protections than the federal courts. Ten, twenty, or thirty years ago, the Center would almost certainly have pursued the case in the federal court system.

The second fundamental error is to presume that every legislative effort necessarily alters individuals' basic liberties. That is, every statute is presumed to be a superstatute that establishes a new normative framework for understanding state policy and individual rights. Indeed, a superstatute often has implications "beyond the four corners of its plain meaning" (Eskridge and Ferejohn 2001, 1216) but what about the bulk of legislative statutes? The bulk of legislative statutes are rather mundane affairs with limited impact on policy outcomes. Most proposals make incremental, not fundamental, shifts in policy. Just as an overly romantic view of the law and legal interpretation is unwise, an overly fretful view of legislative bodies is unwarranted because few legislative proposals are superstatutes. Indeed, to limit opportunities for judicial review, a legislature might purposefully avoid sweeping statutes. Pro-choice advocates might reasonably argue that the incremental legislative proposals examined in this book do alter women's rights. Indeed, incremental efforts may have a cumulative effect, but we are making a comparative claim. Compared to the U.S. Supreme Court, has the U.S. Congress been more or less protective of women's rights? Compared to the Supreme Court, has the U.S. Congress been more or less attentive to the concerns of pro-life advocates or pro-choice advocates?

THE EVOLUTION OF THE U.S. HOUSE
OF REPRESENTATIVES AND ABORTION POLITICS

The backdrop for abortion policy is incredibly complex (e.g., Critchlow 2001) and much of that complexity is reflected in the U.S. House. As noted by John Aldrich and David Rhode (2001), the U.S. House has changed dramatically during the period we are studying. Specifically, Aldrich and Rhode note that, prior to the 1980s, the sorting of ideologies and political parties was blurred. The Democratic Party had Southern Democrats who were far more conservative than many Republicans and the Republican Party contained Northeastern Republicans who were more liberal than some Democrats. The inability to sort members by ideology and partisanship meant that many House members had to act independent of their party to get elected and reelected. Party, as a brand name label, was weak.

Using data on the ideology of members of Congress (DW-NOMINATE Scores), Aldrich and Rhode show that, in the 91st Congress, there were Democrats in each decile of the ideological spectrum. Although a large percentage of Democrats were on the liberal end of the spectrum, a sizable fraction of the party was in the most conservative four deciles. By the 105th Congress, there were no Democrats in the conservative deciles and only a small fraction of Republicans (less than 5 percent) were in a liberal decile. The primary electorates of each party have come to resemble their general election electorates as each party has become more ideologically homogenous.

More effective ideological sorting has allowed the leadership of the majority party in the House to exert more control over the chamber and over their rank and file members (Finocchiaro and Rohde 2008). The House leaders have become more powerful because the ideological opinions in their caucuses have become more homogeneous and the divisions between the parties have become more stark. The preference congruence within each party and the growth in the ideological distance between the parties has created conditions whereby party leaders have been given more power to govern the House. The abortion debate discussed in this book has occurred during the transition from a House with parties that were not ideologically homogenous – the House that David Mayhew wrote about in *The Electoral Connection*, where members were "on their own" when trying to get reelected – to one where parties have become much more powerful and important to the operations of the chamber and the management of congressional elections. In addition, there is evidence that candidates who win on their own electorally remain independent as they legislate (Collie 1989). When eyeballing the table in the Appendix to Chapter 3, we do see some sorting of the most active members involved in the abortion debate. In the early Congresses, Democrats and Republicans were both quite active on the pro-life side of the debate. In the most recent Congresses, Republicans are the most active pro-life members, and Democrats are the most active pro-choice members. That being said, the recent efforts of Rep. Bart Stupak (D-MI) to ensure that the health insurance reform legislation did not allow for abortion funding illustrates that, even in a changed congressional environment, some Democratic members still play a critically important role on the pro-life side of this debate. Lawrence Evans (2001, 217) argues that legislators sometimes address an issue "to neutralize it as a partisan campaign issue."

THE EFFECT OF ABORTION ON OTHER ISSUES

However one feels about the roles of courts and legislatures, it is clear that legislatures do affect abortion policy. There is one other critique of the mixing of legislatures and abortion policy, which we address in this section. Some scholars have argued that abortion-related legislative proposals clog the legislative system and prevent Congress from addressing other important issues. That is, legislative stalemates and legislative gridlock may emanate from a calendar clogged with abortion-related proposals. Does abortion so dominate the legislative agenda during some Congresses that it forces other issues off the agenda? Single-issue politics has been criticized for skewing electoral results, but it may also affect legislative output. Ronald Dworkin has argued that abortion politics drives other economic and social issues from the legislative agenda.[1] Do the shouts associated with single-issue advocates create negative externalities for the legislative agenda? Dworkin has argued that "the sudden

---

[1] Dworkin is not alone in these sentiments, but he was one of the more prominent scholars in the public view to make such claims. Dworkin's extended discussion on abortion highlights other aspects of the abortion debate, and it does not repeat the claim that the abortion debate prevents Congress from addressing other important issues (1993). See Graber (1996) for more details on Dworkin's claims about the connections between legislative productivity and abortion debates.

dominance of the abortion issue" has "driven crucial economic and social issues from the political agenda" (Graber 1996, 28).

There is reason to believe that abortion might constrain the legislative agenda because there is some evidence that more interests and more groups lead to less clout (Gray and Lowery 1995; Salisbury 1990). Imagine the agenda becoming more crowded and the trade-offs and compromises more complex as there are more and more interests. On the other hand, abortion could be just one more interest within a system that promotes all interests and limits none (see, e.g., Lowi 1969). Decisions may be balkanized to such an extent that one interest seldom contends directly with any other interests. Committee systems and legislative norms of behavior reinforce a live and let live system in many policy areas, and abortion policy may be no different. Finally, abortion may crowd the legislative agenda if abortion proposals create a contagion effect, with one abortion proposal leading to numerous other abortion proposals. Whether or under what circumstances majority party leaders would allow each side in the debates to offer proposals or amendments remains to be determined.

Although we are not well positioned to address the political agenda in the broadest sense, we can address whether the overall agenda in the U.S. House of Representatives is affected by abortion politics. A wide range of scholars and practitioners are concerned about the potential effects of abortion on the legislative agenda, including political scientist Elizabeth Oldmixon. In a recent study, she interviewed a wide range of members and staffers on Capitol Hill about abortion policy. Oldmixon records a Republican legislative director saying that "'[Y]ou have some conservative members that are just zealots ... it's often easier for [Majority Leader Tom] Delay ... to just schedule a vote'" (Oldmixon 2005, 167–168). A Republican legislator interviewed by Oldmixon admitted that "'We used to have umpteen votes on abortion ... in '95, '96, ... family planning issues, Mexico City policy – you name ... [it].... [T]he leadership has been trying to ... limit the number of votes. Let's decide these are the critical abortion issues'" and avoid the rest (Oldmixon 2005, 168). Oldmixon's interview data from Republican operatives on the Hill seems to corroborate Dworkin's concerns.

We address the legislative agenda issue from a different angle. Our data on abortion-related proposals spans three decades. During this same period, many political scientists have studied legislative gridlock and legislative workload issues. One group of scholars (Howell, Adler, Cameron, and Reimann, 2000, HACR hereafter) assesses legislative workloads during all but the last couple of Congresses that we evaluate. HACR provide four measures of legislative workload. First, they use a measure drawn from David Mayhew's classic study (1991) of landmark legislative enactments. Numerous scholars have built from Mayhew's original set of landmark enactments as well as his methodology for determining whether a legislative enactment qualifies as being landmark (e.g., Binder 2003). Second, HACR develop a measure that includes the major enactments that secured significant print media coverage. Third, they use a measure from records of ordinary enactments, including all other enactments noted in *Congressional Quarterly* summaries of a Congress. Fourth, HACR measured all minor enactments, including commemorative legislation.

In Table 4.1, we use HACR's four measures as dependent variables in a set of simple bivariate regressions to assess the effect of different measures of abortion-related activity on workload in the House. In this analysis, we are trying to determine – in a simple way – how abortion affected workloads in Congress during these eleven Congresses. In the top half of Table 4.1, we examine whether the total number of pro-life proposals affects legislative workloads and in, the bottom half of the Table 4.1, we examine whether the total number of abortion-related proposals addressed on the House floor affects workloads. The last two columns in Table 4.1 display the results from the HACR measures after those measures are corrected for the increased of omnibus legislation.

With only eleven Congresses to assess, one must be careful about over-interpreting the results in Table 4.1. That said, when looking at the number of pro-life abortion-related proposals sponsored in a Congress and each of the four workload measures, the correlations are always positive. For the Major Enactments, the effect of the number of pro-life proposals is readily significant and positive. An increase in the number of pro-life abortion-related proposals correlates with *more* major enactments. Indeed, for the Landmark Enactments, Corrected Major Enactments, and Minor Enactments, the effect of the number of pro-life proposals is very close to traditional one-tailed measures for significance. The results in the top half of Table 4.1 make it hard to accept the notion that pro-life proposals stymied legislative activity.[2] Although only eleven Congresses are evaluated, the results suggest that more legislatively active Congresses are more active across many issues – including abortion.

---

[2] Some readers will no doubt argue that we should have used some sort of count regression model rather than ordinary least squares. Count models, including Poisson and negative binomial regressions, are well suited for nonnegative integer-valued dependent variables. We avoid count models at this juncture to facilitate an easier interpretation of the coefficients. Negative binomial regressions yielded the same general results, with no evidence of over- or under-dispersion.

TABLE 4.1. *OLS Regression Results for Legislative Workload and Abortion-Related Proposals, 93rd–103rd Congresses*

	Dependent Variable Representing Types of Legislative Enactments					
	Landmark Enactments	Major Enactments	Other Enactments	Minor Enactments	Corrected Landmark Enactments	Corrected Major Enactments
No. of pro-life proposals	.07* (.05)	.21** (.07)	.70* (.43)	2.12 (3.00)	.49 (.73)	1.74* (1.04)
Constant	5.14 (2.55)	1.59 (3.94)	29.27 (23.49)	375.45 (163.11)	91.13 (39.99)	70.73 (56.35)
	Adj R^2 = .13	Adj R^2 = .42	Adj R^2 = .14	Adj R^2 = .	Adj R^2 = .	Adj R^2 = .15
No. of abortion-related proposals addressed on the House floor	-.25** (.11)	-.38* (.23)	-1.91* (1.11)	-4.22 (7.91)	-.68 (1.95)	-3.56 (2.86)
Constant	11.95 (1.45)	16.92 (3.03)	87.89 (14.67)	534.76 (104.53)	124.45 (25.78)	202.41 (37.78)
	Adj R^2 = .30	Adj R^2 = .15	Adj R^2 = .16	Adj R^2 = .	Adj R^2 = .	Adj R^2 = .05

Each cell contains coefficients and standard errors. *$p < .15$; **$p < .05$

The bottom half of Table 4.1 uses a different measure of abortion-related proposals. In the bottom half, we measure the number of abortion-related proposals that received attention on the floor of the House. Sponsorship of proposals may be driven by very different factors that are largely unrelated to floor activity (Schiller 1995; cf. Woon 2008). The results in the bottom half of Table 4.1 indicate a negative relationship between abortion activity on the floor and workload measures; all coefficients are now negative rather than positive. This means that, as the number of abortion-related proposals addressed on the House floor increases, the number of enactments decreases. For Landmark Enactments, the negative coefficient is statistically significant. For Major Enactments and Other Enactments, the abortion variable is very close to traditional levels of significance for one-tailed tests. Statistical significance, however, does falter when we use the workload measures corrected for omnibus legislation, as noted in the last two columns in Table 4.1.

One's interpretation of Dworkin's claims – that abortion politics drives other issues from the legislative agenda – partly depends on how one views abortion-related proposals in the U.S. House. The total number of sponsored proposals generally has a *positive* impact on most measures of legislative productivity. Whether one examines Mayhew's measures of landmark legislation or other measures commonly used, it appears as though more abortion-related proposals are correlated with more measures passed in a Congress. If one uses the same dependent variables but examines the impact of abortion-related proposals that are addressed on the floor of the House, the outcome is reversed. As more abortion-related proposals are addressed on the floor, there are fewer landmark enactments.

What is the true story: the top half or the bottom half of Table 4.1? The results are mixed. Although twenty-two years are covered, our data are organized by Congress, leaving us with only eleven observations. That said, the effects from the sponsorship of abortion-related proposals seem to be very different than the effect of abortion-related proposals addressed on the House floor. One interpretation of the results in Table 4.1 is that abortion activity is driven entirely by clever incremental advances that are attached to a wide variety of bills. That is, abortion may not supplant other issues; abortion may invade and color other issues. Indeed, Chapter 6 on referrals addresses this issue directly.

A slightly different interpretation of the negative coefficients in the bottom half of Table 4.1 requires a slight digression. Some types of issues may be hard to address whenever abortion amendments are ready to be attached. Abortion-related activity might loom over some legislative

proposals, acting akin to killer amendments or fundamental game chang-
ers in the legislative process. A brief discussion of killer amendments
might help clarify this interpretation. Several scholars have explored killer
amendments, but the single most famous killer amendment in the political
science literature is Adam Clayton Powell's amendment to a 1956 school
aid proposal in the U.S. House.[3] Powell, a Harlem Democrat, argued that
only those districts abiding by the Supreme Court's *Brown v. Board of
Education* decision should be granted federal school aid. Powell's amendment split the Northern and Southern legislators in the Democratic Party
and led to the ultimate defeat of the school aid proposal. The question
relevant here is why Powell pursued his amendment knowing it would
kill the bill.[4] The late William H. Riker studied the amendment more
closely than anyone (e.g., DRS 1985; Riker 1986). Riker argued that
Powell's amendment was aimed at the leadership of the Democratic Party.
Amendments akin to Powell's could be offered to any piece of legislation
that affected the distribution of federal largesse. Districts that failed to
abide by *Brown v. Board of Education* could lose all types of federal aid.
Powell sought to alter fundamentally the direction of the Democratic
Party leadership – moving it clearly away from Southern Democrats.[5]

Fast forward for a moment. Could abortion-related issues permeate so
many different proposals? As we will discuss here and in later chapters,
abortion-related issues were addressed by many committees, including the
Appropriations Committee – which of course plays a prominent role in the
distribution of federal largesse. Party leaders seldom whip – that is, actively
seek the votes of members – on the abortion issue. Generally, party leaders
simply let members vote as dictated by their conscience. There are times,
however, when abortion becomes problematic for party leaders. Abortion
riders may kill or weaken any number of legislative proposals. Party leaders do engage in whipping to gather information related to whether or
not an abortion rider might kill a proposal that is much broader in scope
than abortion policy (Oldmixon 2005, 172–177). For example, in 2002,
Senators Patty Murray (D-WA) and Olympia Snowe (R-ME) sought to lift

---

[3] Wilkerson (1999) and Krehbiel and Rivers (1990) argue that there are few opportunities
for, and fewer instances of, sophisticated voting, which is necessary for a killer amendment to undo a legislative proposal.

[4] Numerous party leaders warned the Democrats that a vote for the Powell amendment
would doom the school aid proposal. Indeed, Representative Richard Bolling (D-MO)
secured a statement from former President Truman warning Democrats in the House that
Powell's amendment would quite simply kill federal school aid.

[5] With Barack Obama currently in the White House, some younger readers might unwit-
tingly underestimate the extent to which Southern Democrats in the 1950s and 1960s
sought to protect segregationist policies.

the ban on access to abortion services at military bases. Murray and Snowe were particularly concerned about the approximately 100,000 women living on military bases overseas. The question was whether those women could use their own, private funds to secure abortion services on a military base. Snowe stated bluntly, "constitutional rights are not territorial" (Dewar 2002, A5). Opponents noted that taxpayer funds would still be used for basic services and physical plant facilities tied to the abortion. Regardless of how one feels about that narrow aspect of the abortion debate, the Murray–Snowe proposal illustrates how abortion-related proposals, whether pro-life or pro-choice, can be tied to a broad range of legislative proposals. Senator Sam Brownback (R-KS), a staunch antiabortion advocate, stated that the Murray–Snowe tactics held "America's armed services hostage to abortion politics" (Dewar, 2002, A5).

Consider the following media headlines:

- "Politics of Abortion Delays $15 Billion to Fight Global AIDS,"
- "Abortion Issue Stalls U.N. Family Planning Funds,"
- "Abortion Deadlock Stalls D.C. Funding,"
- "House Health Bill Scuttled by Abortion Rider," or
- "Bankruptcy Bill, Caught in Abortion Dispute, Dies in Congress."[6]

In the first instance, abortion affected attempts to address one of the deadliest epidemics of the last fifty years. In the second, abortion derailed legislation addressing family planning services in foreign nations. The third headline appeared when Congress could not resolve basic funding issues for the District of Columbia. The fourth headline occurred when abortion stymied legislation funding health clinics that played no direct role in abortion services. The fifth instance occurred when an abortion amendment killed legislation that would have tightened bankruptcy standards. Abortion does indeed permeate a wide range of legislative proposals. Sometimes pro-life advocates use other issues to leverage advantages on the abortion issue, and sometimes pro-choice advocates do the same.

THE RANGE OF ABORTION-RELATED PROPOSALS

Incremental Efforts

In the previous section, we found that the evidence of abortion-related proposals affecting the legislative agenda is mixed. In this section,

---

[6] These headlines are taken from, respectively, Stolberg 2003a; Eilperin 2002; Pianin and Phillips 1988; Eilperin 2001, and Shenon 2002.

we explore a wide range of proposals that addressed abortion policy. Although we have argued that incremental proposals are more easily passed than nonincremental proposals, not all incremental efforts to alter abortion policy were successful. Incremental efforts to change abortion policy have come in many guises and met varied success. The ability of abortion to permeate a wide range of proposals is seen both in the development of new agencies and programs as well as in the regular authorization and appropriations procedures for existing programs and agencies. Consider, for instance, one of the earliest incremental efforts in our dataset. When it was created as a stand-alone agency in 1974, the Legal Services Corporation was forbidden from taking on abortion litigation (Public Law 93–1039). Abortion was unlikely to consume much attention from the Legal Services Corporation in any event but, as the statute was written, any attention to abortion was precluded. This Legal Services legislation did not fundamentally alter abortion policy, but it did affect it. Virtually any new program or agency or any reauthorized program is vulnerable to some sort of abortion-related language. For existing programs and agencies, the appropriations process has also allowed the abortion debate to enter into many diverse policy areas.

Hyde Amendments

In 1974, amendments were offered in both the House and the Senate to the Labor and the Health, Education, and Welfare (HEW) appropriations bills as well as other agencies' appropriation bills that would have "prohibited the use of any funds in the bill to perform abortions or to encourage the performance of abortions except to save the life of the mother" (*CQ Almanac* 1974, 106).[7] The House amendment was defeated, but the Senate amendment passed. In conference committee, the Senate amendment was deleted. The House did pass an abortion-limiting amendment on the floor during consideration of the reauthorization of the Economic Opportunity Act (EOA). Much like the Labor–HEW amendment, the EOA amendment would have barred program funds to be used for abortions or supplies for abortions. Again, the amendment died in conference.

---

[7] This legislation became known as the Hyde amendment, after the late Henry Hyde (R-IL) who served in the U.S. House from 1975 to 2007. Hyde Amendment restrictions on Medicaid funding did not affect all states evenly because states already had considerable flexibility in their implementation of Medicaid programs and services, and some states did not offer abortion services through Medicaid.

In 1976, House members were finally successful in attaching an amendment to the Labor–HEW appropriations bill that banned the use of funds in the bill to pay for or promote abortions (CQ *Almanac* 1976, 790). Although the amendment was deleted from the bill in the Senate, the House voted to insist upon their position when the bill was being considered in conference. The argument made by members supportive of the amendment was simple: Regardless of whether you support or oppose access to abortion services, taxpayers should not fund the actual practice. The conference committee did choose to alter the language of the amendment to provide for specific exceptions when federally funded abortions would be permissible. Each chamber assented to the new language, and the legislation became law when Congress overrode President Ford's veto, which was based on the high cost of the overall bill, not the abortion language.

The 1977 debate over the Labor–HEW appropriations bill had a similar dynamic as the 1976 debate and a similar outcome. Although the dynamic for 1977 was not unique, two excerpts from *Congressional Quarterly's* coverage of the issue deserve consideration, as they point to the strategic efforts of abortion opponents in the legislative realm. First, CQ reported that "[t]o some extent, the right-to-life movement focused on the issue of taxpayers' funds for abortion *as an interim strategy*, because Congress has so far ignored its pleas for passage of a constitutional amendment outlawing abortion altogether" (CQ *Almanac* 1977, 296, emphasis added). The Hyde amendments maintained the pressure for fundamental policy change. Pro-life advocates pursued incremental efforts simply because it would be easier to secure incremental changes to existing policy than to win passage of their overriding goal, a constitutional amendment outlawing abortion.

The second important fact noted by CQ in their coverage of the issue is that the pro-life groups had decided that their strategy in Congress should be to write narrow provisions restricting abortion and to attach amendments to the Labor–HEW appropriations bill and similar legislative vehicles. In 1978, pro-life forces attached restrictive language to the Labor–HEW appropriations bill, the Department of Defense appropriations bill, and legislation related to the Peace Corps. All of these changes in policy were made through floor amendments in the House.

After making these incremental changes to abortion policy in 1978, Congress passed more funding restrictions in a relatively short timeframe, attaching funding restrictions to appropriations bills covering everything from the District of Columbia to foreign aid. Members were, in essence, voting to change the same type of policy, federal funding for abortion, over and over, in every venue at home and abroad. Although they were moving the status quo toward the pro-life position, the members may not have viewed their decision in this manner. Once members voted to restrict the use of federal funds for abortions in one area, restrictions in other areas (e.g., Department of Defense or the Peace Corps) were hardly different. Although no abortion-related appropriations bills had been enacted prior to the 95th Congress, eighteen such bills were passed into law from 1979 through 1985. Legislators pursued the incremental strategy through the 1980s and into the 1990s. In the last years of the George H. W. Bush administration, the more liberal Congress attempted to pass appropriations bills that deleted these abortion-limiting policies. Obviously, not all incremental efforts in the Appropriations Committee were in the pro-life direction. President George H. W. Bush vetoed all those appropriations bills that attempted to remove limits on abortion, and the status quo policy of constrained federal funding for abortion remained. After his election in 1992, Democratic President William "Bill" Clinton did not work aggressively to move the status quo policy on abortion funding. Throughout this period, all of the changes in funding policy were incremental by nature; there were no fundamental changes in the policies related to the federal funding of abortion.

China and Abortion Policy

The Hyde amendment strategy had proven successful across a wide range of issues. The Hyde restrictions also proved to be rather popular, and removing these restrictions has proven to be exceedingly difficult. As pervasive as the Hyde strategy was, elected officials found other, new ways to address the abortion issue. Indeed, pro-choice advocates were seeking (and finding) novel ways to inoculate themselves from antiabortion electoral pressures (e.g., Evans 2001; Sulkin 2005).[8] In her discussion of "issue uptake," Tracy Sulkin argues that legislators frequently pursue policies to neutralize their potential challengers. Both pro-choice and

---

[8] Hillygus and Shields (2008) find a similar dynamic in presidential elections. Hillygus and Shields argue that wedge issues – such as abortion – can attract voters from the opposition party without forsaking one's own partisans. Indeed, for Hillygus and Shields (2008), the persuadable voters are most readily swayed with wedge issues where ambivalence is high and the issue domain is narrow. In addition, enhanced targeting technologies have increased the tendencies to employ wedge issues.

pro-life legislators sought means to address abortion policy in order to retain supporters while neutralizing opponents. Some legislators simply wanted to appear "reasonable" when it came to abortion policy, making it more difficult for challengers to make abortion a centerpiece of their electoral battles.

China's "one child policy" created a new set of opportunities for pro-choice advocates to address abortion policies. Established by Deng Xiaoping in 1979 to address China's population growth, the one child policy limited couples to one child, with a variety of measures (fines, pressure to abort, and forced sterilization) applied whenever there were subsequent pregnancies. The policy was applied more strictly in urban areas, and often couples could pay fines or special taxes if they sought larger families (see, e.g., Legge and Zhao 2002). Although some changes and modifications of the policy have occurred over time, an overall effect of the policy has been to foster an acceptance of abortion – an acceptance beyond the simple recognition of its legality. At times, the implementation of the one child policy approached direct promotion of abortion and forced abortion procedures. Even in its gentler, amended forms, China's one child policy was at odds with the attitudes of many Americans. For pro-life Americans, the use of abortion as a population control measure is clearly abhorrent. For many pro-choice Americans, the control that China's one child policy exerts over women and their bodies is similarly objectionable. Forced abortions and sterilizations are clearly antithetical to choice and procreative autonomy.

Congressional legislation related to both abortion and China included the Forced Abortion Condemnation Act, which would have "prohibited the Secretary of State from issuing any visa to, and the Attorney General from admitting to the United States, any Chinese national (including any Communist Party official or Chinese Government official) that [sic] has been found to have been involved in the enforcement of population control policies resulting in a woman being forced to undergo an abortion against her free choice, or resulting in a man or woman being forced to undergo sterilization against his or her free choice."[9]

At times, the Democrats used abortion-related issues to split the Republican opposition. Improving relations with China was a priority for Republican Party leaders from the 1970s onward. President Richard Nixon's rapprochement with China followed by George H. W. Bush's

---

[9] From H.R. 2570, sponsored by Representative Tilly Fowler (R-FL), 1997), http://thomas. loc.gov/cgi-bin/bdquery/z?d105:HR02570:@@@D&summ2=m&.

service as (informal) ambassador to China set the tone for better U.S.–China relations. China's one child policy and the Republican Party's interest in maintaining good relations with China allowed Democrats to split the Republican Party on several issues related to China, including most favored nation status, family planning and population control issues, and immigration. In 1989, President George H. W. Bush vetoed legislation sponsored by Representative Nancy Pelosi (D-CA), which would have adjusted immigration requirements for Chinese nationals. The legislative summary for the bill H.R. 2712 states that "careful consideration [is to] be given to all applications for asylum, withholding of deportation, and refugee status filed by nationals of the PRC [People's Republic of China] who express a fear of persecution upon return because of such country's 'one couple, one child' policy." It further stated "that applicants who establish that they have refused to abort or be sterilized shall be considered to have established a well-founded fear of political persecution upon return to the PRC."[10]

Pelosi has been consistently pro-choice throughout her career. Numerous Republican legislators had sought to limit the promotion or acceptance of abortion in foreign nations. The China legislation allowed Pelosi to address the abortion issue and tweak Republicans for being unwilling in this instance to address abortion issues in the increasingly important China. Though forced procedures are less commonplace today, the use of abortion for family planning and sex selection certainly extends beyond China.[11] Evidence suggests that abortion for sex selection purposes has even entered the United States. Sam Roberts (2009) reports, "more boys than girls are born in the United States, by a ratio of 1.05 to 1. But among American families of Chinese, Korean, or Indian descent, the likelihood of having a boy increased to 1.17 to 1 if the first child was a girl ... [and] if the first two children were girls, the ratio for a third child was 1.51 to 1 – or about 50 percent greater – in favor of boys." For some American families with one or two daughters, the likelihood of the next child born being male increases substantially.

---

[10] http://thomas.loc.gov/cgi-bin/bdquery/z?d101:HR02712:@@@D&summ2=m&.

[11] The U.S. Supreme Court accepted forced sterilization procedures in 1927. Writing for the Court, Justice Oliver Wendell Holmes, Jr., wrote that it is "'better for all the world' ... 'if instead of waiting to execute degenerate offspring for crime, or to let them starve for their imbecility, society can prevent those who are manifestly unfit from continuing their kind'" (Gerson 2009). State sterilization programs waned in the 1950s and early 1960s. The authors know of no programs in the United States ever being linked to forced abortions.

Partial-Birth Abortion

The most important incremental change in abortion policy to be recently voted on in Congress has been the legislation to criminalize a specific type of abortion procedure commonly known as partial-birth abortion.[12] The issue was highly salient and, for eight years, served as a rallying point for antiabortion legislators and activists. Supporters first introduced a bill to ban partial-birth abortion in June 1995. The bill, which passed both the House and Senate in March 1996 (286–129 in the House, 54–44 in the Senate), prohibited physicians from performing "an abortion in which the person performing the abortion partially vaginally delivers a living fetus before killing the fetus and completing the delivery." A physician who failed to comply would be subject to prosecution, risking both fines and prison time. The bill allowed exceptions only when the mother's life was endangered "by physical disorder, illness, or injury." President Clinton vetoed the bill, noting particularly the lack of an exception in cases where the mother's health – not only life – was threatened. The House voted successfully to override the veto (285–137) but, despite the work of key ban-supporter Rick Santorum (R-PA), the veto override failed in the Senate (57–41). In Chapter 2, we argued that incremental proposals are easier to pass than nonincremental proposals. However, when legislation is vetoed, it takes on nonincremental attributes, requiring supermajorities for passage. Incremental efforts do not always prevail.

The 105th Congress reenacted this story, passing a nearly identical partial-birth abortion bill in March 1997 (296–132 in the House, 64–36 in the Senate). Seeking to gain support and to alleviate concerns about physician responsibility for possibly unintended acts, the bill's authors included a further definition of the procedure being banned, noting that "'vaginally delivers a living fetus before killing the fetus' means deliberately and intentionally delivering into the vagina a living fetus, or substantial portion thereof, for the purpose of performing a procedure the

---

[12] Some readers might argue that the partial-birth abortion ban was not incremental at all because it regulated medical procedures, thereby inserting the state between the doctor and patient. We offer three counterpoints. First, the phrase "partial-birth abortion" is not a medical term. It is generally thought to address the use of intact dilation and extraction procedures, but the phrase has greater political content than medical content. Second, numerous abortion-related proposals in our dataset have placed the state between the patient and her doctor, by limiting funding or by mandating counseling procedures. Third, novel approaches to altering abortion policy may only incrementally affect the number of abortions performed. As we have noted elsewhere, the partial birth ban will affect a very small percentage of abortions.

physician knows will kill the fetus." In a further accommodation sought by the American Medical Association, the bill also allowed accused physicians to seek a hearing before the State Medical Board to review whether the procedure had been necessary to save the mother's life.

The bill, however, still failed to provide exceptions in cases where the mother's health was in danger, and President Clinton again vetoed it. A successful veto override in the House (298–132) was rendered meaningless by another failed override vote in the Senate (64–36). Supporters of the ban repeatedly rejected the need for a provision to protect the mother's health, asserting that a partial-birth abortion would never be necessary in such cases, and that other, acceptable procedures could be used. Opponents countered that decisions about what procedure is appropriate should be left up to the patient and her physician. In the veto override debate, opponents of the ban also stressed the potential for the ban to be the first step toward eroding abortion rights more generally (*CQ Weekly* 9/19/1998).

Democrats attempted to find a compromise, offering an alternative proposal that would ban all types of late-term abortion (those performed after the fetus is considered viable), with exceptions for threats to the mother's life or health. However, supporters of the partial-birth abortion ban countered that the proposal would still allow partial-birth abortions prior to viability and that the health exception was too broad and unnecessary.

During the 106th Congress, a third attempt to pass the ban was complicated by the involvement of the Supreme Court on the issue. States have played a steady, regular role in abortion regulations, and numerous states toyed with their own versions of partial-birth abortion bans. When Nebraska sought to ban partial-birth abortion procedures, it made no exclusion for the life of the mother. In April 2000, the Court heard a case involving the Nebraska partial-birth abortion law. Although both the House and Senate passed bills, further consideration was halted when the Supreme Court ruling in *Stenberg v. Carhart* struck down the Nebraska law because it did not include an exception to protect the mother's health and because the definition of the prohibited procedure was too broad (*CQ Weekly* 7/1/2000). Debates about the constitutionality of abortion limits have frequently altered the course of abortion policy (Schonhardt-Bailey 2008). Congress did not take up the issue again until July 2002, when the House again passed a ban. However, at that time the Democrat-controlled Senate did not take up the issue.

The first post-9/11 election strengthened the Republican Party's position in both the House and Senate. Although the party that controls the

White House typically loses seats in congressional midterm elections, 2002 was an exception to the rule. The new, 108th Congress had eight more Republican representatives and two more Republican senators than the 107th. For the party that controls the White House to gain seats in a midterm is highly unusual but the post-9/11 environment had barely settled back to anything close to normalcy by November 2002. In 2003, Republicans found themselves controlling both houses of Congress and the executive branch, and by June 2003, both the House and Senate had passed new versions of the partial-birth abortion ban (282–139 in the House, 64–33 in the Senate). A lengthy move toward a conference was needed to obtain agreement between the legislative bodies, because the Senate bill contained Democrat-backed language affirming the *Roe v. Wade* ruling as guaranteeing a right to abortion. In October 2003, the conference committee rejected that language and the abortion ban was passed by both the House and Senate. The bill passed, as before, without an exception for threats to the woman's health, but with language making it clear that the act must be intentional, deliberate, and overt on the part of the physician.

As expected, President Bush signed the bill into law on November 5, 2003. This legislation represents the first time that Congress has voted to outlaw a specific abortion procedure. The importance of this legislation for the present discussion is its incremental nature. The legislation does not attempt to ban all late-term abortions; rather it only attempts to ban one very specific procedure.[13] However, the intent of this incremental strategy is, no doubt, to create a foothold for directly assaulting the *Roe v. Wade* decision, and the earliest supporters of the ban are explicit about their incremental strategy. "We've got to start somewhere. *We have to take this one step at a time*" (*CQ Almanac* 1995, emphasis added), said Robert Dornan (R-CA).

PRO-LIFE NONINCREMENTAL FAILURES

There have only been nonincremental failures in the efforts to have abortion policy codified by law or constitutional amendments. Pro-life efforts began in 1975, when the Senate Judiciary Subcommittee on Constitutional Amendments voted not to report out a series of

---

[13] Of course, limits on technology also limit the ability to perform any late-term abortions. However, the ban is, strictly speaking, on the procedure, so new technologies and procedures could be developed and used.

constitutional amendments related to abortion. In 1976, Senator Jesse Helms (R-NC) used a procedural mechanism to bring forth a constitutional amendment guaranteeing unborn children the right to life. Helms was a life-long antiabortion advocate and archconservative by most standards. However, the Senate voted to table the Helms amendment and not start formal debate on the issue. Helms's human life amendment (HLA) faced long odds during Democratic control. In 1981, with Ronald Reagan in the White House and the Republican takeover of the Senate, the Senate Judiciary Committee voted on a constitutional amendment to restrict severely or to ban abortions, but these amendments were never considered on the floor. In 1983, Senators Orin Hatch (R-UT) and Thomas Eagleton (D-MO) altered the HLA tact. The Hatch–Eagleton amendment simply stated that "A right to abortion is not secured by this Constitution." The Hatch–Eagleton proposal would have left the states responsible for all issues tied to abortion and the U.S. Constitution would be silent. Hatch and Eagleton were the only legislators able to secure a floor vote on any sort of constitutional amendment tied to abortion. Their efforts, however, failed. The Hatch–Eagleton amendment secured only forty-nine of the necessary sixty-seven votes.

One major change that has occurred in pro-life side of nonincremental abortion politics during this time is that the wording of these proposals has become more settled. In the 94th and 95th Congresses, there were numerous variations on the structure and wording of abortion-related constitutional amendments. Some examples of the types of proposals from the 95th Congress include the following:[14]

- House Joint Resolution 5 (H.J. Res. 5) would have extended due process and equal protection to the individual from the moment of conception and prohibit deprivation of life on account of age, illness or incapacity;
- H.J. Res. 88 would have prohibited abortion except under laws permitting medical procedures required to save the life of the mother endangered by the continuation of the pregnancy;
- H.J. Res. 89 would have permitted any State or the Congress to enact laws with respect to the life of an unborn child from the time of conception;

---

[14] The summary of each law is taken from the Congressional Research Service summary of the legislation, as reported in the "Bill Summary and Status" section of the *Thomas* database. http://thomas.loc.gov.

- H.J. Res. 115 would have deemed every human being to be a person from the moment of conception; and
- H.J. Res. 133 would have prohibited abortions after the fetus's heart begins to beat, except to save the life of the mother.

Today, there is a relatively common three-part form for the constitutional ban for abortion. First, the common form for constitutional bans defines the unborn as a person with Fifth and Fourteenth amendment protections. Second, it prohibits depriving the unborn of their right to life. Third, it allows for the life of the mother to be balanced against the life of the unborn should the health of the mother be in question during pregnancy. The selection of more uniform wording for a constitutional amendment to ban abortions has done little to improve the prospects for passage of such legislation, but it has provided a clear statement of position on the issue for the pro-life side of the debate.

None of the subsequent efforts to ban abortions through passage of a constitutional amendment have been successful. The basic HLA has been modified in numerous ways and has been offered numerous times, but such a bold step faces considerable hurdles. As it happens, Senator Helms did manage an incremental success in the abortion field. When President Clinton nominated William Weld (former Republican governor of Massachusetts) to be the ambassador to Mexico, Helms blocked Senate work. Helms linked his opposition to the nomination to Weld's support of abortion rights. However, it is interesting to note that, during the period January 2003 to January 2007, when Republicans controlled all three branches of government, there were no votes on constitutional amendments to ban abortions, even though the Republicans controlled the agendas in both chambers of Congress.

PRO-CHOICE NONINCREMENTAL FAILURES

Just as the pro-life advocates have failed in their efforts to enact a pro-life amendment to the Constitution, the pro-choice side has also seen efforts to either codify their views into law or pass a constitutional amendment to allow abortions to fall flat. In 1993, with the election of President Clinton and with Democrats in control of Congress, pro-choice groups attempted to craft legislation that would codify into federal law a woman's right to an abortion. Their hopes for success were buoyed by the fact that, on his second day in office, President Clinton signed a series of executive orders that made incremental changes in abortion policy that favored pro-choice groups, such as ending a prohibition on abortion counseling and referrals at federally funded family planning clinics. Both the House and Senate Judiciary Committees crafted measures that codified a woman's right to access into law. However, neither bill was brought to the floor during the 103rd Congress. *Congressional Quarterly* reported that

> Clinton proved unwilling to spend political capital on the divisive abortion issue. As a result, the bill was left to languish ... Leaders were concerned about ... fending off amendments that would weaken [the bill] to the point where its organizational backers would consider it worse than no law at all. (*CQ Almanac* 1993, 349)

Clinton's concerns highlight three aspects of this type of bill. First, because of its non-incremental nature, its passage would require great effort, including considerable presidential attention and strong leadership. Second, leaders were worried that repeated incremental attacks on the bill, via floor amendments, might so weaken the legislation that it would reverse the nature of the legislation and become unpalatable to pro-choice interest groups. This point can be seen as an implicit recognition of the effectiveness of incremental legislating; many of the floor amendments were likely to be successful, altering the bill in ways that Democrats would not appreciate. Third, the legislation sought by abortion rights groups would put moderately pro-choice legislators in a very awkward situation, forcing them to vote on difficult issues, such as ending 24-hour waiting periods and parental notification for minors. Some members did not want to have to defend their votes on these rather popular restrictions. For some legislators, the inoculation against antiabortion challenges would be entirely lost if these restrictions were reversed (see, e.g., Sulkin 2005).

Representative Jesse Jackson, Jr. (D-IL) has proposed a constitutional amendment that would clearly enshrine the *Roe* decision and the woman's right to choose an abortion in the Constitution. Starting in 2003, he introduced an amendment that would ensure that (1) equality of rights under the law shall not be denied or abridged by the United States or by any State on account of sex; and (2) reproductive rights for women under the law shall not be denied or abridged by the United States or any State. Jackson's amendment, like the pro-life amendments that have been introduced since *Roe*, was not considered by the Judiciary Committee. With a Democratic president and a new Democratic majority controlling both chambers of Congress, it is fair to speculate as to whether a new, comprehensive Freedom of Choice Act might be passed. Given the full policy agenda that President Obama has faced, he has not expressed a desire for quick passage. Other issues are more pressing. Even some pro-choice groups are backing away from any sort of drive toward quick passage. Cecile Richards, president of the Planned Parenthood Federation of America, is surprisingly reserved. "We're going to be smart and strategic ... The Freedom of Choice Act is very important ... but we have a long list of things to get done ... that are immediate concerns" (Meckler 2008, A5).

SYMBOLIC POLITICS

In this analysis, we are defining success as the ability of lawmakers to shepherd a piece of legislation through the Congress and get it passed by both chambers. The history of nonincremental abortion legislation is one where the legislative difficulties associated with it have proved too daunting to overcome, but this has not thwarted members of Congress from proposing constitutional amendments. The rationale for continuing to do so is that introducing nonincremental policy proposals, such as constitutional amendments, serves to promote a member's political interests to signal to constituents and interest groups their position. Mayhew (1974) notes that members use such activities as position taking and credit claiming to promote themselves and enhance their reelection prospects. For the member, the success of a legislative proposal is not critical for the member to be able to engage in credit claiming; sponsoring or cosponsoring are low-cost means to signal a position to constituents. Such signaling is strategic: A member is quite "conscious of, and sensitive to, the consequences of their positions and statements" on their constituents and other political supporters (Kessler and Krehbiel 1996, 555). Members can engage in signaling through both nonincremental and incremental proposals.

Legislating can be either purposeful or symbolic. In politics and policy decision making, symbolic politics can be used for a variety of reasons. Symbols often help an individual or group – such as the political parties in Congress – to tell a story. Examples of symbolic politics abound (see, e.g., Condit 1990; Stone 2001). Deborah Stone (2001) identifies four types of symbolic devices that are often used in defining problems. These devices include stories of decline or stories of conspiracies; synecdoche, where small "horror stories" are used to discuss a larger whole; metaphors that compare different policy problems; and ambiguity, which allows different people to view a policy from different perspectives and support the policy for different reasons. The use of these symbolic devices in problem definition is a part of a larger problem definition process. For example, Stone (2012, 175–176) explicitly notes that the Supreme Court, in *Roe* as well as in subsequent decisions, began quantifying abortion rights within the context of the terms of a pregnancy. By dividing pregnancy into segments of viability, it allowed the problem and possible solutions to be defined within a specific context.

Symbolism has the potential to play a huge role in politics. Issue advocates often gain by identifying the "bad guys." Psychologists (e.g., Kahneman and Tversky 1979) and interest group scholars (e.g., Hansen 1985) have known for many years that mobilizing supporters is much easier when losses loom. Small legislative gains make it harder to identify the "bad guys." Incremental changes are more apt to inoculate one from opponent's attacks and nonincremental changes are more apt to mobilize your opponents.

In the context of legislation on abortion, all legislation in this area can be viewed through this lens of symbolism. Any member can use the bill sponsorship and cosponsorship process as a means to achieving a symbolic goal. Although both incremental and nonincremental legislative proposals have signaling – and potentially symbolic – purposes, the reduced likelihood that a nonincremental bill will be enacted suggests that these bills are likely to be introduced primarily for their symbolic value. A member who wants his or her opinion on abortion politics to be unquestionable can achieve this by either sponsoring or cosponsoring a constitutional amendment to either ban or facilitate access to abortion. This symbolism may also be less costly than an incremental proposal because constitutional amendments carry heavy burdens that must be overcome in order to be enacted. Therefore, the member is able to stake a position without having to live with the consequences of its enactment because such an outcome has a low probability of success. The chances of passage in the chamber are low, the chances of passage in the Senate are low, the chances of presidential approval are often low, and the chance of the federal courts upholding the legislation may be low. Given all of these hurdles, the likelihood of successful implementation is extremely low. By contrast, incremental legislation, which tends to be more purposeful in nature, may require a member not only to stake out a position but also to live with the political consequences of its enactment, since such an outcome bears a much lower threshold for achievement.[15] In Chapter 2, we explored the trade-off between votes for a proposal and actual policy

[15] See Woon (2008) for a game theoretic representation of this phenomenon.

gains. Here, we see the power of symbolic efforts versus the possibility of actual legislative gains.

The use of nonincremental politics as symbolism can be seen directly in the case of the constitutional amendment to require a federal balanced budget. Both Democrats and Republicans used the amendment as a means to score points in the political debate over the federal budget. For the Republicans, the message they were attempting to communicate was simple: Republicans are fiscally prudent and Democrats are not. As Andrew Taylor of *Congressional Quarterly* (1997, 577) noted:

Majority Leader Trent Lott, R-Miss., declined to switch his vote to "no" to permit him to call up the [balanced budget constitutional] amendment at any time for a revote. To have done so would have interfered with the GOP message of the day: All 55 Republicans supported the measure, and its defeat came at the hands of Democrats who broke campaign promises to back the idea.

Democrats likewise offered an amendment to the legislation exempting Social Security from the balanced budget provision in an attempt to put Republicans on record as supporting a raid on Social Security finances to balance the budget. The balanced budget amendment debate allowed both sides to score political points with the knowledge there was a very low likelihood that either side would actually have to live with the consequences of the proposal. Moreover, because the Senate considered the amendment before the House, Senators were further insulated from having to worry about the impact of the amendment's enactment. Unless the proposal passed in the House perfectly mirrored the one passed in the Senate, the amendment had several additional hurdles to overcome before being sent to the states for ratification. In short, the symbolic attributes of the debate far outweighed any policy outcomes that members may have ultimately wanted.

ABORTION TRENDS – 93RD THROUGH 108TH CONGRESSES

We examine the sources of incremental activity regarding abortion measures using data collected on over 1,000 measures (bills and amendments) introduced in the U.S. House of Representatives from 1973 to 2004. The information collected on these measures includes sponsorship, the incremental or nonincremental nature of the measure, and the direction the proposal would move the status quo, either in the pro-choice or the right-to-life direction. Legislation codifying the right of women to have broad access to abortion and proposing amendments to the

Constitution to ban abortion practices were deemed nonincremental. Proposals such as those restricting abortion funding affecting waiting periods and requiring notification procedures for minors were deemed incremental. In addition to the characteristics of each individual abortion measure, the internal legislative and external political environments were also analyzed. Internal legislative environment variables include party control of the chamber as well as NOMINATE ideology scores for the chamber median and key legislators.[16]

In addition to collecting data on abortion activity in Congress, we also collected information about the external political environment affecting abortion politics. Numerous scholars have noted that "morality issues tend to be more widely salient" among the public and that morality policies are more likely to reflect public sentiments (see, e.g., Mooney and Lee 1995, 600, 615). Here, we use measures of public opinion and the level of media attention given to group activity surrounding the abortion issue. Public opinion data was obtained from the Gallup Poll. More specifically, we used the percentage of respondents in the survey indicating that abortion should be "legal under some circumstances." Group activity concerning the abortion issue was measured by a surrogate: the amount of media coverage received. Surrogate measures always have shortcomings, but media mentions of groups related to the abortion issue do provide a good measure of the visibility and salience of the groups' activities and of the abortion issue in general. Some pro-life activists felt that "by threatening chaos, direct action goaded legislators to adopt pro-life measures" (Maxwell 2002, 202). That is, direct group action was thought to complement and reinforce legislative actions.[17] By some accounts, "Operation Rescue turned what had been a small, ragtag group of easily ignored protestors into a genuine movement, an aggressive national campaign that put the anti-abortion cause back onto *America's Page One*" (Risen and Thomas 1998, 220, emphasis added). With these sentiments in mind, we collected the total number of articles reporting on group

---

[16] NOMINATE scores are ideology measures that have been developed for every member and senator for every Congress. Unlike interest group scores, NOMINATE scores facilitate comparisons over time. See Poole and Rosenthal (1997) for a complete description of the data and its development.

[17] Direct action typically meant protests and vigils, but there have been literally hundreds of violent actions taken against abortion clinics and individuals working in and around them. Since the 1970s, there have been over 200 arsons, over 100 attacks with acid, over 600 anthrax letter threats, numerous bombings and shootings, and several deaths. Wichita, Kansas, a center for antiabortion protests, made over 2,000 arrests in just one month in the summer of 1991.

activity regarding either side of the issue by conducting a Lexis-Nexis search of the headlines and leading paragraphs of the two leading newspapers of record, the *New York Times* and *The Washington Post*. In addition to measuring group activity, we also recorded the group's policy stand: seeking to protect the standard set forth in *Roe v. Wade* or seeking to limit abortion access.[18]

During the period of our study, most abortion activity, as measured by bills or amendments to bills, originated in the U.S. House of Representatives. On average, the House accounted for just over 75 percent of all abortion-related activity. At no time has the House accounted for less than 56 percent of all abortion-related congressional activity and, for a few Congresses, the House has accounted for more than 80 percent of all abortion-related activity. To understand better the dynamics of legislative abortion policy, therefore, our focus will be on the House. Legislative activity on abortion has been most prominent during four Congresses: the two immediately after the *Roe* decision was reached, the last Congress of the George H. W. Bush administration, and the 104th Congress, which marked the first Republican takeover of Congress in decades.

We start our examination of the trends in abortion politics by considering both the number of nonincremental abortion proposals that have been made in each Congress and the percentage of all abortion-related proposals that are nonincremental. Table 4.2 shows both of these aspects of nonincremental abortion politics during three periods of our study. Clearly, we see that Congress quickly moved to propose a vast number of nonincremental proposals to ban abortion in the immediate aftermath of the *Roe* decision. In the 1970s, the percentage of abortion-related legislative proposals that were nonincremental exceeded 60 percent in every Congress up to 1980. The number of nonincremental proposals reached its peak in the 94th Congress (at 97 percent). The number of nonincremental proposals began to decline with the 97th and 98th Congresses (nonincremental proposals represented 47 and 38 percent, respectively, of all abortion-related bills) and continued to decline thereafter.

Since the *Roe* decision, nonincremental abortion activity in the House has consistently declined. In the 94th Congress, less than 4 percent of all abortion activity was incremental, but by the 97th Congress, 53 percent

---

[18] Key search terms for pro-choice groups included references to Planned Parenthood, NOW, NARAL, and EMILY's List. Key search terms for pro-life group activity included references to the National Right to Life Committee, Operation Rescue, and Susan B. Anthony's List. We also searched "abortion." All data were grouped by Congress.

TABLE 4.2. *Incremental and Nonincremental Proposals*

Congress/Year	Incremental	Nonincremental	Total
93–98 (1973–1984)	137 (30.8%)	308 (69.8%)	445
99–102 (1985–1992)	163 (76.5%)	50 (23.5%)	213
103–108 (1993–2004)	303 (87.1%)	45 (12.9%)	348
Total	602 (59.8%)	403 (40.2%)	1006

of abortion activity was incremental. For the 101st through the 108th Congresses, the percentage of incremental activity in the House has never been below 78 percent. The raw numerical data portrayed in Figure 4.1 reveal the expected patterns of incrementalism in this area of single-issue politics. Both the number and the percentage of "all-or-nothing" proposals declined as incrementalism became the preferred strategy.

The increase in incrementalism is clear, but the causes of incrementalism demand more careful study. One might speculate that such incrementalism was due to the counteractive lobbying efforts of opposing groups. That is, one force may have resisted an opposing force. Perhaps each side mobilized to counter the activity of the other so that no sweeping changes were obtained. Directly measuring group mobilization is difficult, but this issue will be further explored in the following chapters. Although we address this issue more extensively in Chapter 6, at this stage, it is safe to say that countervailing forces were more successful at killing nonincremental proposals and less successful at killing incremental proposals.

About 80 percent of the abortion-related proposals in our data are in the pro-life direction. One might think there would be more incremental and more nonincremental pro-choice activity in the House. However, the pro-choice community was reasonably satisfied with *Roe*, which meant that its efforts would be mostly defensive. After the initial attempts at a constitutional amendment banning abortion in the 93rd and 94th Congresses, pro-life groups quickly moved to change abortion through incremental means. For each Congress, approximately 72 percent of pro-life abortion activity has been incremental and, in half of the Congresses examined, more than 80 percent of pro-life efforts have been incremental. Incremental abortion activity has been dominated by measures that move toward the right-to-life position.

Not only is much of the incremental abortion activity dominated by the pro-life position, but these incremental attempts to limit abortions through federal action are frequently successful. After initially failing to achieve any success in the 94th Congress, pro-life forces have generally

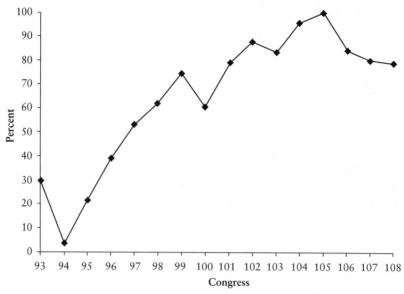

FIGURE 4.1. Incremental abortion proposals as a percent of all abortion-related proposals.

seen between 25 and 35 percent of their incremental efforts to restrict abortion enacted into law. In fact, in only one Congress since the 95th have they failed to get 25 percent of their incremental legislative agenda passed into law. These success rates are based on fairly regular levels of activity over the period studied. On average, there were eight successful pro-life incremental measures per Congress, four congresses with six or fewer measures and four with ten or more.

Figure 4.2 illustrates how the House's median NOMINATE score tracks the pro-life abortion-related activity in the House. Generally, increases in the rate of pro-life activity correspond with increasingly conservative NOMINATE scores, and decreases in the rate of pro-life activity correspond with increasingly liberal NOMINATE scores. Although the trend lines generally track one another, there are perturbations along the way. In the 94th, 95th, and 98th Congresses, the House became more liberal – with more negative NOMINATE scores – but the rate of pro-life activity remained quite steady. In four Congresses – the 101st, 104th, 105th, and 108th – the trend lines move in opposite directions. Obviously, pro-life forces take advantage of opportunities to counter liberal Congresses and pro-choice forces see opportunities to counter conservative Congresses.

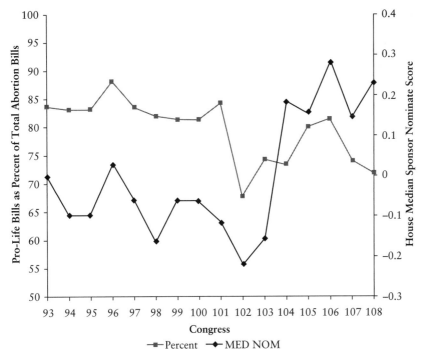

FIGURE 4.2. House NOMINATE score and rate of pro-life abortion activity.

Public opinion over this period remained steady and supported the general notions behind regulations on access to abortions. According to the Gallup Survey, for each of the years in our study, a slim but steady majority of Americans found federal regulatory policies limiting abortion access acceptable. Around 50 percent of respondents agree that abortion should be "legal under some circumstances." These public opinion scores suggest that policy advocates could engage in incremental activity in the pro-life direction without encountering fierce opposition. Indeed, legislators could reasonably suggest that incremental activity in the pro-life direction was generally representative of constituents' desires. In short, public opinion was not constraining incremental pro-life activity. Legislators had considerable "wiggle room," especially in the 1970s and 1980s. Neither the pro-life nor the pro-choice advocates held sway with the larger public (see, e.g., Alvarez and Brehm 1995).

Importantly, members of *both* political parties took advantage of this wiggle room provided by public opinion. To be certain, Republicans appeared to take the greatest advantage of this wiggle room after their

TABLE 4.3. *Pro-Choice and Pro-Life Abortion-Related Proposals by Party*

Party	Pro-Life	Pro-Choice
Democrat	73.6%	26.4%
Republican	85.6%	14.2%

takeover of the House, but the Democrats were increasingly willing to engage in incremental pro-life activity during much of this time. As Table 4.3 indicates, the vast majority of Republican-sponsored legislation regarding abortion (86 percent) involves placing regulations or restrictions on *Roe*, which should not be surprising.

Analysis of Democratic legislators, however, demonstrates that they too have been far more likely to sponsor legislation in the right-to-life direction (74 percent) than in the pro-choice direction (26 percent). Given the nature of public opinion in this area, legislators from both parties can take advantage of the opportunity to legislate in this area of single-issue politics without much threat of constituency "punishment."

CONCLUSION

Many observers of politics consider abortion as more emblematic of single-issue politics than any other political issue. Years ago, the abortion issue seemed to stand apart from other political issues. There was politics as usual, and then there was abortion. Today, abortion is wrapped up with many issues, some of which are themselves highly charged. Abortion politics today may indeed be a condensational issue (Fried 1988), representative of a wide array of prominent concerns. In this chapter, we conducted a broad, aggregate level exploration of abortion politics in the U.S. House of Representatives. Regardless of the incredible din surrounding many abortion debates, abortion provides an example of single-issue politics that is most successful when small changes to existing policy are made. Attempts by Senator Jesse Helms to establish Constitutional grounds to ban all abortions in the late 1970s and early 1980s repeatedly failed. In the 103rd Congress, the Freedom of Choice Act, which would have codified a woman's right to abortion, also failed. Even with a Democratic House and a filibuster-proof Democratic Senate, President Obama has backed away from his earlier calls for a quick passage of the Freedom of Choice Act. Even when circumstances appear especially favorable, legislators and presidents often back away from sweeping proposals.

Although sweeping changes have failed, numerous pieces of abortion-related legislation from various committees have incrementally moved abortion policy. Indeed, the range of proposals is so broad and the volume so great that some commentators worry about the effects of abortion-related legislation on the overall congressional agenda. The first section of this chapter assessed the claims made by Dworkin that the focus on abortion policy limited congressional attention to other important issues. The empirical results for Dworkin's claim are inconclusive, but we can note that abortion language does get attached to numerous legislative vehicles from numerous committees. The range of policy changes affected by abortion has been tremendously broad. Legislation concerning U.S. military funding, Peace Corps funding, and most favored nation trading status for China have all been affected by abortion politics. At times, legislators consider how to respond to the practice of forced abortions and, at times, they consider how to regulate physical access to abortion clinics.

Within the wide range of abortion-related proposals, numerous legislators appear quite active. Both Democrats and Republicans are actively engaged on both sides of abortion policy. Abortion attitudes among members of Congress are not always neatly separated along party lines or tightly clustered only toward the ends of the ideological spectrum. "A pro-life Republican representative notes that 'even some people that have a full-blown position in support of abortion rights, who have had a consistent record in support of abortion rights, have had some trouble dealing with partial birth abortion, and that's why we ended up getting as many votes ... as we did'" (Oldmixon 2005, 39–40). Since *Roe*, a wide array of abortion-related issues was addressed in the U.S. House, but most abortion-related legislation was predominantly pro-life and predominantly incremental.

In the remainder of this book, our analysis is increasingly focused on the individual level. We rely less and less on aggregate level analyses and focus on the individual sponsor level or the individual proposal level. In Chapter 5, we look at sponsors of incremental and nonincremental abortion-related proposals. Most studies of abortion focus on the incidence of abortion policy activity. Such studies might consider which legislators are most likely to enter into the abortion debate and which are less likely. In Chapter 5, we focus only on those legislators active in the abortion debate. Among those involved in sponsoring abortion-related legislation, are some legislators more likely to pursue incremental strategies? Are some more likely to pursue a nonincremental approach? In Chapter 6, we explore the committee referral of abortion proposals. Our focus in Chapter 6 is at the individual proposal level. The sixth chapter also explores those abortion-related proposals that are most successful at wending their way through the legislative process.

PART II

ABORTION IN THE HOUSE

5

Sponsors of Abortion Policies

Bill sponsorship "is a strong indicator of which issues he or she wants to be associated with and the reputation he or she wants to acquire among colleagues." (Schiller 1995, 187)

INTRODUCTION

If your average, politically astute person was asked the question, "Who has been the most prolific sponsor of constitutional amendments that would ban abortions?," she might name Chris Smith, the Republican representative from New Jersey or the late Henry Hyde, a former Republican member from Illinois. If she could not guess the member of Congress by name, she would almost certainly guess that the person was a Republican and a conservative. Alas, the guess would be completely wrong.

The most prolific sponsor of constitutional amendments to ban abortion has been Representative James Oberstar, a Democrat from Minnesota and a stalwart liberal. Oberstar was one of the first sponsors – going all of the way back to the 94th Congress – of abortion legislation that would institute a constitutional ban on abortions. Oberstar has introduced the same constitutional amendment on abortion every Congress for the past thirty years. Although his amendments have never gone beyond being referred to the House Committee on the Judiciary, this legislation and Oberstar's persistence is deeply symbolic. Looking at Representative Oberstar's biography, it is easy to see possible roots of such efforts: Oberstar is a devout Catholic. Elizabeth Oldmixon (2005) finds that religion is an important factor in legislators' attitudes and decision making surrounding a wide array of morality issues, such as abortion. Barry Burden (2007) argues that the personal experiences and the individual characteristics of legislators have direct effects on legislative decision making, even after controlling for the usual suspects in social science analyses of legislative votes.

In the first half of this chapter, we consider the characteristics of the sponsors of pro-choice and pro-life legislation. We are especially interested in how the characteristics of sponsors has changed over time, as the political parties have become more closely affiliated with specific positions on abortion. Our analysis illustrates that, within Congress, sponsorship activity on the abortion issue is not as predictable among certain types of legislators as might have been expected. Although each party does tend to favor a given position, there are members in each party who deviate from the traditional storyline that Democratic Party members are pro-choice and Republican Party members are pro-life. We see that this was especially true before 1988 but it is still true today.[1] Although ideology plays a role, its impact on sponsorship might not reflect preestablished biases about which legislators pursue abortion politics.

In the second half of this chapter, we explore an entirely different aspect of legislative sponsorship. To wit: we empirically assess whether legislators are more apt to sponsor incremental abortion-related proposals under some circumstances. What internal, legislative and external, electoral environments promote abortion-related legislative activity? Are certain types of abortion-related proposals favored more under some conditions? In particular, rather than simply assessing what leads to sponsorship activity, we evaluate when sponsors pursue incremental rather than nonincremental legislative proposals.

PRO-CHOICE AND PRO-LIFE SPONSORS

Who sponsors pro-choice and pro-life legislation? Is Oberstar reflective of the typical pro-life legislator or is he anomalous? It seems perfectly reasonable to expect that pro-life members would be Republicans and conservative and that pro-choice members would be Democrats and liberal. As we see in Table 5.1, neither stereotype is entirely true. Before considering the partisan and ideological component of the analysis, note

---

[1] Representatives who feel cross-pressured by partisanship and personal preferences may coincidentally reflect constituents who feel similar cross-pressures. Even strong Democrats and strong Republicans sometimes have trouble toeing the party line (see, e.g., Hillygus and Shields 2008).

TABLE 5.1. *Pro-Life and Pro-Choice Proposals, 94th–108th Congresses*

		Pro-Life Bills	Pro-Choice Bills
Totals		79.9%	20.1%
		(803)	(202)
Partisanship	Democrat	73.6%	26.4%
		(356)	(128)
	Republican	85.6	14.2
		(447)	(74)
Ideology (Sponsor's NOMINATE Score)	Most Liberal (<–0.5)	68.1	31.9
		(92)	(43)
	Liberal (0 to –0.5)	74.2	25.8
		(270)	(94)
	Conservative (0 to 0.5)	88.8	11.2
		(364)	(45)
	Most Conservative (>0.5)	79.4	20.6
		(77)	(20)

that the aggregate level of activity across the 94th through the 108th Congresses has been in the pro-life direction. Legislation on abortion has been strongly tilted in the pro-life direction. About 80 percent of all abortion-related proposals are pro-life. This is not surprising when one considers that *Roe* pretty much anchors one end of the abortion policy spectrum. In addition, by favoring the pro-choice position, *Roe* made room – and we argue – more opportunities to engage in strategic incrementalism in the pro-life direction.

When we do consider the partisanship question, we see that *both* Democrats and Republicans are much more likely to sponsor pro-life legislation instead of pro-choice legislation. To be certain, Republicans sponsor more abortion-related proposals, and those proposals are most likely in the pro-life direction. However, 44 percent (356/803) of all pro-life proposals had Democratic sponsorship, and 37 percent (74/202) of all pro-choice proposals had Republican sponsorship. Put in slightly different terms, Democrats sponsored almost three pro-life proposals for every pro-choice proposal and Republicans sponsored just over six pro-life proposals for every pro-choice proposal. Between Democrats' and Republicans' sponsorship of abortion-related proposals, there is a clear difference in degree, but among the legislators active in this policy area, the pro-life direction dominates each party.

In the bottom half of Table 5.1, we shift from partisanship to ideology. As with partisanship, for all levels of ideology – from liberal to

conservative – most sponsorship activity has been in the pro-life direction. However, in the aggregate, some of these results are stunning: The
most liberal sponsors of abortion legislation sponsored more than twice
as many pro-life pieces of legislation as they did pro-choice pieces of legislation. For individuals who are moderately liberal, we see a three to one
bias toward the introduction of pro-life legislation. Equally as interesting, twenty of the ninety-seven abortion-related bills introduced by the
most conservative members of Congress were pro-choice. The conservative and most conservative members are more likely to introduce pro-life
than pro-choice legislation, but the more moderately conservative legislators are particularly active and more pro-life. We also note that the
most conservative members are roughly twice as likely to sponsor pro-
choice legislation as their slightly less conservative counterparts (11.2
percent as compared to 20.6 percent). In regards to abortion policy, the
most conservative members are closer to liberals than to conservatives.
Perhaps the libertarian instincts among the most conservative members
may affect their willingness to protect procreative autonomy and choice.
Or perhaps the most conservative members are so demonstrably conservative that they do not need to engage in abortion-related legislative
activity to signal to their constituents.

Given that the Democratic Party platform has expressed a more pro-
choice stand since 1976, when the party platform included language
opposing a constitutional amendment banning abortions, the fact that
Democrats have been the sponsors of so many pro-life pieces of legislation
may seem somewhat incongruous. To remind readers about the clarity of
each party's position on abortion during this time, in Table 5.2 we quote
the party platforms in 1980 and again in 2000.[2] The Democratic Party
position may have represented the views of its party activists and elites,
but it failed to reflect the diversity of the views of many of the Democratic
members of the House of Representatives who were active in abortion
politics. Some readers might argue that the *Roe* decision had so anchored
the extreme pro-choice end of the policy spectrum that most activity in
Congress – by default – was on the other side of the debate. Regardless
of one's attitudes toward *Roe*, its trimester framework all but precluded
procreative autonomy throughout a pregnancy. If they chose, states could
play a role in the second and third trimesters of pregnancy. In addition,
issues of funding abortion procedures or disseminating information about

---

[2] The 1980 position is taken from Granberg and Burlison (1983). The 2000 positions are
taken from www.ontheissues.org.

TABLE 5.2. *Platform Positions of Democratic and Republican Parties on Abortion*

	Democrats	Republicans
1980	We wholly recognize the religious and ethical concerns which many Americans have about abortion. We also recognize the belief of many Americans that a woman has the right to choose whether and when to have a child. The Democratic Party supports the 1973 Supreme Court decision on abortion rights as the law of the land and opposes any constitutional amendment to restrict or overturn that decision. [The platform also approved Medicaid funding for abortion.]	There can be no doubt that the question of abortion, despite the nature of its various issues, is ultimately concerned with equality of rights under the law. While we recognize differing views on this question among Americans in general – and in our own party – we affirm our support of a constitutional amendment to restore protection of the right to life for unborn children. We also support the congressional efforts to restrict the use of taxpayers' dollars for abortion.
2000	Democrats stand behind the right of every woman to choose. We believe it is a constitutional liberty. This year's Supreme Court ruling shows us that eliminating a woman's right to choose is only one justice away. Our goal is to make abortion more rare, not more dangerous. We support contraceptive research, family planning, comprehensive family life education, and policies that support healthy childbearing.	We say the unborn child has a fundamental right to life. We support a human life amendment to the Constitution and we endorse legislation that the Fourteenth amendment's protections apply to unborn children. Our purpose is to have legislative and judicial protection of that right against those who perform abortions. We oppose using public revenues for abortion and will not fund organizations that advocate it. We support the appointment of judges who respect the sanctity of innocent human life.

abortion services affect the impact of *Roe*. In short, we see no reason to presume that *Roe necessarily* anchors an extreme end of the abortion debate. *Roe* may create political strategic limits, but it does not create conceptual limits. Absolute procreative autonomy would require a decision much stronger than *Roe*. There is, therefore, room on each side of *Roe* and on each side of the larger abortion debates for considerable legislative activity, but most activity has been in the pro-life direction.

TABLE 5.3. *Percent and Volume of Pro-Life Legislation Over Time, 93rd–108th Congresses*

	Democrats	Republicans	Most Liberal	Liberal	Conservative	Most Conservative
93–98	78%	78%	77%	83%	87%	84%
(1973–1984)	(202)	(171)	(46)	(156)	(136)	(32)
99–102	77	88	71	79	83	75
(1985–1992)	(108)	(59)	(30)	(79)	(40)	(15)
103–108	55	92	39	50	94	80
(1993–2004)	(46)	(217)	(16)	(32)	(147)	(59)
N	356	447	92	267	323	106

When we examine abortion sponsorship over time in Table 5.3, we see a trend toward liberal and Democratic members sponsoring more pro-choice legislation, but substantial pro-life sponsorship continues. In the period from 1973 to 1984, the most liberal sponsors of abortion legislation sponsored more pro-life pieces of legislation than the most conservative members of the House. Similarly, during that period, Democrats sponsored more pro-life legislation than Republicans. The (sometimes large) Democratic majorities during that period clearly played a role, but the larger lesson drawn from the first row in Table 5.3 is that there were not great party or left–right ideological differences across the legislators engaged in pro-life abortion policy. Seventy-eight percent of the abortion-related proposals sponsored, whether by Democrats or Republicans, were pro-life. For members who were liberal but not among the most liberal members of Congress during this period, we also see a tremendous volume of pro-life legislation. Indeed, liberals produced the greatest volume of pro-life legislation from the beginning of our study to 1992. During the period 1985 to 1992, Republicans became less active in sponsorship but they were more pro-life when they did sponsor legislation. Although they were becoming slightly more pro-choice during this period, Democrats and liberals still produced the most pro-life legislation.

The starkest changes occur when we move into the last period from 1993 to 2004, when the partisan and ideological divides on abortion came into sharper contrast. During this period, Democratic sponsorship of pro-life legislation falls dramatically, and Republican sponsorship is at its highest levels ever. The legislation sponsored by the Democrats is still overwhelmingly in the pro-life direction, but there is much less activity. Almost all of the Republican activity in this time period is pro-life. Republicans sponsored more than 200 bills during this period, but only 17 were pro-choice. Republican pro-choice legislators were virtually silent (or nonexistent) in the last third of the timeframe studied. From 1993 to 2004, Republican pro-life activity far outstrips Democratic activity *for the first time*, with Republicans sponsoring more than four times as many pro-life bills as Democrats. The four rightmost columns in Table 5.3 divide the legislators by their ideology rather than their partisanship. The pro-life sponsorship among liberal and most liberal legislators is at its nadir during the last period of out study. In stark contrast, the conservative and most conservative legislators are more active than they have ever been. During the last third of our study, sponsoring abortion legislation may be an easy way for conservative members of Congress to signal to their constituents that they are truly distinct from their more liberal counterparts.

INCREMENTALISM AND ABORTION-RELATED PROPOSALS

In the previous section, we showed that both Democrats and Republicans have been regular sponsors of pro-life legislation. The data in Table 5.4 show that both Democrats and Republicans have, in the aggregate, favored over the last thirty years an incremental strategy to change abortion policy. Both Democratic and Republican sponsors of abortion-related legislation are similarly likely to pursue an incremental strategy. The figures in the top half of Table 5.4 run contrary to the idea that Republicans are narrowly focused on trying to ban abortions though constitutional amendments. Here, we see that both Republicans and Democrats are much more strategic in their legislative activity, introducing abortion-related legislation that incrementally alters abortion policy.

Among those legislators who sponsor abortion-related legislation, we see that members across the entire ideological spectrum have pursued an incremental strategy more often than a nonincremental one. Just over 55 percent of abortion-related legislation introduced by conservative members and 70 percent of abortion-related legislation introduced by most conservative members has been incremental. For the liberal and most liberal legislators, those numbers are almost identical, with 60 percent of the legislation tied to liberal legislators being incremental and 68 percent of the legislation tied to the most liberal legislators being incremental. When we focus on bill sponsorship, the more mainstream conservative and liberal legislators are least likely to pursue an incremental strategy.

TABLE 5.4. *Incremental and Nonincremental Bills by Party and Ideology, 93rd–108th Congresses*

	Party	Incremental Bills	Nonincremental Bills
Party	Democrat	60.5 %	39.5%
		(293)	(191)
	Republican	59.8	40.2
		(312)	(209)
Ideology	Most liberal	68.1	31.9
		(92)	(43)
	Liberal	60.2	38.8
		(219)	(145)
	Conservative	55.1	44.9
		(226)	(185)
	Most conservative	70.1	29.9
		(68)	(29)
	Total	605	401

Those legislators at the extremes of the ideological spectrum are most likely to pursue an incremental strategy to change abortion policies.

When we examine incrementalism and nonincrementalism over time in Table 5.5, we see that nonincremental activity was at its apex during the first third of our study. In those Congresses immediately after *Roe*, Democrats and Republicans and legislators from across virtually the entire ideological spectrum were most likely to pursue nonincremental means to change abortion policy. Only the most liberal legislators have consistently favored incremental proposals throughout the entire time period. Save for the most liberal legislators, nonincremental legislation was by far more common than incremental legislation during the earliest Congresses under study. Again, as noted in Table 5.4, it was the conservative – not the most conservative – members who were the most prominent sponsors of nonincremental legislation.

For the twenty-year period from 1985 to 2004, there was less nonincremental legislation sponsored than for the period from 1973 to 1984. Both Democrats and Republicans introduced three times as much nonincremental legislation during the first eleven years studied here than in the remaining twenty years. Since the 103rd Congress, there has been a marked increase in the volume of incremental legislative activity among conservative members and the most conservative members of the House. In general, the volume of incremental activity linked to Democrat legislators is steady over time, but the volume for Republicans shifts dramatically

TABLE 5.5. *Incrementalism and Nonincrementalism During Different Time Periods, 93rd–108th Congresses*

Incremental Bills

	Democrats	Republicans	Most Liberal	Liberal	Conservative	Most Conservative
93–98 (1973–1984)	39% (93)	22% (44)	52% (32)	38% (71)	11% (18)	41% (16)
99–102 (1985–1992)	78 (108)	75 (56)	79 (33)	78 (79)	76 (37)	65 (13)
103–108 (1993–2004)	88 (92)	87 (212)	78 (32)	94 (61)	90 (152)	80 (59)
N	293	312	97	211	207	88

Nonincremental Bills

	Democrats	Republicans	Most Liberal	Liberal	Conservative	Most Conservative
93–98 (1973–1984)	61 (147)	78 (160)	48 (28)	62 (117)	89 (140)	59 (23)
99–102 (1985–1992)	22 (31)	24 (19)	21 (9)	22 (22)	24 (12)	35 (7)
103–108 (1993–2004)	12 (13)	13 (31)	22 (9)	6 (4)	10 (16)	20 (15)
N	191	209	46	143	168	45

over time. Republicans increased their volume of incremental legislation almost fivefold – from 44 to 212.

RELIGION AND ABORTION

Religion and abortion have been tied closely together in the political arena. During the period of our study, the Roman Catholic Church and numerous conservative Protestant denominations have taken strong stands against abortion.[3] Many scholars have argued that the rise of the Christian Coalition was linked to the abortion debate. The abortion debate is also tied to the general movement of many (conservative) Roman Catholics toward the Republican Party over the past twenty years (e.g., Abramowitz and Saunders 2006). Religious groups have almost uniformly focused on the moral aspects of the abortion debate, arguing that abortion involves the taking of life.

Tables 5.6 and 5.7 portray sponsorship activity across legislators' faiths and denominations. In Tables 5.6 and 5.7, we display the self-ascribed religious affiliation of the sponsors of abortion-related proposals. Legislators' self-ascribed religious affiliations are Catholic, Baptist, Methodist, Presbyterian, Protestant, and Jewish. We realize that the Protestant category is a bit of a catchall, but these affiliations are self-ascribed by the legislators themselves, not judged by us. Of those legislators who chose to engage in abortion-related legislative sponsorship, across all faiths and denominations, Roman Catholics are by far the most active. This finding ties in closely to the strong view of the Roman Catholic Church on the abortion issue. Throughout the period we examine, the Church has repeatedly stressed its views on abortion in written and verbal statements (Dillon 1993b). As John Dilulio (2006, 7) summarizes,

Not all Church teachings with relevance to present-day political issues are plain, but the Church's teachings against abortion could not be plainer. The Catechism of the Catholic Church condemns and forbids abortion from just about every theological, philosophical, and moral angle imaginable. The first entry in the subject index says it all: "Abortion: condemnation in the early Church; excommunication as penalty; inalienable right to life; protection of human life from the moment of conception." If the Catechism is not enough, there are many papal encyclicals, notably Pope John Paul II's *Evangelium Vitae* ("The Gospel of Life"),

---

[3] To be certain, there were times when the Catholic Church's stand on abortion was quite different. For instance, evidence of the ensoulment of the fetus was often tied to the first quickening. That said, during the period of our study, the Church has been emphatic: Life begins at conception, and abortion involves the taking of life.

TABLE 5.6. *Pro-Life or Pro-Choice Bills by Representative's Religion, 93rd–108th Congresses*

Representative's Religious Affiliation	Pro-Life Bills	Pro-Choice Bills	Incremental	Nonincremental	Total
Catholic	89%	11%	47%	53%	375
	(333)	(42)	(177)	(198)	
Baptist	94	6	73	28	86
	(81)	(5)	(62)	(23)	
Episcopalian	73	27	83	17	59
	(43)	(16)	(49)	(10)	
Jewish	36	64	90	10	67
	(24)	(43)	(60)	(7)	
Protestant	65	35	65	36	99
	(65)	(34)	(64)	(34)	
Christian	89	11	67	33	36
	(32)	(4)	(24)	(12)	
Methodist	89	11	50	50	94
	(84)	(10)	(47)	(47)	
Presbyterian	88	12	63	38	97
	(85)	(12)	(60)	(36)	
Other	63	37	74	26	46
	(29)	(17)	(34)	(12)	
None	62	38	57	43	47
	(29)	(18)	(27)	(20)	

that proclaim the same staunchly and compassionately pro-life message about abortion. In addition, Catholic scholars, notably Princeton University's Robert P. George, have fashioned more purely philosophical and legal arguments against abortion that do not depend on shared religious principles.

Church leaders, as well as Catholic lay scholars, have spoken and written of the moral, philosophical, and legal failings of ready abortion services. For some Catholics representatives, such strong Church stands against abortion might be reflected in their legislative activity. When we consider specific members of Congress who are or have been prominent in the abortion debate, we see that Roman Catholicism links Representatives Christopher Smith (R-NJ), James Oberstar (D-MN), and the now deceased Henry Hyde (R-IL).

Baptists are often viewed as being closely tied to the abortion debate and the Christian Coalition. The late Jerry Falwell was one of the most prominent Baptists of his era and was one of the original leaders of the

TABLE 5.7. *Pro-Life Nonincremental Legislation Over Time, by Religious Affiliation, 93rd–108th Congresses*

	Pro-Life Percentage					
	Catholic	Baptist	Methodist	Presbyterian	Protestant	Jewish
93–98	90%	88%	86%	95%	69%	41%
(1973–1984)	(176)	(22)	(44)	(40)	(33)	(7)
99–102	98	100	91	80	61	30
(1985–1992)	(84)	(18)	(10)	(8)	(14)	(7)
103–108	77	95	94	84	64	36
(1993–2004)	(73)	(41)	(30)	(37)	(18)	(10)
N	333	81	84	85	65	24

	Nonincremental Percentage					
	Catholic	Baptist	Methodist	Presbyterian	Protestant	Jewish
93–98	78	56	84	62	52	38
(1973–1984)	(153)	(14)	(43)	(26)	(25)	(6)
99–102	37	0	27	40	9	0
(1985–1992)	(32)	(0)	(3)	(4)	(2)	(0)
103–108	14	21	3	14	25	4
(1993–2004)	(13)	(9)	(1)	(6)	(7)	(1)
N	198	23	47	36	34	7

Christian Coalition. Falwell was also staunchly antiabortion. However, Baptist sponsors of abortion-related legislation do not dominate the issue. When members who are Baptist do sponsor abortion-related legislation it is almost always in the pro-life direction (94 percent). However, for sponsors of abortion-related proposals who are Methodist or Presbyterian, we see similar pro-life stances (89 and 88 percent, respectively) and greater volume of pro-life legislation compared to Baptists. The abortion-related activity among Methodists and Presbyterians is interesting because there is a split among the Presbyterian organizations regarding whether abortions are permissible, and the Methodist Church has viewed abortion as a choice since before the *Roe* decision and was instrumental (along with the Presbyterian Church USA) in the creation of the Religious Coalition for Abortion Rights. We know of no Christian denomination that advocates abortion, but denominations do approach the abortion and choice issues very differently. Catholics who sponsor abortion-related proposals generally mirror their church's stand, more so than the typical Catholic voter (Dilulio 2006). Methodists who sponsor abortion-related proposals are more staunchly pro-life than their church's stand. When assessing the figures in Table 5.6, it is crucial to keep in mind that we are only looking at the sponsors of abortion-related proposals. Many Methodist legislators might reflect their church's stand on abortion but choose not to sponsor abortion-related legislation. However, of those Methodists who choose to address abortion policy, most are pro-life.

Among those legislators who pursue abortion policy, Jewish members have been most likely to be pro-choice. Among those members who sponsored abortion-related proposals, Jews comprise the only religious group in Congress that has sponsored more pro-choice bills than pro-life bills; 65 percent of abortion-related bills sponsored by Jewish members have been pro-choice. To repeat an earlier cautionary note, we cannot say that Jews are more pro-choice than legislators of other faiths, but we can say that those Jewish members of Congress who pursue abortion policy tend to be more pro-choice than legislators of other faiths who pursue abortion policy.

Abortion is a complicated issue in Jewish tradition and law.[4] Abortion is neither banned nor allowed on demand. The clearest injunction is that abortion may be used to save the life of the mother. Such clarity on the importance of safeguarding the life of the mother is similar to the position taken by the United Methodist Church. Though we do not mean to make this a comparative study, we do note that abortion is legal in Israel. However, despite its legality, abortions can be difficult to obtain in areas within Israel where religious authorities have greater authority (Wilder 2007). Indeed, there is such a myriad of positions and explanations relating to the appropriateness of abortions under specific circumstances that some Jewish scholars argue that each potential abortion requires a consultation with a rabbi or halachic authority.

Clearly, different faiths have very nuanced views on abortion. Some Protestant denominations have changed views over time, which may allow members of the same religion to follow their religions tenets on abortion differently at different times. That said, Table 5.7 indicates that Baptist sponsors of abortion-related legislation are most consistently pro-life. Baptists do not, however, dominate the sponsorship activity related to abortion. Until the most recent period – from 1993 to 2004 – Catholics were the most staunchly pro-life. Even in the 1993–2004 period, over

---

[4] Halacha – the body of Jewish religious law – includes Biblical, Talmudic, and rabbinical injunctions. In addition to these formal writings, customs and traditions play a role in Jewish law.

75 percent of all Catholic-sponsored legislation was pro-life. Measured by the raw number of bills introduced, Catholics play a more prominent role than all other faiths. There are, however, interesting variations. Catholic activity has dropped over the period of our study, and their tendency to favor pro-life proposals peaked in the middle period. The volume of legislation tied to Catholics peaked in the first period of our study (176 proposals) and was at its lowest in the last period (73 proposals). The percent of the proposals sponsored by Catholics that were pro-life peaked in the middle period at 98 pieces of legislation. Across all other Christian denominations, the middle period represents the nadir in sponsorship activity.

Catholics also introduce the most nonincremental legislation. For nonincremental sponsorship, as we have noted earlier, there is a general movement away from sweeping proposals and toward incremental proposals. For Baptists and Protestants, the last period of our study saw a demonstrable increase in nonincremental proposals. Given that Catholic nonincremental proposals dropped from 153 between 1973 and 1984, to 32 between 1985 and 1992, to 13 between 1993 and 2004, it is interesting to see that Baptist nonincremental activity vacillates from 14 in 1973 and 1984, to 0 between 1985 and 1992, to 9 between 1993 and 2004 and that Protestant nonincrementalism shifts from 25 (1973–1984) to 2 (1985–1993) to 7 (1994–2004). The general shift away from nonincrementalism is not reflected across all faiths. Legislators of different faiths pursue different types of policy – pro-life or pro-choice – and they also favor different strategies – either incremental or nonincremental.

Personal politics are not easy to write about, but we know that Catholics, Jews, and various Protestant denominations think very differently about the myriad issues entwined with the abortion debates. Legislators with different religious affiliations adopt different strategies. Of course, legislators with the same religious affiliation may also adopt different strategies under different legislative environments or when faced with different external pressures. In the next section, we explore some of these issues more rigorously using multivariate analyses.

SPONSORING INCREMENTAL OR NONINCREMENTAL ABORTION-RELATED PROPOSALS

In Table 5.8, we present the results of an analysis in which we try to determine the factors that affect the introduction of incremental or nonincremental pro-life and pro-choice legislation by members.[5] In these analyses, we examine three types of factors that may affect the decision to introduce either incremental or nonincremental legislation. First, we consider factors related to the external environment in which the member is functioning. These factors are (1) the number of pro-choice media mentions in the year the bill was introduced, (2) the number of pro-life media mentions in the year the bill was introduced, (3) the percent of individuals answering "it depends" to questions related to abortion in public opinion polls, (4) if it is an election year, (5) the member's margin of victory in the last election, and the interaction between election year and public opinion.[6]

Second, we look at factors related to the internal environment – the environment within the Congress – in which the member is introducing a bill. Here, we are interested in (1) the number of cosponsors that the member has on the introduced bill, (2) the ideology of the median House member, and (3) the ideology of the median member of the majority party. The ideological medians (measured using the NOMINATE score) of the majority party and the House structure the strategic opportunities for legislators. The cosponsorship variable allows us to assess whether there is any substance to the claim that legislators seek political cover for some types of abortion-related activity by securing a large number of cosponsors. Finally, we consider the personal attributes of the member, including (1) the member's own ideology and (2) if the member is either Catholic or Jewish.[7]

---

[5] We use logit models to analyze this question because we have a dichotomous dependent variable. The regression analyses in Table 5.8 use a cluster option, which allows us to weaken the traditional assumptions about independent observations and secure robust standard errors. Within a Congress, legislators experience the same internal and external environments, so their sponsorship activity may not be entirely independent from one another. The cluster option weakens the independence assumption for activity within a given Congress. Observations across Congresses are still presumed to be independent. The standard errors are generally increased whenever one uses a cluster option, and our standard errors are marginally increased. One could argue that we should cluster on any number of other variables, such as member or religious affiliation. The basic results are only marginally affected. Clustering yields robust standard errors, which is good, but choosing which variable to cluster on is partly subjective.

[6] For the External Environment, our independent variables are Pro-Choice and Pro-Life Media, Public Opinion, a dummy variable for election years, and an interactive term between Public Opinion and the election year variable. All variables are measured in the same manner as they were in earlier chapters. For instance, Public Opinion is the proportion of respondents answering, "it depends," when asked whether abortions should be permissible.

[7] The Personal, Political Environment includes three variables. There are two dummy variables: one to denote Catholic affiliation and the other to denote Jewish affiliation. The

TABLE 5.8. *Logit Regressions: Sponsoring Incremental (1) v. Nonincremental (0) Pro-Life and Pro-Choice Abortion-Related Proposals*

		Pro-Life: Incremental (1) v. Nonincremental (0)			Pro-Choice Incremental (1) v. Nonincremental (0)		
		Summary	Coefficient	Significance	Summary	Coefficient	Significance
External environment	Pro-choice media	Not significant	0.04	0.10	Not significant	-0.05	0.10
	Pro-life media	Not significant	-0.41	0.52	Significant, nonincremental	-2.55	0.02
	Public opinion ("it depends")	Not significant	-0.11	0.56	Significant, nonincremental	-0.62	0.05
	Election year	Significant, incremental	1.09	0.00	Not significant	0.26	0.75
	Margin of victory in last election	Significant, incremental	0.02	0.05	Not significant	0.02	0.54
	Public opinion in election Year	Not significant	0.01	0.44	Significant, incremental	0.05	0.02
Internal, legislative environment	Number of cosponsors	Not significant	0.01	0.25	Significant, nonincremental	-0.02	0.04
	House median NOMINATE	Significant, incremental	20.57	0.00	Significant, incremental	27.05	0.03
	Majority party NOMINATE	Significant, nonincremental	-7.98	0.01	Significant, nonincremental	-15.85	0.01
Personal, political environment	Sponsor's NOMINATE	Not significant	-0.46	0.15	Not significant	-0.29	0.40
	Catholic (1 = Y, 0 = N)	Significant, nonincremental	-1.03	0.00	Not significant	0.03	0.97
	Jewish (1 = Y, 0 = N)	Significant, incremental	1.93	0.01	Significant, incremental	1.32	0.05
	Constant	Not significant	4.09	0.68	Significant	34.53	0.05
		$N = 717$ Pseudo $R^2 = 0.37$			$N = 153$ Pseudo $R^2 = 0.23$		

If we know key information about the external political environment, the internal dynamics of the Congress, and the personal attributes of a member, what can we say about the likelihood of a piece of legislation being incremental or nonincremental?

Starting first with the external environment, we see in the top of Table 5.8 that the amount of pro-choice media has only a slight affect on incremental or nonincremental activity. More pro-choice media may slightly increase the likelihood that pro-life legislation will be incremental and that pro-choice legislation will be nonincremental. By contrast, the amount of pro-life media does not affect incremental activity on the pro-life side, but more pro-life media mentions are associated with more pro-choice nonincremental activity. Whether pro-choice media mentions promote incrementalism depends on the direction of the proposed abortion policy. When we consider public opinion, we see that it has a demonstrable effect on whether a pro-choice proposal will be incremental, but it is not a statistically significant factor in the pro-life model. When there are more respondents saying, "it depends," pro-choice abortion-related proposals are less apt to be incremental.

Election years promote incrementalism in the pro-life proposals, but election years do not significantly affect the type of pro-choice legislation that is introduced. The greater the percentage of votes that a member secured in the last congressional campaign, the more the election promotes incrementalism in the pro-life model, but that percentage does not have an effect on the pro-choice side. As the last electoral margin gets bigger, incrementalism is favored, or, to put it slightly differently, after tight races, pro-life proposals offered by members of Congress are more apt to be nonincremental. Addressing the abortion issue might inoculate an incumbent from some challengers but – among those legislators involved in abortion politics – incumbents surviving tight races are more apt to pursue nonincremental strategies, and incumbents who secure wider electoral victories are more apt to pursue incremental strategies. Nonincremental proposals have considerable symbolic content, especially since their chances of success are extremely low. When we examine the interaction of an election year and public opinion, we find that it

excluded category includes all non-Catholic Christian affiliations as well as any faiths beyond the Judeo-Christian tradition. We fully recognize that across the Protestant denominations the variations in attitudes are at times tremendous. Indeed, there are schisms even within certain Protestant denominations. Given that we are only looking at legislators who are active in abortion politics within the House, these issues are somewhat muted.

is positively correlated with incrementalism in the pro-choice measures. Although public opinion has no independent effect on the incidence of pro-choice incrementalism, during election years, as the set of "it depends" respondents increases, incrementalism is favored by sponsors of pro-choice legislation.

Next, we consider the three factors associated with the internal legislative environment in which members of Congress are operating as they make a decision regarding how to address the abortion question. Here, we find that, as the House becomes more conservative, both pro-life and pro-choice abortion-related proposals are more likely to be incremental. This effect is very strong and clearly present in both the pro-life and pro-choice models. By contrast, when we examine the ideology of the majority party, we find just the opposite effect. A more conservative majority party increases the likelihood that abortion proposals are nonincremental. The party effect is strong and clearly present in both the pro-life and pro-choice models. A conservative majority promotes more nonincremental proposals on the pro-life side *as well as* on the pro-choice side. Pro-life and pro-choice advocates respond in a similar strategic fashion, pursuing incremental or nonincremental proposals under similar House environments. The motivation behind and the symbolic content of such nonincremental pursuits are likely to be very different but the House environments are very similar. Cosponsorship is negatively associated with incrementalism in the pro-choice model but has no significance in the pro-life model. Put slightly differently, nonincremental, pro-choice proposals are more likely to have a large number of cosponsors than incremental pro-choice proposals.

Given the overall focus of this chapter, we are very interested in the personal, political factors that explain which members introduce incremental and nonincremental legislative activity. The three factors we consider are more tightly focused on the sponsors themselves. The first factor – the sponsor's NOMINATE score indicating the member's ideology – is insignificant in both models. A sponsor's ideology has no significant link to an incremental or nonincremental legislative strategy. However, the two variables that measure religious affiliation provide us with more interesting results. We find that Catholic and Jewish legislators are significantly different from each other and from the set of all other religious affiliations in the pro-life model.[8] Jewish affiliation is also

---

[8] The Catholic and Jewish variables are dummy variables measured 0 or 1. The coefficients for dummy variables are interpreted in relation to the *excluded category*. In this instance, any legislator who is not a self-ascribed Catholic or Jew is in the excluded category. The

significant in the pro-choice model. For those legislators active in abortion politics, Catholics are less likely to sponsor incremental pro-life proposals than Protestants, our excluded category. In contrast, Jewish legislators are more likely to offer incremental pro-life proposals than Protestants. We also see that Jewish members of Congress are also more likely to offer incremental pro-choice proposals than Protestants.

Two issues deserve careful attention. First, our findings are based on data that are organized by abortion-related proposal, so we are looking only at those legislators who are active in abortion policy. The Catholics active in abortion policy may or may not accurately reflect the set of all Catholic House members. Likewise, Jewish legislators active in abortion politics may or may not reflect the set of all Jewish House members. Our analysis of legislative sponsors allows us to say, "Among those legislators active in abortion politics, Catholics are less likely to offer incremental proposals and Jewish legislators are more likely." The second issue we need to address is the relative substantive effect of the factors that we identified in Table 5.8 that influence the decision to introduce either incremental or nonincremental pro-choice or pro-life abortion legislation.[9] In order to interpret the data in Table 5.8 more effectively we need to ask, all else being equal, how important is a given factor compared to the others? For example, what happens to the likelihood that pro-life or pro-choice abortion legislation will be incremental when we change the House median ideology from being solidly liberal to being solidly conservative? In Table 5.9, we examine the most statistically significant variables to ascertain their substantive impact for both pro-choice and pro-life legislative activities.

Table 5.9 displays only the most statistically significant variables from Table 5.8. The columns are labeled by religious affiliation – Catholic, Jewish, or Other, which consists of all non-Catholics and non-Jewish members. The two numbers in each cell represent changes in the predicted probabilities of a proposal being incremental during nonelection and then election years.[10] Consider the bottom row in the top panel of Table 5.9.

---

coefficient for Catholics is interpreted in relation to all of the Protestants in the excluded category. The Jewish–Catholic comparison is possible only because they are each significantly different than zero and they have opposite signs.

[9] In linear regression models, direct interpretation of coefficients is much easier than in nonlinear models. In nonlinear, maximum likelihood models, such as the logit regressions we are using, direct interpretation of coefficients is dangerous because the substantive impact of a variable is affected by the levels of the other variables. In short, statistical significance does not ensure substantive significance.

[10] In this analysis, all continuous variables are set at their means.

TABLE 5.9. *Changes in Predicted Probabilities of Sponsoring an Incremental Proposal (Nonelection Year, Election Year)*

Pro-Life Proposals	Other Affiliation	Catholic Affiliation	Jewish Affiliation
External environment			
Pro-choice media p25, p75	(.19, .10)	(.22, .18)	(.05, .02)
Election year Nonelection to election year	(.16)	(.25)	(.04)
Last election % p25, p75	(.05, .02)	(.06, .05)	(.01, .01)
Internal, legislative environment			
House median NOMINATE p25, p75	(.76, .57)	(.85, .75)	(.41, .24)
Majority party NOMINATE p25, p75	(−.83, −.76)	(−.80, −.83)	(−.63, −.48)
Personal, political environment			
Sponsor's NOMINATE p25, p75	(−.06, −.03)	(−.08, −.07)	(−.02, −.01)

Pro-Choice Proposals	Other Affiliation	Catholic Affiliation	Jewish Affiliation
External environment			
Pro-choice media p25, p75	(−.08, −.05)	(−.10, −.06)	(−.03, −.02)
Pro-life media P25, p75	(−.97, −.97)	(−.97, −.97)	(−.96, −.95)
Public opinion	(−.17, −.16)	(−.18, −.16)	(−.06, −.07)
Election year* opinion p25, p75	(.98, .98)	(.98, .98)	(.98, .98)
Internal, legislative environment			
cosponsors p25, p75	(−.07, −.07)	(−.07, −.07)	(−.02, −.03)
House median NOMINATE p25, p75	(.74, .73)	(.71, .70)	(.56, .52)
Majority party NOMINATE p25, p75	(−.94, −.94)	(−.91, −.92)	(−.88, −.87)

When we hold all other variables at their mean, as Sponsor's NOMINATE shifts from the 25th percentile to the 75th percentile (from the liberal side of the spectrum to the conservative side), the predicted probability that a proposal is incremental goes down. For Catholic members, the probability of one of their sponsored proposals being incremental declines by 8 percentage points during nonelection years and by 7 percentage points during election years. Interpreting the results in Table 5.9 in this manner allows us to explore a number of interesting issues.

In Table 5.9, we see that Jewish members are less affected by changes in the amount of pro-choice media coverage. In the face of increases in the pro-choice media coverage, the probability of pro-life legislation being incremental increases by no more than 5 percentage points for Jewish legislators and by as much as 22 percentage points for other legislators. In a similar fashion, Jewish legislators are less affected by election year status. Although this variable was statistically significant in Table 5.8, we see that, for Jewish legislators, an election year is not a substantively important factor, increasing the likelihood of incremental legislation by only 4 percentage points. In contrast, we note that during an election year Catholic legislators increase their probability of sponsoring incremental proposals by 25 percentage points. The margin of victory in the last election has minimal substantive impact on the likelihood of offering incremental legislation. It is never more than 6 percentage points, and its effect practically disappears for Jewish legislators. If electoral margins affect legislators' interests in the type of abortion policy to pursue, it is greatest for Catholics and Others.

Turning to the two internal legislative factors that were significant in the pro-life model – the House median NOMINATE score and the majority party NOMINATE score – we see that both are important for members regardless of their religious affiliation. However, Jewish legislators are less apt than other legislators to alter their abortion sponsorship strategies as ideologies shift. Across all religious affiliations, an increasingly conservative House median promotes incrementalism, but an increasingly conservative majority party promotes more nonincrementalism. Conservative House medians prefer incremental efforts that have a greater chance of passing than nonincremental efforts. Conservative majority party medians promote both pro-choice and pro-life nonincremental efforts to alter abortion policy. Conservative majority parties are more closely tied to efforts that are largely symbolic, whereas more conservative House medians promote incremental efforts that have, as we will see in the next chapter, some chance of being adopted.

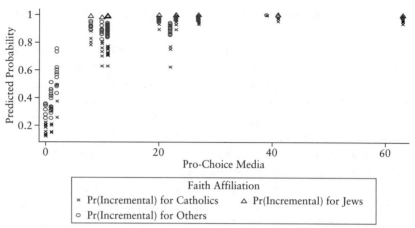

FIGURE 5.1a. Predicted probability of incrementalism for pro-life proposals (election years).

Figures 5.1a and 5.1b present some of the same information displayed in Table 5.9. In each figure, the predicted probability of incrementalism is on the vertical axis. The number of pro-choice media mentions is represented along the horizontal axis. Each observation represents a pro-life proposal and the religious affiliation of its sponsor. Figure 5.1a displays our results for election years, and Figure 5.1b provides results for nonelection years. All other independent variables are held at their average values. Clearly, Jewish legislators almost always prefer an incremental approach to pro-life abortion policy, regardless of media attention. Catholic legislators dominate the lower tier of observations. Those legislators who are neither Catholic nor Jewish dominate the middle tier. For Catholics and Others, increases in pro-choice media mentions have a very clear effect, increasing the likelihood that their pro-life abortion proposals are incremental.

The bottom half of Table 5.9 explores shifts in the predicted probabilities of pro-choice legislative proposals being incremental. Generally, there are fewer differences across faith affiliation in legislators' adoption of strategic incrementalism on the pro-choice side of the abortion debate. Once again, the variation in predicted probabilities for shifts in the internal, legislative environment deserves special attention. Consider a shift in the House median NOMINATE value from its 25th to its 75th percentile – thereby moving the House from being more liberal to more conservative. The predicted probability of a pro-choice proposal being incremental when a legislator with Catholic or Other affiliation sponsors

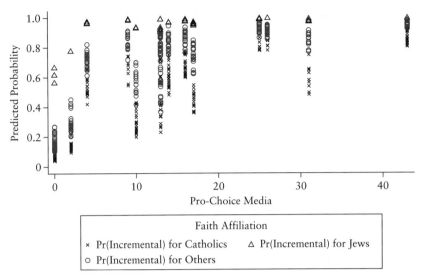

FIGURE 5.1b. Predicted probability of incrementalism for pro-life proposals (nonelection years).

it increases by at least 70 percentage points. For Jewish legislators, those changes in predicted probabilities are much smaller but are still large, at over 50 percentage points. Clearly, there are differences across these faiths but it is also true that the ideology of the House median member has a tremendous impact on legislators across all faith categories. The number of pro-life media mentions and the majority party NOMINATE values similarly affects all faiths. An increase in the number of pro-life media mentions is linked directly to a precipitous drop in the likelihood of a pro-choice proposal being incremental. To express this point slightly differently, as there are more pro-life media stories, legislators across all faiths are much more likely to sponsor nonincremental pro-choice legislation. In a similar fashion, a conservative majority party promotes less strategic incrementalism among sponsors of pro-choice legislation.

SUMMARY

Legislative sponsorship can serve many different purposes for legislators. For an issue heavily laden with moral implications, such as abortion, one immediately considers the symbolic content of legislation. Clearly, there is multifaceted symbolism in many abortion-related proposals. One might also consider the personal political environment of the legislators themselves. A sponsor's ideology has no demonstrable affect on her pursuit of strategic incrementalism. Some factors, such as the margin of the member's last election, that appear statistically significant for pro-life activity have little substantive impact. A legislator's last electoral campaign might affect her willingness to pursue abortion policy, but it does not demonstrably affect whether that pursuit is incremental or nonincremental. A legislator's religious affiliation, a most personal declaration arguably far removed from day-to-day politics, does have an effect on the type of pro-life proposals one pursues. Catholic members of Congress are least apt to adopt strategic incrementalism with their pro-life proposals and both pro-life and pro-choice Jewish members are most likely to pursue strategic incrementalism with their proposals. Those legislators who are neither Catholic nor Jewish occupy the middle ground.

The internal, legislative environment is also very important when legislators consider whether to sponsor incremental or nonincremental abortion-related proposals. Interestingly, an increasingly conservative party median has the same effect on both pro-choice and pro-life sponsorship. As party control becomes more conservative, fewer legislators pursue strategic incrementalism, and both pro-choice and pro-life advocates pursue the nonincremental approach. For the ideology of the House median member, the effects are just the opposite. A more conservative House median member is linked to more strategic incrementalism.

The decision of whether or not to introduce abortion-related legislation and whether that legislation will be incremental or nonincremental is the first step in the legislative process for House members. In the next chapter, we explore where abortion proposals are referred and how abortion proposals fare. The strategy of incremental versus nonincremental legislating can, in part, play an important role in shaping where legislation is referred.

6

Playing the Field

Committee Referrals of Abortion-Related Proposals

> Perhaps the most important thing to know about committees in the House
> of Representatives ... is that they are **jurisdiction-specific** subunits of their
> parent chamber. (Shepsle 1978, 4, emphasis in the original)

> Pick any twenty pages in the Congressional Record or watch an hour of
> C-SPAN, and you will see telltale signs of jurisdictional intrigues. (King
> 1997, 1)

INTRODUCTION

How well established are committee jurisdictions? Are multifaceted
policies readily constrained to just one or two committee jurisdictions?
As we noted in Chapter 3, abortion lies at the intersection of many fundamental human motivations, not the least of which are sex and procreation.
Those fundamental motivations and advances in medical technologies
and health services sometimes fail to mesh in a smooth, consistent, or
coherent fashion. Views on abortion are intertwined with views on the
definition of life, individualism, privacy, womanhood, and feminism, as
well as morality and religion and the roles of the church and state in
our lives. How is a policy with such a dramatic impact on our senses of
being handled by Congress? How do policies with such dramatic content
affect the staid traditions and established procedures of the U.S. House
of Representatives? Issues related to clinic access or the free speech
rights of physicians or demonstrators might readily find their way to the
Committee on the Judiciary, but many abortion-related proposals are far
removed from traditional constitutional concerns. For instance, regulations on scientific procedures and commercial research and development

might find a more natural home in the Commerce Committee and funding issues are naturally the province of the Appropriations Committee.

David Price (1978) notes that committee activity varies by policy. That is, within committees, not all issues are treated similarly. Committee members typically seek high-salience issues with low conflict. With lower salience, there is little ability to claim credit for legislative efforts, and with higher conflict, the risks of angering an important set of players by addressing the policy are greater. Underlying much of Price's analysis is the notion that committee decision making reflects various environmental forces like those discussed in the previous chapters. We are interested in determining how the extant literature on committee jurisdictions and members' decision making apply to abortion politics. Specifically, conflict and salience are both present in abortion politics, but are incremental and nonincremental abortion-related proposals affected similarly? Conflict and salience may vary not only by issue areas but also by the breadth of a proposal.[1]

Paul Schulman's (1975) critique of incremental policy making encompasses an astute analysis of decision making within established institutions. Incrementalism may be a "vision problem," but it can also be an institutional and jurisdictional one. That is, the institution, and not just legislators' preferences, may affect the incremental or nonincremental nature of policy outcomes.[2] Established rules and procedures are central to strong institutions (e.g., Polsby 1968). Schulman claimed that incrementalism encourages small changes *within existing* institutional and jurisdictional shapes. This raises the question as to whether incrementalism is institutionally staid and whether abortion activists – on either side of the issue – are unable to envision new alternative routes to policy change. If Schulman's view defines one end of a spectrum, the other end is characterized by unorthodox or chaotic lawmaking.[3] Given that lawmakers have the ability to suspend or completely rewrite the rules that structure their chamber, how do basic House rules affect the referral of abortion-related proposals? In this chapter, we examine how abortion

---

[1] Some of the best recent work in this area is by Adler and Wilkerson (2008; 2009), which we address directly later in this chapter.
[2] Those readers interested in an extended discussion of the connections between preferences and institutions are encouraged to read Riker's 1980 article.
[3] Barbara Sinclair's *Unorthodox Lawmaking* (2000), Thomas Mann and Norm Ornstein's *The Broken Branch* (2008), and Glen Krutz's *Hitching a Ride* (2001) all discuss the recent breakup of traditional lawmaking and the rise of chaotic, unorthodox legislative practices over the past twenty years.

policies have been addressed within the U.S. House, focusing specifically on committee referrals of abortion-related legislation. Are the referrals of abortion-related proposals planned and strategic, or chaotic, flexible or ineffective? More importantly, do different referral strategies create different opportunities for success?

The scholarly arguments about the original rationale for establishing clear committee jurisdictions often focus on efficiency concerns or distributive rewards. In a series of works, Thomas Gilligan and Keith Krehbiel (1989; 1990) have argued that committees are given jurisdictional claims by the House to facilitate efficiency (see also Krehbiel 1992). Members of committees with strong jurisdictional claims have greater incentives to gather information and master complicated policy. The benefit for the chamber is that the development of expertise in the committees helps the entire chamber make better decisions. If committee proposals are overturned (or rolled) on the floor, then committee members have less of an incentive to gather information – which is a costly activity – as they structure policy. In an earlier series of works, Kenneth Shepsle (1978; 1979) and Shepsle and Barry Weingast (1984; 1994) argued that committees with jurisdictional claims provided distributional rewards to their members. Firmly established committee jurisdictions coupled with an implicit agreement to logroll across committees allow members to dominate policy on issue dimensions of greatest concern to them. A wide array of scholars entered into the debates about the purpose and nature of committees. More recently, scholars have explored whether committees are representative and somehow beholden to the floor median or the majority party (Cox and McCubbins 2005; Rohde 1991; cf. Maltzman 1995). All of these authors generally presume that committee jurisdictions are fixed.

One can question, however, if it is reasonable to presume that committees have fixed jurisdictions. Does a committee reflect the interests of the floor or majority party by resisting an encroachment on committee turf or are its members narrowly self-interested? A committee may *relinquish* turf on a policy if there are no rewards linked to the policy. For example, suppose the majority party or the floor maintains a very tight rein on the policy. Losing committee turf may be of little consequence to the policy-minded committee member. If a policy-minded committee member (e.g., Fenno 1973) is actually prevented from affecting policy, then he or she might reduce burdensome duties by encouraging turf loss so that some other committee can act as a delegate reflecting the floor or majority party preferences. If a committee has a high conflict issue, then loss of that issue to some other committee might be favored, not resisted. Indeed, everyone might favor the shift in turf control if the issue that is high conflict for one committee is low conflict for the other committee, suggesting that changes in committee jurisdictions might increase the overall efficiency of the chamber.

Many elements of turf control have yet to be explored by congressional scholars. Is it reasonable to argue that committees guard their turf if those committees are forced to reflect the floor or majority party? Do committees compete in their (obsequious) efforts to reflect the floor or the party? Every aspect of legislative decision making is affected by committee turf control, but that does not mean that turf battles are inevitable. Incentives to gather information are affected by a shift in turf control. The ability to gain distributive rewards is affected by the loss of turf. If there are readily available electoral rewards tied to policies, one might presume that legislators will engage in turf wars. However, in the absence of narrow electoral rewards, Adler and Wilkerson (2008) suggest coordinated efforts for policy change are tied to jurisdictional reforms.

As noted in Chapter 4, extremely sharp debates over fundamental rights so far have failed to translate into sustained constitutional debates in the U.S. House, even among the staunchest advocates in the abortion policy area. Consider that abortion politics has been a prominent feature of the clamorous backdrop of American politics for over thirty-five years. A strong antiabortion stand has been a cornerstone of the ideological right's earliest forays into politics. Demands from highly charged voters from beyond the Washington, D.C., beltway for constitutional limits on access to abortion services have been incessant, but congressional activity on constitutional limits has been more sporadic. Despite the external demands, members of Congress have promoted much more subtle and, as we argued in the previous chapters, much more incremental policy changes. If you look at the numbers, abortion politics today is clearly not about constitutional amendments to outlaw the procedure nor is it about amendments to codify the right to abortion articulated in the *Roe* decision. The more subtle, incremental approach marks a significant shift from the mid 1970s, when abortion politics in Congress was so often about constitutional amendments.

As abortion politics inside the U.S. House has become more subtle, the legislative procedures used to handle abortion-related proposals have also changed. In this chapter, we note that, although abortion proposals are less sweeping today, there is no lack of abortion-related legislative activity. Indeed, by one important measure, abortion-related policy is more pervasive – even if less sweeping in nature. To wit: a wide array of committees address proposals related to abortion. The Judiciary Committee no longer dominates abortion policy as it once did. Activity occurs across a spectrum of committees, starting with Judiciary but quickly moving to Appropriations, International Relations, Commerce, and others. In this chapter, we explore what characterized the internal House environment as legislators offered abortion-related proposals that did not receive Judiciary Committee referral. In short, "What prompted the changes in referrals and what type of legislator was most apt to violate traditional turf norms?" The last sections of the chapter evaluate the success rates of proposals emanating from different committees and consider how the changes in turf control affected success rates?

REFERRALS IN CONGRESS

Over time, members' knowledge of abortion procedures has changed, and the technical issues surrounding abortion have changed. Such changes might lead to a natural realignment of committee jurisdictions. Technical issues were important to jurisdictional change in other policy areas (e.g., King 1997) and, certainly, abortion policy has been complicated by legal, ethical, and technical concerns. Although new technological issues may lead to new jurisdictions, new strategies may also lead policy advocates to new committees. That is, the strategic concerns of policy advocates may drive the changes in jurisdiction as much or more than the technical issues themselves (e.g., Baumgartner and Jones 1993; Sabatier and Jenkins-Smith 1993; Shipan 1992). There is also a distinct possibility that strategic concerns and technological issues interact one with the other. That is, by playing committees off one another, abortion policy advocates may simply be using technological changes and concerns about committee turf to create the most hospitable niche within the committee system to secure policy goals.

A final possible explanation for shifts in turf control is that policy advocates may deem the movement in policy to be more important than any protection of committee turf. That is, legislators seeking a similar abortion policy may allow one another to encroach on established committee jurisdictions simply out of a desire to see policy changes come to fruition. There may even be coordinated actions across the committees to enhance party control of abortion politics. There is evidence that party leaders try to get the right blend of abortion advocates on committees. Elizabeth Oldmixon records a former staffer to a former member of the

Republican leadership: "'we requested members' right-to-life scores, and that way we could make sure that if we put them on a committee that had jurisdiction over abortion, we knew that we could keep a prolife majority ... the last thing you want to do is put a prochoice majority on the Armed Services Committee and have them pass an amendment overturning current law, thus allowing abortions on military installations overseas'" (Oldmixon 2005, 177). Concerns about the composition of committees are warranted if committee jurisdictions are firmly set. Party coordination across the committees may also facilitate greater electoral rewards for individual members who feel they may benefit from pursuing abortion politics.

Sensitivity to committee composition is less warranted if committee jurisdictions repeatedly shift, and, by some accounts, the House is not shy about making jurisdictional changes. Scott Adler and John Wilkerson (2008) note that there have been almost 150 formal changes in jurisdiction since 1973, the year of *Roe v. Wade*. When important new issues arise, government officials often seek to realign committee jurisdictions. For instance, the 9/11 Commission recommended a realignment of committee jurisdictions to reflect better the needs of homeland security.[4] Indeed, clear and well-demarcated committee jurisdictions are often linked to legislative effectiveness. Adler and Wilkerson note that the concerns about ill-defined jurisdictions becoming "'so scattered that the House's effectiveness is sharply reduced'" are widespread (2008, 89).

David King, however, is barely swayed by the formal jurisdictions outlined in House rules. For King, jurisdictions are ever changing, affected more by statutory complexities and electoral concerns than major congressional reforms. Opposition to congressional reforms is typically tied to reelection concerns (Adler 2002). Legislators want to be able to affect policies important for their own constituents. Though he looks at jurisdictions broadly, John Hardin (1998) notes that external environmental forces affect the array of issues pursued by committees. Frank Baumgartner and Bryan Jones (1993) echo King's view of committee jurisdictions.

Our work builds on the work of scholars who study committee turf (e.g., Adler and Wilkerson 2008; King 1997), focusing on how the bill strategies employed by members have evolved over time. However, the nature of our dependent variable is very different from King's or Adler

---

[4] Although the 9/11 Commission made this recommendation, no effort was made on the part of Congress to implement such a change.

and Wilkerson's. King focused on House members' entrepreneurial efforts to stake claims and expand turf, and Adler and Wilkerson were most concerned about the effects of jurisdictional reforms. We focus on the actual committee referral, which jurisdictional reforms ought to affect (Evans 1999). Specifically, we consider under what circumstances abortion-related measures are referred to Judiciary and under what circumstances such measures are referred to other committees. We also examine how staunch abortion policy advocates pursue committee turf claims. Some members are clearly symbolic actors who make abortion a point of rhetoric, but others act to affect abortion policy, working strategically to find new niches in which to promote their position and achieve legislative success. Our analysis allows us to determine how congressional context facilitates the movement of abortion politics away from the Judiciary Committee.

Technological Advances and Committee Referrals

Initially, abortion politics was associated with the House Judiciary Committee. This is not surprising for two reasons. First, abortion became a major political issue following the Supreme Court's *Roe v. Wade* decision, and the Judiciary Committee has jurisdiction over proposed amendments to the Constitution and similar legal matters tied to free access and free speech. However, the term "abortion" itself does not appear in the formal rules for the House, so no committee has been formally granted authority over this issue. Of course, as noted by King (1997), formal rules alone do not determine the assignment process, but the rules do establish the default referral for the standard-issue legislative proposals. Indeed, the textbook institutionalist view of politics in Congress is one in which committees have fixed and clearly delineated jurisdictions. This textbook view can lead to the conclusion that all abortion politics in Congress is Judiciary Committee politics. Viewed from the "turf wars" perspective of committee competition over jurisdictional issues, movement in abortion politics away from the Judiciary Committees and toward other committees could be viewed as a loss of jurisdictional power by Judiciary. The failure of the Judiciary Committee to capture all abortion referrals would be seen as a loss of control over an issue by the committee.

Given the medical and technological advances affecting the abortion debates, changes in committee jurisdiction might also be interpreted as an attempt by members to secure efficiency gains. Debates over stem cells and their use in medical research highlight the role of technology and innovation in the evolution of the abortion debate in the House. Embryonic research has captivated scientists for thousands of years. Aristotle, the first known scholar to engage in systematic embryonic research, recorded his studies of embryo development by opening a chicken egg during each of the 21 days of incubation (Smith and Daniel 2000, 17, 43–44). Embryonic research tied to humans is much newer and much more controversial. Human fetal research became a prominent issue in 1987 and 1988, when the Reagan administration ordered the National Institute of Health to discontinue research using tissue from aborted fetuses. The debate pitted abortion opponents, who feared such research would lead to more abortions, against medical researchers, who saw the fetal tissue research as holding potential treatments for diseases such as Parkinson's, diabetes, and certain forms of cancer.

With the decision by the Reagan administration to ban the National Institute of Health from doing research on fetal tissue research – and the subsequent decision by the Clinton Administration to rescind the ban – action in Congress became a competition to either codify the president's decision or to overturn it. Representative Henry Waxman (D-CA) was a major advocate for fetal tissue research and Representative Chris Smith (R-NJ) was a major opponent of such research. Not surprisingly, Waxman was most active on this issue during the Reagan and Bush administrations, as he worked to overturn the bans on research, and Smith was most active during the Clinton years, attempting to reimplement the ban. All of this activity occurred in the Commerce Committee, as a debate over medical research. The Judiciary Committee played no role.

During the 1990s, there continued to be a tremendous debate over this issue, but the debate has changed as the science of fetal tissue research has changed. Consider two innovations. First, scientists began to do fetal stem cell research on unused embryos that were created in test tubes for couples undergoing fertility treatments, not on tissue from aborted fetuses. Currently, fertility treatment requires the creation of many more embryos than will actually be implanted. The remaining embryos are typically frozen and stored. By some counts, there are about half a million such embryos in cold storage across the country. The use of test tube embryos allowed some pro-life members of Congress to consider supporting fetal tissue research, as the tissue was not coming from aborted fetuses but from tissue that had never been implanted in a woman's uterus.

Second, the issue of fetal tissue research changed as the potential of stem cells – which are extracted from fetal tissue – became better understood. In 1998, with a breakthrough in the ability to culture stem cells, it became clear that stem cells might provide potential cures for an ever-increasing variety of diseases, such as Parkinson's, Alzheimer's, Huntington's, spinal cord injuries, and diabetes. As it became more clear that this research would likely provide medical benefits to millions of Americans and could be conducted using embryonic tissue from fertilization clinics – and not fetal tissue taken as a by-product of abortions – this became more of a public health issue focused on medical benefits and less of an abortion issue. Clearly, some members continued to press a staunchly pro-life position on fetal tissue research, focusing their attention on the fertilization not the implantation. Other pro-life members supported the research.

Whether one views the Commerce Committee's foray into stem cell issues as illustrating a loss of jurisdictional turf for the Judiciary Committee may very well depend on how one views embryos – whether implanted or not. If the destruction of an embryo is akin to the abortion of an implanted embryo, then one might argue that Judiciary lost turf. Our point is less dramatic. Simply put, technological change may affect committee jurisdictions. Constitutional issues typically handled by Judiciary become entwined with technological issues often handled by Commerce.

Strategic Advocates and Committee Referrals

Battles over jurisdiction often arise when new technologies or new policies arise that fit somewhere in-between the existing jurisdictions of two or more committees, as happened with energy policies in the 1970s and 1980s.[5] However, it is also possible that advocates of a particular type of abortion policy may adapt to changing opportunities within Congress. The older committees of jurisdiction may not be well suited or well positioned for new strategies because of ideological shifts surrounding the issue. Changes in issue framing may occur as a response to changes in public opinion or other changes in the congressional or electoral environment. Framing effects inside of Congress may not be the same as framing effects outside of Congress. Inside of Congress, a particular frame may very well affect other institutional rules and procedures. For instance, when abortion policy is interpreted from different angles, emphasizing, say, health, technology, or rights, committee referrals are directly affected. Issue reframing affects congressional rules, structures, and procedures. In

---

[5] King notes that this also occurred with the development of the magnetic levitating trains (King 1997).

contrast, a frame for public opinion probably has few constraints on it. Depending on the frame, different people will be mobilized but the basic rules or norms operating within the society are left unchanged. Framing by an interest group may have some constraints because of internal group dynamics and previous stances taken on related issues. No group wants to scare away members or donors, so groups do have some constraints on their abilities to reframe an issue. For instance, whether a group empha- sizes parents' rights (and obligations) to protect their young daughters or daughters' rights to choose depends on the group's previous deci- sions and its members' interpretations of the issue. Abortion policy is not unique in this fashion. Numerous policies are interpreted differently over time and handled differently by Congress over time. For example, Frank Baumgartner and Bryan Jones (1993) note that the way Congress handles nuclear power and drug policy changed dramatically over time. As the issue framing changed, so did the salience of the issue for different committees.

Paul Sabatier and Hank Jenkins-Smith (1993) have noted that the coalitions involved in a given policy niche evolve over time as the over- all knowledge about the policy changes. As new studies are conducted and new information becomes available, various policy actors change their strategies on how to address an issue. For example, views on the issue of air quality and global warming have changed over time, based on changes in scientific knowledge, social contexts, and technology. Support for methods of lowering airborne toxins from cars depends on whether there is an energy crisis, the relative cost of the technology that will be used to eliminate these toxins, and our knowledge of the benefits that will accrue from making such changes. Such profound changes in the policy-making environment often strain established partisan divisions on an issue.

As with the case of air quality and global warming, knowledge about abortion has changed since 1974, as have the ways in which members of Congress, interest groups, and the media frame the abortion issue. Recall that, for the period toward the beginning of our study, abortion was simply not mentioned in polite company and that abortion was not central to the rise of the women's movement in the 1960s. Earlier, hushed discussions have certainly been replaced with open and often rancorous debates. Open debates have altered our knowledge of abor- tion and abortion-related issues during the period of under study. The framing of abortion has also changed during the period of our study; however, the impact on a policy-making environment of technological changes, framing effects, or more widespread knowledge can never be fully separated from legislators' strategic concerns. We contend that numerous changes in the policy-making environment provide incentives for changes in the referral process but demands for policy changes must be reflected clearly within the legislators' relevant environments. That is, policy change and the referrals that promote policy change must be supported within the legislative environment. Technological changes may be fortuitous, rather than determinative.

In the preceding chapter, we saw how the internal and external environments affected bill sponsorship. For committee referrals and proposal success rates, the internal congressional politics must be conducive to policy change. Without support for policy change, changes in established congressional procedure are harder to justify. We contend that it is the ideological shifts in Congress that allow technological changes and framing effects to alter committee jurisdictions. That is, the ideological makeup of the House as well as its parties and committees affect the incentives to attempt to reframe an issue to secure a new committee venue. Incentives (bolstered by ideology) and opportunities (bolstered by technological changes and shifts in issue framing) are both necessary conditions for legislators' strategic maneuvering.

As we showed in Chapter 3, there is wide variation among committees in their interparty ideological differences. In addition, there are differences in the relationships across committee-floor ideologies and majority party committee and majority party caucus ideologies. These dynamics affect how members plan to shape an abortion proposal. A member may want to have his bill considered by a specific committee with a specific ideological dynamic or relationship with the floor of the House. As Oldmixon's (2005) work shows, parties sometimes work carefully to affect the abortion balance on a wide array of committees.

THE RISE AND FALL OF THE CONSTITUTIONAL AMENDMENT

The strength of the Judiciary Committee's claim over abortion policy, at least initially, was predicated on the fact that abortion was considered a constitutional issue. Given that the national debate over abortion arose, in large measure, from the Supreme Court's *Roe v. Wade* decision – which found that the constitutional right to privacy that grants women autonomy over their bodies extends to abortion – pro-life critics of *Roe* likewise looked to a constitutional solution. Legislators – especially House members – initially saw abortion as being a constitutional issue.

In the early years, about 70 percent of Judiciary referrals were constitutional amendments. In the years following the Supreme Court's decision, members of both parties introduced many constitutional amendments aimed at banning abortion. Each of these constitutional amendments was assigned to the House Judiciary Committee, where they languished.

During the Reagan era, there was a dramatic shift away from the constitutional amendment strategy. In the House, more constitutional amendments related to abortion were introduced from 1975 through 1980 than were introduced in the remainder of the years examined. This is a somewhat odd finding, given that Ronald Reagan resided in the White House from 1981 to 1989, a period when abortion politics remained at the forefront of many individuals' political agendas. Even the presidency of one of the key figures for the ideological right failed to generate an increase in constitutional broadsides on abortion policy. Similarly, the Republican takeover of Congress in 1994, which brought an influx of new, more conservative members, did not move the constitutional amendment to the fore.

For many in the pro-life movement, the human life amendment was the guiding principle maintaining their focus and uniting their efforts (Cassidy 1996). Movement away from the human life amendment was interpreted as a willingness to accept and even legitimize some abortions. Many pro-life advocates simply could not accept any compromise. To be certain, there were deep divisions within the antiabortion movement (Cassidy 1996), but a large segment feared the loss of the moral cornerstone of the movement. From an ideological perch closer to the pro-choice side of the debate, these differences may seem minor, but, within the movement, there were "enormous tensions" and "bitter internal rows" (Cassidy 1996, 145).

The number of abortion-related constitutional amendments continued to decline in the House, accounting for less than 10 percent of all abortion-related activity in the 1990s. Now, there are a limited number of legislators in the U.S. House who are the keepers of the pro-life constitutional amendment flame. The most consistent member in this regard is Representative James Oberstar (D-MN), who has introduced a pro-life constitutional amendment in every Congress since the 94th and whose interest in abortion politics is almost entirely focused on the symbolic. Representative Oberstar has not introduced any other form of abortion-related legislation since 1979.

The Judiciary Committee was affected by the fact that, early in the debate over abortion, pro-choice and pro-life members of Congress moved to a much more incremental strategy on abortion. Instead of undertaking grand, sweeping efforts on abortion policy that are the focus of constitutional amendments, they moved to change abortion policy more gradually. Moving away from constitutional amendments allowed House members to move away from the Judiciary Committee. Although the Rules of the House defining committee jurisdictions give Judiciary control over proposed amendments to the Constitution, Judiciary held no formal lock on more incremental abortion-related proposals. Without a formal lock on abortion proposals, Judiciary was bound to lose some turf due to incremental proposals.

Although some turf loss was probably inevitable, nothing precluded Judiciary from pursuing its own incremental efforts. As the absolute number of abortion-related constitutional amendments declined, so too have abortion amendments as a percentage of all abortion legislation considered by the Judiciary. Indeed, the Committee on the Judiciary has always addressed issues related to abortion that were far removed from constitutional reach or constitutional claims. Before 1981, constitutional amendments constituted 88 percent of the abortion legislation considered by Judiciary. During the 1980s, constitutional amendments constituted approximately 64 percent of all abortion legislation Judiciary considered. However, during the 1990s, there were only twelve abortion-related constitutional amendments introduced in the House, less than 29 percent of the Judiciary Committee's workload that related to abortion.

THE ABORTION STRATEGY SHIFT: NEW VENUES

The seeds for the decline in importance of the abortion-related constitutional amendment were sown during the first Congress after the *Roe* decision as a few members initiated incremental efforts to limit abortion. Some of these early incremental efforts were successful, prompting emulation. In fact, the success of a certain type of incremental activity – restricting federal funding of abortions – was seen by many as having shifted abortion from being a Judiciary Committee issue to being an Appropriations Committee issue. This success began in 1976, when House members amended the Labor–HEW appropriations bill to ban the use of funds in the bill to pay for or promote abortions (*CQ Almanac* 1976). The legislation passed after a congressional override of President Ford's veto.

As we reviewed in Chapter 4, the success achieved on the Labor–HEW appropriations bill led pro-life members of Congress to write narrow amendments restricting abortion and attaching them to similar appropriation legislation vehicles. In 1978, pro-life forces attached restrictive language to the Labor–HEW appropriations bill, the Department of Defense appropriations bill, and legislation related to the Peace Corps. Soon thereafter, funding restrictions were added to appropriations bills covering everything from the District of Columbia to foreign aid. Pro-life forces benefited from the fact that once a member voted to restrict the use of federal funds for abortions in one area, restrictions in other areas were hardly any different. Thus, by 1980, abortion politics was often enmeshed in appropriations politics. In the 1970s, there was a small but significant number of abortion-related bills coming from the Appropriations Committee, approximately 6 percent of all abortion activity. By the mid-1980s, Appropriations Committee referrals accounted for around a quarter of all abortion-related legislative activity and remained consistently at this level into the 1990s.

As Table 6.1 shows, trends in the House have led to increasingly diverse committee venues for abortion policy advocates. Although over time the abortion-related proposals were less sweeping and more likely to be incremental, abortion politics became more pervasive, affecting many committees throughout the House. The shifts in abortion-related legislative activity occurred in the late 1970s and 1980s and gave greater emphasis to the work of committees other than Judiciary. By the mid- and late 1980s, Appropriations and Energy and Commerce each constituted approximately a quarter of all abortion proposals. International Relations and all other committees combined for another quarter. Judiciary's dominance in the issue area dropped from over 60 percent to less than 25 percent. Although the House Judiciary Committee is the venue for many important debates over abortion politics, members quickly determined it was not necessarily the best place for substantive policy change. Interestingly, the late Representative Hyde (R-IL) – an early innovator of incremental abortion politics – was a member of the Judiciary Committee. However, Hyde's most lasting impact on abortion policy occurred on the Appropriations Committee, not the Judiciary Committee. Strong, vocal advocates on both sides of the abortion issue sat on Judiciary, but their presence did not mean that Judiciary controlled all abortion-related turf.

Two examples illustrate how the issue has changed over time. First, beginning in the late 1970s, members of Congress began to see abortion not only as a domestic issue but as an international one as well. This can be seen in bill referrals to the House International Relations Committee.

TABLE 6.1. *All Types of Abortion Bills Introduced into Congress by Committee*

	Judiciary	Appropriations	Commerce	International Relations	Other	Total
1973–1984	64%	11%	11%	2%	11%	99%
	(223)	(39)	(38)	(8)	(37)	(345)
1985–1992	22%	22%	27%	10%	19%	100%
	(49)	(49)	(62)	(23)	(44)	(227)
1993–2004	25%	29%	19%	9%	18%	100%
	(38)	(38)	(45)	(14)	(21)	(156)
Total	43%	17%	20%	6%	14%	100.0%
	(310)	(126)	(145)	(45)	(102)	(728)

Beginning in 1978, the House International Relations Committee began to have bills related to the use of international aid for health, population control, and family planning referred to it. Specifically, pro-life members wanted to ensure that federal aid would not go to programs or organizations that provided abortions or forced sterilizations. Concerns about forced abortions were also raised on repeated occasions. Interest in legislation related to overseas abortions increased the role for the International Relations Committee, allowing it to expand its turf into the abortion policy area. As seen in Table 6.1, International Relations now controls 9 to 10 percent of all abortion-related measures, whereas in the late 1970s it controlled about 2 percent of abortion measures. This case also illustrates the power of issue framing because it was difficult for some pro-choice legislators to support family planning programs in which forced procedures were sometimes employed. Beyond some sort of Orwellian realm, force and choice do not dovetail smoothly.[6]

Second, in the 1980s and 1990s, the actions of the appropriators affected other committee's turf. After disallowing the use of federal fund for abortions, the House Energy and Commerce Committee had many bills related to Medicaid funds for abortions referred to it. Bills related to the teaching of abortion procedures in medical schools that receive federal funds were also sent to Energy and Commerce. In more recent years, the

---

[6] Pressure to secure an abortion is seldom discussed in the United States, but there are an increasing number of anecdotes in which women discuss the pressure they felt to obtain an abortion. Saletan (2003) devotes an entire chapter of *Bearing Right: How Conservatives Won the Abortion War* to the issue of boyfriends, husbands, and parents pressuring women to obtain an abortion.

House Energy and Commerce Committee has been ground zero for the debate over fetal tissue research because medical research falls within the committee's jurisdiction. Both pro-choice and pro-life members have introduced bills related to whether federal medical research funds can be used to fund research on fetal tissue and stem cells. The technological changes in the area of fetal tissue research have strained parts of the established abortion coalitions. In particular, issues and debates surrounding fetal tissue research changed as the potential of stem cells – which are extracted from fetal tissue – became better understood. Technologies and politics interacted as the public health issues tied to stem cell research created some strains in the pro-life coalition.

We conclude this section with three points. First, abortion politics has never been completely monopolized by the Judiciary Committee but the move away from the Judiciary Committee has been sharp. Second, as indicated in Table 6.1, the Appropriations Committee has never dominated the abortion policy area. The so-called Hyde amendments received considerable media attention in the 1970s and 1980s, but the movement away from Judiciary was not perfectly matched by a movement toward Appropriations. Finally, not all Judiciary Committee activity dealt with proposed constitutional amendments, even in the mid-1970s. Judiciary had always handled an array of different abortion measures, so abortion policy advocates could have abandoned the constitutional amendment strategy without forsaking Judiciary. In the next section, we use a logit regression to analyze Judiciary's loss of turf. In particular, we explore how members' personal ideologies and the congressional environment affected turf claims and abortion politics.

WHAT EXPLAINS THE LOSS OF CONTROL BY JUDICIARY?

Turf battles are often sharp in the House. In the House, jurisdictions matter to all aspects of a legislator's professional life. Recognized committee turf allows committee members to control policy more effectively, which can enhance one's reputation within the House as well as increase one's reelection prospects. Committee turf is central to Richard Fenno's classic argument (1973) that legislators use committees to seek policy gains, reelection, and a good reputation within the chamber. Committees may facilitate gains from trade as legislators allow one another to dominate those policy areas about which they feel most strongly. Of course, while allowing dominance in one policy area, legislators secure dominance for themselves in another policy area. Alternatively, committees may be ultimately controlled by the median on the floor. Committees structured under the median legislator's influence likely enhances the information available to the chamber. Considerable amounts of ink have been spilled in the debates circling about congressional committees. Here, we note that in both the Shepsle and Weingast and Krehbiel views of congressional committees, turf control is presumed. In virtually every model of congressional committees, turf is crucial.

Considering Pro-Life Proposals

Given the importance of committees to legislators, the House parliamentarian generally adheres to the formal rules of the House for bill referrals. Any referrals that fall beyond the reach of the House rules are watched closely as precedents. Our regression analysis in this section focuses exclusively on committee referrals of pro-life incremental abortion measures in the House. If we look at both incremental and nonincremental measures, the results are similar, but it is worth noting that *all* nonincremental measures – whether constitutional amendments or not – are referred to the Judiciary committee. Turf loss for Judiciary only occurred with incremental measures. The dependent variable simply reflects whether an abortion measure was referred to Judiciary (coded as 1) or some other committee (coded as 0). We highlight the Judiciary Committee because as previously shown it was the committee losing the turf battles.

As we noted in Chapter 3, the political environment in Congress has changed dramatically over the past thirty years. Here, we determine how some of those changes affected committee referrals of abortion-related proposals. We view the independent variables as falling into one of two broad categories: sponsorship dynamics and strategic opportunities within the House. *Sponsorship Dynamics* subsumes personal characteristics related to the sponsor in the chamber and the sponsor in the electorate. The absolute value of the difference between the sponsor's NOMINATE and the House median NOMINATE falls within this category. Legislators more removed from the House median may be more apt to stretch the standards and traditions of the House, or they may be the most stalwart in both their policy preferences and the means they follow to secure their preferred policies. The number of cosponsors may also affect committee referrals. When a sponsor has numerous supporters, movement away from Judiciary, the traditional home of abortion-related proposals, may be easier. The presence of cosponsors may affect the course of a turf battle, and we predict that turf renegades will run in larger packs. We also include a variable representing the sponsor's party affiliation (with Democrats coded 1 and Republicans coded 0). Finally, we include a dummy variable for election years and another variable reflecting the sponsor's percentage of votes in the last election.

In addition to the sponsorship dynamics, legislators are also sensitive to their *Strategic Opportunities* in the House. Those legislators working in the abortion policy area inevitably must ask themselves whether or not Judiciary would be a hospitable committee for a particular measure. Of course, the actual referral is determined by the House parliamentarian, a nonelected public official who serves at the pleasure of the speaker, but David King makes clear that the parliamentarian is "most closely associated with the median position of the whole House" (1997, 8). If King is correct, which we think is the case, then the parliamentarian's referrals reflect commonplace political concerns of legislators. Legislators are also aware of the referral procedures. If necessary, legislators can craft abortion measures so that the "weight of the bill" leads the parliamentarian to consider venues other than the Judiciary Committee. Independent variables reflecting the strategic opportunities within the House include NOMINATE scores for the Judiciary Committee median, the ranking minority Judiciary member, the House majority party median, and the House median.

For the logit regression, we employ a clustering option by Congress, which ensures that we have robust standard errors.[7] The clustering option allows us to weaken the assumption of independent observations within a Congress. Our observations are organized by measure but our observations within a particular two-year Congress may not be fully independent from one another because legislators within the same Congress face the same strategic opportunities within the House. However, observations across Congresses are assumed to be independent. Generally, a clustering option increases the standard errors for a model's independent variables, thereby reducing levels of significance, which is indeed the case for our models.

The model reported in Table 6.2 is very strong, with a pseudo R^2 of .30. All variables, except for the last election percentage and the House median NOMINATE, are strongly significant. A quick review of the variables in Table 6.2 suggests that Republican sponsors and sponsors far removed from the House median favor the Judiciary Committee. Referrals during election years are more likely to move away from the Judiciary

---

[7] Long (1997) remains a good reference for logit regression models.

TABLE 6.2. *Logit Regression: Judiciary (1) v. Nonjudiciary (0) Referral For Incremental Pro-Life Abortion Measures*

		Coefficient	Significance
Sponsorship Dynamics	Sponsor's party (D = 1, R = 0)	−1.216	0.04
	Last election percentage	0.026	0.10
	Absolute value sponsor – House median	2.221	0.00
	Election year	−0.755	0.05
	Number of cosponsors	0.025	0.00
Strategic Opportunities	Judiciary median NOMINATE	−6.592	0.10
	Ranking minority Judiciary NOMINATE	17.526	0.00
	Party control (D = 1, R = 0)	−15.970	0.00
	House median NOMINATE	9.417	0.16
	Constant	8.816	0.01
	N = 413 Pseudo R^2 = 0.30 Wald chi^2 = 109.29, p > chi^2 = .000		

Committee. As the number of cosponsors increases, referrals are likely to remain within Judiciary, something we did not anticipate. The strategic opportunities within the House also affect referrals. As the Judiciary Committee median becomes more conservative, members appear to craft legislation to secure referrals to other committees. As the ranking minority member on Judiciary becomes more conservative, Judiciary referrals are again favored.

Statistical significance may or may not signify substantive significance for two reasons. First, we are using a nonlinear regression model, which makes substantive interpretations slightly complicated. For linear regression models, the impact of any particular variable is constant, regardless of the value of the other independent variables. For nonlinear models, the impact of any particular independent variable is not constant and instead depends on the values of the other independent variables. The second issue complicating the interpretation of coefficients is more general and directly tied to the nature of statistical significance. A statistically significant variable has a small standard error relative to its coefficient value. The statistical significance of a variable with a very small coefficient is not necessarily a good thing. If the coefficient of a statistically significant variable is so small as to have little impact on the dependent variable, then the associated variable can be safely ignored. Consider the number of cosponsors in Table 6.2. It is strongly statistically significant, but its coefficient value suggests that it may not be substantively important because it is unlikely to affect the value of the dependent variable. That is, the effect of the number of cosponsors on a proposal may be negligible and have no demonstrable effect on the referral decision even though the variable itself is statistically significant.

Table 6.3 provides information about the substantive impact of the variables in our referral model. While holding all continuous variables at their means, we can assess the impact of a change in the dependent variable under eight different scenarios. First, we separate our analyses by Democratic or Republican control of the House. Next, we separately analyze the referral of proposals by Democratic and Republican sponsors. Finally, we consider these scenarios during nonelection years and election years.

Our logit model yields predicted probabilities for the likelihood of a referral to the Judiciary Committee. Table 6.3 displays the changes in those predicted probabilities as independent variables shift in value. Generally, we shift the value of independent variables from the lower percentiles to higher percentiles. For ideology scores, these shifts indicate a conservative shift. For sponsorship dynamics, we shift the variables from the 25th percentile to the 75th. For the variables subsumed by our *Strategic Opportunities* category, we shift from the 25th to the 50th percentile or the 50th to the 75th percentile, depending on the variable analyzed. One immediately notes that during periods of Democratic control of the House none of the independent variables demonstrably shift the dependent variable. A check of our data indicates that, during Democratic control, the Judiciary Committee receives most of the referrals of abortion-related proposals, and nothing else really matters. During periods of Republican control, the sponsorship dynamics have minimal impact. Legislators with larger electoral margins favor the Judiciary Committee over others. Legislators with ideologies well removed from the House median favor the Judiciary Committee. Those proposals with a larger number of cosponsors are also more likely to be referred to Judiciary. However, for each of these variables, the effects on the likelihood of a Judiciary referral are very small, never shifting the probability of a Judiciary referral by more than .03. The substantive effects are insubstantial even though the coefficients themselves are statistically significant.

The strategic opportunities in the House during Republican control are key to understanding the referral of abortion-related proposals. As

TABLE 6.3. *Changes in Predicted Probabilities of a Judiciary (1) v. Nonjudiciary (0) Referral for Incremental Pro-Life Abortion Measures (Nonelection Year, Election Year)*

		Democratic Control			Republican Control	
		Dem Sponsor	Rep Sponsor		Dem Sponsor	Rep Sponsor
Sponsorship Dynamics	Last election percentage (p25, p75)	0.00, 0.00	0.00, 0.00	Last election percentage (p25, p75)	0.01, 0.02	0.00, 0.01
	Absolute value sponsor – House median (p25, p75)	0.00, 0.00	0.01, 0.00	Absolute value sponsor – House median (p25, p75)	0.02, 0.03	0.01, 0.01
	Number of cosponsors (p25, p75)	0.00, 0.00	0.00, 0.00	Number of cosponsors (p25, p75)	0.01, 0.01	0.00, 0.01
Strategic Opportunities	Judiciary median NOMINATE (p25, p50)	0.00, 0.00	0.00, 0.00	Judiciary median NOMINATE (p50, p75)	−0.11, −0.16	−0.05, −0.09
	Ranking minority Judiciary NOMINATE (p50, p75)	0.00, 0.00	0.00, 0.00	Ranking Judiciary NOMINATE (p25, p50)	0.89, 0.94	0.77, 0.86
	House median NOMINATE (p25, p50)	0.00, 0.00	0.00, 0.00	House median NOMINATE (p50, p75)	0.05, 0.08	0.02, 0.04

169

the Judiciary Committee becomes more conservative, other committees are more likely to receive referrals. The likelihood of a Judiciary referral decreases by 11 percent to 16 percent, depending on whether we focus on election or nonelection years and Democratic or Republican sponsors. A favorable Judiciary environment alone does not lead to more Judiciary referrals. As the Judiciary Committee becomes more conservative, other committees may have even more favorable settings to pursue changes in abortion policy. More conservative Judiciary Committees may favor some loss of their own turf to solidify gains in abortion policy across a wide range of committees.

The ranking minority legislator on Judiciary plays an interesting role, especially given our discussion of vote maximization in Chapter 2. During periods of Republican control, the ideology of the ranking Democrat is very important. As the ideology of the ranking Democrat shifts to a more conservative stance, the likelihood of a Judiciary referral increases dramatically, from 77 percent to 94 percent. Although dramatic across the board, the shift is greater during election years and among Democratic sponsors. A more conservative House median also improves the chances of a Judiciary referral, but the impact is not nearly as dramatic, never more than .08.

Accounting for Symbolic Proposals

In Table 6.4, we look more closely at the fates of abortion-related proposals during periods of Democratic control versus Republican control. Some abortion-related proposals are meant for purely symbolic purposes, meaning that the importance of the sponsorship far outweighs the importance of moving forward through the legislative process. Although it would be foolish to think that legislators know ahead of time which proposals might pass from committee, it is not hard to imagine that legislators know which of their own proposals are sponsored for symbolic purposes and will never set forth beyond the committee. If legislators are guided by symbolic reasons, they may largely ignore referral issues. Sponsorship matters – but referral does not.

To account for some of the effects of symbolic sponsorship, we separate failed proposals from passed proposals. For present purposes, a failed proposal dies in committee, and a successful proposal is voted onto the floor. Are referrals handled differently for those proposals that ultimately die in committee as opposed to those that ultimately pass? Every textbook reminds us that 90 percent of all legislation dies in committee.

TABLE 6.4. *Logit Regression: Judiciary (1) v. Nonjudiciary Committee Referral (0) for Incremental, Pro-Life Abortion Measures (by the Proposal's Committee-Level Success and Partisan Control of the House)*

	Successful Proposals		Unsuccessful Proposals	
	Democratic Control	Republican Control	Democratic Control	Republican Control
Judiciary	−10.83	4.04	−3.24	5.47
median	$p < 0.068$	$p < 0.00$	$p < 0.547$	$p < 0.02$
House	50.89	−19.97	6.75	5.98
median	$p < 0.007$	$p < 0.00$	$p < 0.803$	$p < 0.08$
Constant	−0.29	.48	−1.90	−5.39
	$p < 0.739$	$p < 0.193$	$p < 0.547$	$p < 0.00$
	N = 120	N = 110	N = 104	N = 79
	$R^2 = .11$	$R^2 = .02$	$R^2 = .01$	$R^2 = .04$
	Pr>chi^2 = 0.02	Pr>chi^2 = 0.00	Pr>chi^2 = 0.83	Pr>chi^2 = 0.00

In Table 6.4, we assess whether the legislation that ultimately died in committee was handled differently than the legislation that ultimately passed from committee.

The models in Table 6.4 include all incremental proposals in the pro-life direction, but we separate our analyses by the success of the proposal and the partisan control of the House. Given our smaller sample sizes, we included only two independent variables – the Judiciary and House medians. As predicted, the results in Table 6.4 are stronger for those models with just successful proposals. Legislators pursuing symbolic rewards from bill sponsorship care little about committee referrals. Except for the unsuccessful proposals during Democratic control, the models in Table 6.4 perform quite well. Generally, as the Judiciary Committee becomes more conservative, it is favored with referrals during periods of Republican control and more apt to be avoided during periods of Democratic control. For the House median, the opposite occurs. A more conservative chamber median leads to more Judiciary referrals during Democratic control and fewer Judiciary referrals during Republican control.[8] These results are especially strong for those proposals that are ultimately successful at the committee level. Those proposals that fail at the committee level

[8] These results are virtually unchanged if we exclude Appropriations bills, which have higher success rates than any other legislation. The results for referrals during periods of Republican control for failed measures shift slightly, making the House median variable insignificant at traditional levels. All other results are largely unaffected.

likely include the bulk of the purely symbolic proposals. Strategic opportunities within the House – as measured by the Judiciary Committee's median and the chamber median – should (and do) mean less for purely symbolic proposals.

ACHIEVING LEGISLATIVE SUCCESSES

Typically, studies of legislative efforts focus narrowly on roll call behaviors. Scholars explore who voted for or against a set of proposals. Recall, however, that our data are organized at the proposal level, so we do not have roll call votes. As Congress avoids roll calls on more and more proposals, simple measures of success will become increasingly important (Clinton and Lapinski 2008). We do have simple measures of proposal success, and the reasons for studying success are straightforward. Policy change can only occur after legislative successes. Legislators' reasons for focusing on success are also straightforward. "[A] more productive Congress is a more popular Congress" (Glosser, Wilkerson, and Adler 2009, 1). John Lapinski (2008, 235) laments that "Congress scholars have focused nearly all of their intellectual energy into studies of rules, procedures, and institutions, leaving the study of policy outputs, particularly the study of specific policy issues, to other subfields." Lapinski hides this statement in a footnote, but the implication is straightforward: Congressional scholars need to explore policy. In this section, we explore both policy and rules and procedures.

Our preliminary evidence suggests that members seek out certain types of committees based on the political environment in which they are operating. As the ideological environment within Congress – especially the Judiciary Committee – changes, members tend to seek out different committees in which to introduce their abortion legislation. If a member views abortion politics as simply being a symbolic act, then the member will be indifferent to the internal, congressional environment in which the debate over abortion is occurring. Given that symbolic legislation is most likely to die, it is unlikely that a legislator cares in which committee it dies. However, if the member is acting strategically and trying to change abortion policy through the legislative process, then the member will be sensitive to various congressional characteristics because these factors affect the likely success of this legislation. Floor dynamics and public pressure for policy change are key determinants of success.

The desire for successful passage creates an incentive to change the way in which an issue is framed and the strategies members employ to pursue their legislative goals. If one were to look across all types of abortion-related legislation – pro-choice and pro-life, incremental and non-incremental – the success rate for the Judiciary Committee would be the lowest among the major committees handling abortion-related proposals. Indeed, more than 90 percent of Judiciary's proposals would die in committee. The success picture changes if one focuses more narrowly on incremental, pro-life proposals but committee referrals are still crucial. The top row in Table 6.5 shows that incremental pro-life legislation has differential rates of success based upon the committee to which the legislation is referred. In the House, of all of the major committees that handle abortion legislation, legislation referred to the Commerce Committee has been the least likely to get out of committee and onto the floor. Its baseline success is just .10. By contrast, the vast majority of abortion-related legislation considered by the Appropriations Committee is considered on the floor of the House (and a majority these items become law).

The success of the bills emerging through the appropriations process is not completely surprising. Appropriations bills inevitably move through the legislative process because of their "must pass" status. Since the success of the original Hyde amendment in the 1970s, there has been a series of successful efforts to limit federal funding for abortion across Appropriations subcommittees – from defense to health to international funding. A blithe reliance on hindsight obscures the fact that the abortion proposals are written by goal-oriented legislators who are sensitive to their legislative and electoral environments. Table 6.5 includes measures of the level of pro-life media mentions and public opinion scores as well as variables related to the internal, legislative environment. We include measures for the sponsor's party (Democrat = 1, Republican = 0), the majority party's median NOMINATE, the House median NOMINATE, and the absolute value of the difference between the sponsor's NOMINATE and the House median. Various scholars note that members close to the chamber median have greater legislative success (Anderson et al. 2003; Volden and Wiseman 2008).

The results in Table 6.5 indicate that different committees are sensitive to different elements of their environment. Pro-life media attention affects the fate of Judiciary Committee proposals but no others. Public opinion affects the International Relations and Appropriations Committees but no others. Even the effect of the sponsor's party affiliation varies across committees. Democrats are generally slightly more successful, except on the Appropriations Committee. Success on the Appropriations Committee was almost entirely driven by Republican sponsorships. Generally, the

TABLE 6.5. *Logit Regression: Committee-Level Success of Incremental, Pro-Life Abortion-Related Proposals (Across Four Committees)*

	Judiciary (Baseline Success = .46)	Appropriations (Baseline Success = .89)	Commerce (Baseline Success = .10)	International Relations (Baseline Success = .38)
Pro-life media	.13 0.03 .42	.01 0.65 .00	−.09 .14 −.04	.06 0.10 .07
Public opinion (depends)	.02 0.91 .02	.45 0.01 .06	−.39 .19 −.06	.24 0.01 .23
Sponsor's party	2.71 0.03 .00	−22.22 0.04 −.87	2.25 .02 .08	1.50 0.11 .29
Absolute value sponsor – House median	−7.02 0.00 −.45	7.63 0.01 .04	−7.82 .00 −.09	−5.99 0.01 −.37
Majority party NOMINATE	−8.41 0.31 −.64	−56.38 0.00 −.99	−3.08 .80 −.09	−14.11 0.06 −.87
House median NOMINATE	26.95 0.18 .74	53.88 0.00 .96	9.85 .70 .23	35.09 0.06 .89
Constant	−2.20 0.83	−9.73 0.08	21.29 .20	−13.85 0.01
	N = 41	N = 176	N = 79	N = 47
	Wald chi²(6) = 44.62	Wald chi²(6) = 243.83	Wald chi²(6) = 44.73	Wald chi²(6) = 30.66
	Prob > chi² = 0.00	Prob > chi² = 0.00	Prob > chi² = 0.00	Prob > chi² = 0.00
	R² = 0.34	R² = 0.33	R² = 0.32	R² = 0.26

Note: Each cell contains the coefficient, its level of significance, and its impact on the dependent variable.

sponsor's extremism hurts a proposal's likelihood of success – unless one looks only at the Appropriations Committee. On Appropriations, the sponsor's extremism is *positively* associated with a proposal's success. As indicated by the majority party's NOMINATE score, Republican-controlled Congresses were less successful than Democratic-controlled Congresses. A conservative House median, however, does promote more success. Unlike the other variables, the effects of the majority party NOMINATE and the House median NOMINATE are fairly consistent across the four committees.

The results in Table 6.5 make it clear that different committees respond differently to opportunities to pass abortion-related proposals. With such small numbers of observations, the reasons for these variations across committees are difficult to pin down. Some differences may occur because of the personalities involved on the committees. Some variations may have more to do with the other committee obligations that limit opportunities to address abortion-related proposals. Nonetheless, two simple points deserve attention. First, when legislators had both the incentives and the opportunities to successfully address abortion-related issues in venues beyond the Judiciary Committee, they took them. Second, just as committees offer very different benefits to legislators, committees are spurred to act under different circumstances.

DISCUSSION

At this point, our measure of success ignores floor activity, but committee support is the crucial first step prior to floor consideration. When we explore floor passage using the same basic model in Table 6.5, the results for the International Relations and Appropriations Committees are virtually unchanged. The same things that prompt committee success prompt floor passage. For the Judiciary and Commerce Committees, the floor passage models are very weak. However, focusing too narrowly on enactments from specific committees can be dangerous. Adler and Wilkerson (2009) make clear that there are key distinctions between policy change, program change, and the success or failure of legislative vehicles. "Existing studies of enactments or the durability of specific laws or programs make valuable contributions ... [but] enactments do not always map directly to policy. Policy is often shaped by multiple laws, which contain multiple provisions" (Adler and Wilkerson 2009, 4).

Abortion policy has changed over the years, but not because of the enactment of a small number of federal abortion programs. Instead, abortion policy has changed over the years because abortion-related issues have crept into a wide range of policy areas across various committees. Abortion policy can be affected by changes in numerous programs. There is no single abortion policy program in U.S. statutes. To help illustrate this fact, consider Temporary Aid to Needy Families (TANF), passed during the Clinton presidency. The immediate predecessor to TANF was the Aid to Families with Dependent Children program (AFDC), which dated from the 1960s. Under TANF, states have considerable discretion. Many of the training and education programs under TANF received considerable media attention, but there were program specifics that affected abortion-related issues as well. Section 403 2c promoted families and discouraged single mothers. A state's eligibility for federal monies depended on its abilities to foster traditional family structures and limit the number of single-parent households. However, out of wedlock births could not be reduced with an increase in the "rate of induced pregnancy terminations" as measured from 1995. In other words, states were encouraged to reduce the numbers of single moms – but not at the cost of increasing abortions. Addressing welfare policy affected basic education and job training programs as well as abortion policy. As seen by the events of 2010, health care reform was directly affected by the abortion debate. Indeed, the recent health care legislation allows states to prohibit insurance exchanges from covering any abortion-related services (Mathews 2010). The abortion debate has remained incredibly resilient and able to affect many diverse issues.

CONCLUSION

Our goal in this chapter was to examine strategic issues related to the referral of abortion legislation. We are used to seeing abortion-related demonstrations on the streets, but abortion politics also plays out in the U.S. Congress, and it is one of the most volatile issues that members of Congress revisit on a regular basis. Given the volatility of the issue, how do members and the chamber itself respond? Though committee referrals are a narrow slice of entire legislative context, they are crucial for setting the agenda as well as the tone of policy debates and for affecting the fates of measures and committees. Recent work on committee jurisdictions clearly indicates that the traditional textbook conception of strictly maintained committee jurisdictional bounds is misguided (e.g., King 1997; Sheingate 2006). Over the period we studied, the reduction in turf for the House Judiciary Committee was dramatic. Such a loss of turf is especially surprising because, as King argues, turf begets more turf, and Judiciary has one of the most expansive jurisdictions in the House (1997, 22). That is, an expansive jurisdiction allows a committee to reach into numerous policy areas. Judiciary's reach did not, however, prevent it from losing ground in the area of abortion politics.

Was the loss of turf a natural occurrence due to substantive technical issues or was there a strategic underpinning to the changing referrals among committees? Certainly abortion policies have become more intricate as they have reflected technological changes. Some natural loss may have occurred with the International Relations Committee, as members addressed abortions overseas. However, there appear to be very prominent strategic underpinnings to abortion referrals. Personal ideologies, legislators' external environments, and the strategic opportunities within the House all correlate with the referral of abortion measures. No doubt, legislators' personal ideologies are important for the sponsorship of abortion measures but legislators' personal ideologies, as measured by their party affiliations and their NOMINATE scores, also affect the referral of abortion measures and sometimes their success.

Did the loss of turf correspond with what we have labeled the changing strategic opportunities in the House? In short, yes. The results are clearest in Table 6.4. Judiciary referrals are affected by the Judiciary Committee median and the House median – but those effects shift as party control of the chamber changes. Those effects are also sensitive to the symbolic content of the proposal. One way to interpret such dichotomous results is that some members sponsor legislation for symbolic purposes without regard to referral issues, while others sponsor legislation because they seek to become true policy entrepreneurs with a record of success. Strategic maneuvering is not necessary for one to receive the benefits of symbolic sponsorship. When legislators do want to affect policy, abortion-related proposals often become attractive. Abortion-related issues touch many diverse programs, so there are numerous legislative vehicles that can be affected by abortion-related proposals. In addition, abortion is an issue area that has not been codified in the House Rules structuring committee jurisdictions, so there is considerable flexibility in the referral process, and when the rules are "'silent or unclear, the [parliamentarian's] office is guided by precedent, logic, or political advantage'" (Adler and Wilkerson 2008, 90).

7

Conclusion

The Activists:
We had a celebratory meeting the next day … the champagne flowed – we were almost delirious. And everybody was ready to disband the networks that had been built. And I said, "No, you can't do this. This isn't the end. This is just the beginning. There will definitely be a counterattack." (Lawrence Lader, NARAL, on post-*Roe* celebrations, Risen and Thomas 1998, 37)

There is a tension … A lot of those people – what we tend to think of as the purists – in essence think that people who would push a more incremental approach are sellouts. I understand that type of zeal, but there is a severe penalty you can end up paying. (Daniel McConchie, Americans United for Life, Davey 2006)

The Legislator:
I'm about 99% pro-choice. (Senator Blanche Lincoln (D-AR) just before voting in support of a ban of partial-birth abortion procedures. (Stolberg 2003b)

The Legal Scholar:
It is perfectly consistent to insist that states have no power to impose on their citizens a particular view of how and why life is sacred, and yet also insist that states do have the power to encourage their citizens to treat the question of abortion seriously. "What is at stake is the women's right to make the ultimate decision, not a right to be insulated from all others in doing so." (Dworkin 1993, 153)

INTRODUCTION

Although each of the four perspectives opening this chapter is unique, they each exemplify the struggles one faces when addressing abortion policy and the role for incrementalism. The legal scholar who recognizes a woman's fundamental right to choose also recognizes the state's rights to affect that decision. Our most sacred rights, such as free speech or free exercise of religious practices, are not walled off from the rest of society or the state. For example, free speech rights designed to ensure open and vigorous debates about terrorism do not extend to all such discussions in any venue. Free speech in airports about bombs or suicide missions is more strictly regulated than most other speech. Free exercise may be regulated if, say, religious practices call for animal sacrifices or drug use. No right is absolute, including the right to privacy. The "image of the rights-bearer as radically free, self-determining, and self-sufficient" is wildly inaccurate (Glendon 1991, 107). Indeed, by most measures, the right to privacy, as the legal scholars Mary Ann Glendon (1991) and Ronald Dworkin (1993) argue, fails to consider an individual's relations to society and sometimes has cold implications. Courts recognize rights and then society demands that all rights bearers be self-sufficient. "Norma McCorvey [the Jane Roe of *Roe v. Wade*] ... won ... the 'right to be let alone.' And let alone she was. No one, apparently, had been willing to help her either to have the abortion she desired, or to keep and raise the child who was eventually born" (Glendon 1991, 58). A right to be let alone, coupled with societal indifference, offers little to the most vulnerable members of society.

The legislator's statement exemplifies the ambivalence that many people hold in regard to their abortion attitudes. Ambivalence, the ability to hold contradictory notions related to the same issue, has always affected abortion attitudes. A person can be pro-choice but, in personal matters, choose life or can be pro-choice but support parental notification laws for minors. Likewise, one can be antiabortion but approve of stem cell research. Absolute clarity or consistency is simply not inherent in many people's attitudes about abortion.[1] Pro-life advocates often remind listeners that Norma McCorvey and Sandra Race Cano, the Mary Doe of the *Roe* companion case *Doe v. Bolton*, have themselves vacillated in their attitudes toward abortion. Both McCorvey and Cano are now staunchly pro-life. Ambivalence suggests less wild vacillation in attitudes but more temperate wavering. The fact is that many people do hold contradictory positions about abortion. "Pro-life respondents *do* value

---

[1] There is no reason to believe that ambivalence might not affect other issues – either mundane or emotion-laden. See Alvarez and Brehm (2002) for a discussion of ambiguity across other policy issues.

personal freedom and autonomy, and pro-choice citizens *do* have some concern for the fate of the embryo" (Cook, Jelen, and Wilcox 1992, 156, emphasis in the original). Senator Lincoln's statement suggests a concern about her own consistency. Perhaps 99 percent consistency is the best one can hope for when addressing an issue rife with such pronounced levels of ambivalence.

The two activists offer their own unique perspectives. From the pro-choice activist, there is a clear recognition that the policy process is ongoing. A court or legislative victory is seldom definitive. The *Roe* decision was drastic enough to create clear losses for antiabortion advocates – losses great enough to inspire concerted countermobilizations. Some activists consider moves and countermoves, but others focus myopically on their immediate goals without consideration of what might come next. The antiabortion activist recognizes the trade-offs inherent in incremental measures. An incremental measure typically cannot accomplish an activist's goals. Activists with strong policy preferences typically pursue fundamental shifts in policy, not incremental changes. Does one constrain goals to increase the chances of passage, or does one remain a stalwart proponent of an all-encompassing policy? Numerous congressional scholars argue that positions taken are more important than policies secured. Most notably, David Mayhew (1974, 132) writes, "the electoral payment is for positions rather than for effects." Morris Fiorina (1973) argues that electoral marginality affects legislators' tendencies to mirror constituents' opinions. In a similar fashion, some interest group advocates insist on maintaining the ideological purity of their positions, but others seek policy gains – even minor, incremental ones.

Just as legislators sometimes favor position taking over all else, the incentives for group advocates to eschew minor gains can be overwhelming. With the rise in public awareness of Supreme Court Chief Justice John Roberts, some people became aware of the group Common Ground Network for Life and Choice. During his confirmation hearings, various media outlets noted that Roberts' wife was involved with the group. At times, Roberts tailored his responses to senators' questions about abortion in a fashion similar to Common Ground statements on abortion. Common Ground emerged in St. Louis after the *Webster v. Reproductive Health Services* decision, which among other things limited the availability of public facilities for clinic space and state funds for abortion services. One of the key leaders of Common Ground was the author of the Missouri law reviewed by the Supreme Court in *Webster*. Other leaders were central figures among the pro-choice advocates in Missouri. Why is Common Ground not more widely recognized? Why has it virtually disappeared? The incremental approach to abortion policy adopted by Common Ground did not garner headlines. "Although Common Ground received accurate, sympathetic, and continuous (although sporadic) ... media coverage between 1990 and 1993, its incremental approach to formulating a new politics of reproduction ... [did] not make headline material" (Maxwell 1995, 14). An incremental approach to policy change is not well suited for garnering headlines and a successful group strategy for garnering headlines does not always correspond with a successful legislative strategy.

In this book, we argued that the incremental approach to policy change appeals to a variety of individuals for slightly different reasons. Legislators value incremental proposals when there is electoral uncertainty surrounding an issue. In the case of abortion, uncertainty initially stemmed from the novelty of the issue for both legislators and society, the ambivalence that many people feel about abortion, and the fact that abortion-related proposals had an uncertain effect on the number and rate of abortions. As abortion proposals moved from committee to committee and touched many policy areas, more and more legislators had to address the abortion issue. For some legislators, abortion has been, and remains, an unwelcome guest on the congressional agenda. For other legislators, abortion-related congressional activity is viewed as an opportunity. Tracy Sulkin (2005) argues that legislators seek to insulate themselves from likely electoral attacks by pursuing certain types of legislation. For some legislators, abortion advocacy is second nature, but for other legislators abortion-related proposals offer insulation – just as Sulkin suggested. In Chapter 5, we also found that the *type* of abortion proposal sponsored is affected by electoral margins. Safer legislators pursue incremental measures, and more vulnerable legislators favor nonincremental abortion-related proposals. In a political sense, some members need to send signals to their base and use abortion for that purpose, but other members have the luxury of crafting policy proposals that are intended to shift policy strategically.

During the "Century of Silence" (Luker 1984, Chapter 3), it was considered impolite to discuss abortion or birth control. Then, barely a decade after *Griswold v. Connecticut*, which ensured greater access to contraceptive devices, and just after *Roe*, members of Congress found themselves addressing the very same issue that so many people had avoided discussing for a hundred years. Indeed, a wide range of individuals sought to distance themselves from all abortion-related issues. Early advocates for greater access to contraceptive devices tried to distinguish their efforts from the abortion access movement. Ties to the abortion access movement, some feared, would undermine the expansion of access to contraception. They sought to separate responsible and widely accepted conjugal acts from less socially accepted acts. The earliest waves of the women's movement largely ignored abortion. Many feminists did not want their efforts to be linked with social issues as much as with economic issues and political freedoms. Although she cofounded the National Association for the Repeal of Abortion Laws in the late 1960s, Betty Friedan's early work largely ignored abortion. Credibility and seriousness demanded that social issues be ignored. One scholar sympathetic to Friedan refers to her 1963 references to sexuality in *The Feminine Mystique* as "almost puritanical" (Tribe 1992, 44).

Kristin Luker (1984) suggests that the prevailing silence on abortion was due to an unwillingness to consider the sexual activity that preceded abortion. By the 1970s, many people in the women's movement had addressed abortion, and it became a centerpiece of the National Organization of Women's (NOW) lobbying efforts. As a nation, we went from never discussing abortion in public to carrying placards in highly publicized marches avowing support for or against abortion access. Even after countless policy proposals, the old tensions revolving around abortion never entirely disappeared. Today, about half of all women's issues handled in the House and Senate address abortion (Wolbretch 2000, 102). Although abortion and women's issues are thoroughly intertwined, about half of all women's issues have nothing to do with abortion. How do legislators – most of whom are male – predict voter reaction to such issues? Abortion is laden with emotional content and complicated by voters' ambivalence as well as society's changing attitudes and mores.

Throughout this book, we have sought to understand how legislators reacted as the nation broke its long silence on the abortion issue. In Chapters 4 and 6, we also saw how abortion permeated a wide array of issues and found a home in many different congressional committees. The demand for policy change – whether from within or beyond the walls of the Capitol – varies across both issues and committees. As seen in Chapter 6, the strategic opportunities to alter abortion policy vary depending on party control of the chamber, public demands for policy change, and the congressional committee of record.

In the remainder of this chapter, we review recent literature on policy change, noting how our understanding of strategic incrementalism differs from recent policy-oriented work. We review the possibility first raised in Chapter 4 that courts, rather than legislatures, should address rights issues. In the last major section of the chapter, we discuss how our work affects standard assumptions and textbook understandings of key aspects of American political institutions.

TYPES OF POLICY CHANGE

Most scholars exploring changes in abortion policy focus on the direction of the policy shift. They wonder whether abortion policy is moving in the pro-life or pro-choice direction. Although we too noted the direction of policy change, more importantly we chose to expand our focus and assess a largely overlooked element of the abortion policy debate. To wit: how do legislators craft their abortion-related proposals – with an eye toward incremental or nonincremental policy shifts? In addition, we explored how incremental and nonincremental abortion-related proposals fare.

When exploring policy change, many scholars have used broad strokes to incorporate the analysis of numerous issues. In his study of legislative enactments and divided government, David Mayhew (1991; 2005) focused on major bills across all types of policy areas. Rather than highlight one or two policy areas, Mayhew focused on major bills regardless of their policy area and ignored the less significant bills. Less significant bills were simply deemed unimportant to the nation's business. For Mayhew, the real question was "When does the U.S. Congress tackle major issues?" Whether one knows beforehand which bills will remain significant over time is difficult to say. Mayhew (1991, 41) recognizes that he ignores incremental approaches as well as the appropriations process.

The breadth of Mayhew's analysis appears to touch on many more issues than we do, but three points deserve attention. First, it would be impossible to describe abortion policy in the U.S. House without including appropriations activity. When it comes to abortion, appropriations and policy are intimately connected. Second, no major abortion-related proposals have passed but numerous incremental measures have. President Ford was generally sympathetic to pro-choice forces, and President Carter was favorably disposed toward pro-life concerns.[2] Neither Ford nor Carter sought to move major abortion-related proposals forward. The human life amendment never gained much ground during the Reagan, George H.

---

[2] Ford did support efforts to move the abortion issue to the state level, but those efforts never secured much headway. Whether such a shift would favor pro-choice or pro-life advocates depends on one's home state. After leaving office, Ford's support for pro-choice policies was more direct.

W. Bush, or George W. Bush presidencies, or after the Republican take-over of Congress in 1994. The Freedom of Choice Act, which stalled during the Clinton years, to date remains untouched by the Obama White House. As we noted in Chapter 2, William Eskridge and John Ferejohn (2001) would include just a small handful of bills within their "super-statute" category. Most legislation is mundane and incremental. Most policies are addressed repeatedly, within numerous statutes.

Third, all of the proposals in our dataset address abortion, but they seldom focus exclusively on abortion. Most of the proposals in our dataset are primarily focused on issues well removed from abortion politics. Changes in abortion policy are not due to a particular piece of legislation or even a small body of congressional statutes. As noted in Chapter 6, many committees have pursued abortion-related proposals. A wide range of proposals and statutes – across many different policy areas and from many different committees – affects abortion policy in the United States. In addition, abortion affects the fate of *other* policies. Consider for instance the health care debates in the House and Senate in late 2009. The fate of the House's health care proposal hinged on its treatment of abortion services, and abortion was a central point of debate in the Senate as well. As noted in Chapter 6, abortion permeates many issues and finds a home in many congressional committees. Also, as we noted in Chapter 5, it should not be surprising that the sponsors of the abortion amendments during the health care debates in the House and the Senate were Democrats, not Republicans.

Forrest Maltzman and Charles Shipan (2008) explore when Mayhew's major laws are *significantly* revised. If the initial legislation is of interest, then subsequent legislation may be as well. Maltzman and Shipan (2008) characterize the partisan environment that favors major revisions in the original legislation. Numerous policy areas are, however, affected by minor changes in a wide variety of programs. Considering abortion, there may be an incentive to use minor legislative vehicles to avoid the limelight. For any given policy, a set of minor legislative vehicles may create substantial changes. In a related fashion, major legislative proposals may become vehicles to move abortion policies incrementally. The major health care proposal or a defense-funding bill provides opportunities for some legislators to attach language that incrementally affects abortion policy.[3] How one chooses to explore the evolution of policy

---

[3] Simon (2009) reports that the abortion language in the initial House health care plan passed in the fall of 2009 would have a limited effect on abortions. "Perhaps the biggest

might be a matter of taste, but many incremental changes can add up to significant policy change over time, and incremental changes to abortion may appear within a wide array of legislative vehicles.

Bryan Jones, Heather Larsen, and Tracy Sulkin (2003) argue that transaction costs (both decision making and informational) create institutional friction that reduces the likelihood of policy changes. More friction leads to more punctuated equilibria. In a very important body of work, Frank Baumgartner and Bryan Jones (1993; 2009) describe punctuated equilibria as those policy outcomes exemplified by small policy changes over long periods of time, until a fundamental disturbance creates pressure for dramatic change. Reduced friction should, therefore, lead to less punctuated policy change and more opportunities for dramatic policy change. In the capstone of their efforts, Jones and Baumgartner (2005, 349) develop a "general punctuation hypothesis." Incremental models, they argue, should predict small, random changes in policy that are normally distributed. The general punctuation hypothesis predicts a much more peaked distribution.[4]

To test their claims, Baumgartner and Jones (2005) follow the path established in the earliest works on incrementalism and look at changes in program budgets. Abortion policy, however, is pursued across many different issue areas and congressional committees, crossing many programs and budgets. Friction in one issue area or on one committee may simply lead to efforts to alter abortion policy in other venues. Legislators may simply move their legislative efforts from committee to committee until they find the right internal environment to pursue policy change. In addition, many of the abortion-related proposals in our dataset have no immediate budget implications.

For Baumgartner and Jones (1993; 2005), the quiet moments in politics allow only incremental policy shifts. Nonincremental change occurs in response to tumultuous times, extraordinary circumstances, and greater feedback providing more information to decision makers (Baumgartner and Jones 1993). Here, we see that abortion politics yields incremental shifts when there is more turmoil. In Chapter 5, sponsorship of incremental proposals was promoted by the electoral environment and pro-choice media coverage. Feedback led to *resistance* to proposals

---

impact of the House bill is that it would bar millions of low-income women who are currently uninsured from obtaining abortion coverage in the future" (Simon 2009, A-4).

[4] Specifically, they predict a larger kurtosis in the distribution of policy outputs. Kurtosis is the fourth moment of a distribution, after mean, variance, and skewness.

for major policy change. One counterexample does not tip the balance against a model. Our intent is to fine-tune the understanding of when different theories of policy change hold true. Our results are not a replication of the Baumgartner and Jones work. Indeed, the differences in analysis are pronounced. Baumgartner and Jones look at actual shifts in policy. We spend considerable time exploring who seeks policy change. We also assess what sorts of policy proposals are sought and when they are sought. Major changes in abortion policy cannot occur in the absence of any sponsorship of major proposals. In short, we look at *efforts* to change policy as well as actual policy shifts. In addition, we explored how members of Congress crafted proposals differently (incrementally or nonincrementally), and we explored how members handled abortion-related proposals procedurally. Critically, we considered how the pursuit of policy goals was entwined with the strategic opportunities across the House committee system.

Strategic Incrementalism

Strategic incrementalism crosses governmental institutions – both the Congress and the executive – and is recognized by group advocates working well beyond the Washington, D.C., beltway. Consider Elizabeth Oldmixon's (2005) interviews of House members. Oldmixon records a Democratic legislator stating that "'I remember there was an attempt ... to codify *Roe v. Wade*, back when we were in charge. I think our leadership was reluctant to bring that out, simply because they knew it would split our caucus ... I'm not sure how much the Republicans operate that way, but I think they have to some extent ... [I]n the Reagan years there was a kind of understanding ... the White House wouldn't push the social and cultural agenda'" (Oldmixon 2005, 170). Oldmixon's interviewee corroborates our notion of strategic incrementalism. A split caucus invites sabotage efforts. If a legislator shifts a proposal to secure greater policy gains, then the set of partisans willing to engage in sabotage increases. Policy gains could be made but votes in favor of the proposal would be reduced, and sabotage efforts would increase.

More recently, George W. Bush presidential advisor Karl Rove was asked when the newly elected Bush would initiate the push to ban abortions. Rove's response indicated the administration's interest in incremental efforts. Rove replied: "'For now, we're focusing on getting the partial-birth abortion ban and doing something about cloning. Let's get those victories before we start making prognostications about what might be years in the future" (Toner 2003).

Is the Obama administration, with Democratic majorities in the House and Senate, poised to pass the Freedom of Choice Act (FOCA)? FOCA would codify *Roe v. Wade* and effectively overturn numerous state laws to ensure greater access to abortion services. We consider FOCA to be nonincremental legislation. The numbers in the House and Senate might suggest that FOCA passage is a done deal.[5] Obama's staunchest and most vocal opponents frequently attack his stands on gun control and abortion – even though no major legislation in either area has advanced. How do pro-choice groups evaluate the chances of the quick passage of FOCA? Cecile Richards, President of the Planned Parenthood Federation of American is remarkably reserved about the chances for FOCA passage. "We're going to be smart and strategic about our policy agenda to bring people together … The Freedom of Choice Act is very important … but we have a long list of things to get done that I think can address problems immediately that women are facing, that are immediate concerns" (Meckler 2008, A5). Richards makes it clear that FOCA, or some other codification of *Roe*, remains an important goal but there are many other incremental advances that are higher on her priority list. Richards is hardly alone in her reserve. "A coalition of nearly 60 liberal and women's groups submitted a list of 15 requests for action in the Obama administration's first 100 days, and FOCA … [was not] on the list" (Meckler 2008, A5).

Strategic incrementalism allows policy advocates to use many different sorts of legislative vehicles to advance their goals. For instance, abortion has already and will continue to affect health care reform efforts (e.g., Eggen and Stein 2009). Issues about federal monies used for abortion, issues about counseling, issues about procedures and notifications all entered into the health care reform debate. Since Richards spoke, as the head of Planned Parenthood, of her interests in pursuing other issues before addressing FOCA, the U.S. House has amended its health care proposal restricting federal funds for abortion services and abortion access.

---

[5] One might argue that two wars and an economic collapse have pushed FOCA from the policy agenda. Two counterpoints deserve consideration. First, abortion has not been pushed from the agenda, as the health care debates indicate. Second, presidents often seek easy wins. If FOCA were easy for Obama and the Democrats to pass, they would have strong incentives to pursue it and claim the easy credit. Likewise, if right-to-life statutes had been easy for Bush, he would have pursued them.

In the face of that defeat, it is hard to imagine how Richards would ever be able to pursue FOCA.

We conclude this section with a brief discussion of two questions typically tied to policy-making models and to incrementalism in particular. The first question is whether or not our admittedly narrow focus on abortion politics limits the general applicability of our results. We cannot dispute the obvious fact that we are exploring one issue in considerable depth. We recorded all abortion-related activity in the U.S. House over the last three-plus decades. Over that period of time, numerous representatives and a wide range of committees addressed abortion policy. We have considerable institutional breadth given that abortion permeated so many committees. In his work on the interplay between the personal characteristics of legislators and their representation function, Barry Burden (2007) argues that a narrow focus on specific issues can highlight important dynamics related to legislators' preferences. Even if our general storyline is accurate, vis-à-vis abortion, one might be concerned about external validity. That is, the decision-making dynamics in other issue areas may be entirely different.

Although his policy areas are broader than abortion alone, John Lapinski (2008) contends that pooling enactments across policy areas can yield incorrect conclusions. That is, internal validity is reduced. What underpins our model of strategic incrementalism as developed in Chapter 2? Our model is preference driven. Legislators recognize the trade-offs between votes for a measure and policy gains. They understand the ever-present blame game and the opportunities for legislative sabotage. Legislators like to maximize votes for legislative proposals to limit blame game opportunities. In addition, proposals that maximize votes rather than policy gains are less vulnerable to sabotage and countermobilizations by opposition groups.

Even though abortion might be considered a "third rail" issue, many Americans hold conflicting or contradictory opinions about abortion. Ambivalence among voters creates uncertainty among legislators. The same voters might react very differently to two pieces of abortion-related legislation. As we argued in Chapters 2 and 3, ambivalence on the part of voters, however, offers legislators wiggle room. Even interest group advocates recognize the dangers of mobilizing opponents by overreaching to secure larger policy gains. In sum, the behaviors of every player within the policy-making environment play a role in strategic incrementalism. Yes, we focus tightly on abortion policy, but the items driving abortion policy are very basic to our general understanding of politics.

Is there some other readily identified issue that might fit our model of strategic incrementalism? Consider health care proposals. Although many readers might recall President Clinton's failed attempt to secure national health care legislation, he was not the first president to consider sweeping health care proposals. Presidents Theodore Roosevelt, Franklin D. Roosevelt, and Harry S. Truman proposed national health care policies. The failure to implement the most sweeping health care policies has not precluded the success of other, more incremental efforts. The late Senator Edward Kennedy (D-MA) lamented his refusal to compromise with President Nixon in 1971 on the single-payer issue tied to a national health insurance proposal. Kennedy wanted more; Nixon wanted less. In the end, Congress passed and Nixon signed the National Cancer Act of 1971, a much more focused health-related proposal. Other health-related proposals recently passed include the Children's Health Insurance Program in 1997 and the Medicare Prescription Drug, Improvement, and Modernization Act of 2003. Indeed, the Children's Health Insurance Program was driven by bipartisan congressional support in the wake of the failed Clinton health care plan. Numerous incremental health care proposals and insurance reforms have passed. More sweeping proposals have not fared nearly as well. It is an interesting thought experiment to consider where health care policy in the United States would be today if advocates for expanded health care in the United States had consistently followed a more incremental process starting thirty-five years ago.

Of course, health care is back in the news. The recently passed health care legislation, as Vice President Joseph Biden noted, is a pretty big deal.[6] Although the Obama White House desperately wanted to secure bipartisan support, they initially garnered single Republican votes in the House and the Senate. Broader Republican support was sought to protect conservative Democrats in 2010 midterm elections. By November of 2009, health care proponents were more concerned about sabotage efforts from conservative Democrats. To maximize votes, single payer and public option plans were modified and abortion coverage was virtually eliminated in both public and private insurance options. "The ultimate irony ... is that both sides argue that they aren't even trying to reopen the debate on federal abortion policy" (Seib 2009). The abortion limits appeared to have broad congressional support even though individuals with private insurers may lose some coverage of abortion-related services.

---

[6] Biden's precise language was slightly more raw.

Do voters have any ambivalence about health care? Is it simply Red States versus Blue States? Andrew Gelman, Nate Silver, and Daniel Lee (2009) suggest that attitudes about health care are fairly easy to explain. The trick is to figure out attitudes toward *Obama's* health care plan. Gelman, Silver, and Lee note that opponents to health care tag the plan with Obama's signature. In states such as Arkansas, there is considerable support for health care reform but much less support for Obama; therefore, Arkansas legislators are cross-pressured. Arkansas was McCain country in 2008, and support for Obama remains thin, but the typical Arkansan would likely benefit from health care reforms. If the Arkansas public interprets health care reform as Obamacare, then Arkansas representatives are less likely to benefit from it. A more incremental proposal would have been easier for the Arkansas representatives to support because there is wiggle room for incremental efforts.

The second question is whether the results of over thirty years of incremental measures are indeed incremental. A large component of the incrementalism storyline is that policy seldom shifts dramatically. Whether repeated efforts at strategic incrementalism do or do not "add up" to major shifts is not a key concern for us, and we do not see the fate of our approach relying on it. That said, the question does deserve some attention. Within the realm of abortion politics, we cannot study shifts in budgets but scholars have studied the impact of abortion policies in other ways. For example Mark Graber (1996, 125) and Kenneth Meier et al. (1996) see little connection between limits on abortion services and the rates and numbers of abortions provided. The number of abortions is a relatively easy measure to understand. However, abortion rates can go up or down independently from the total number of abortions performed as population figures and the number of annual pregnancies change. Of course, any policy is likely to have manifold implications, and assessing the impact of abortion policy by counting the number of procedures may be inappropriate. Perhaps some state regulations, such as waiting periods, are not meant to alter the abortion decision, only the route to that decision. Still, it seems odd that abortion regulations have no demonstrable effect on abortion rates or numbers. Surely, bans on partial-birth abortions are meant to reduce the total number of abortions and not just the type of abortion procedure used. Except, as we noted earlier, in light of the million plus abortions performed each year, very few late term abortions were ever practiced. Even among the late term abortions, the so-called partial-birth abortion ban restricted just one set of procedures.

Perhaps the limits on abortion have a delayed effect. The number of abortions performed did dip below one million in the late 1990s but those numbers climbed back over the one million mark in the early 2000s. The latest measures of the abortion rate, however, are below 20 percent. Helena Silverstein (2007) offers a new interpretation of this issue. In her work on parental notification laws, Silverstein argues that the actual impact of these new requirements may not be that which was intended. Throughout her work, Silverstein argues that the interpretation of law reflects the times and the experiences of those involved. The sound logic of legal reasoning is overwhelmed by the social currents of the times. Simply put, the same laws and regulations have different impact as the times and circumstances change. We are left to conclude that the extant literature on the subject indicates that the most intimate of decisions is made within the purview of the state but that state limitations have little impact of aggregate abortion rates.

Nonincremental Failures

Nonincremental failures are readily found across a wide array of issue areas. Abortion policy has never been fundamentally altered by a nonincremental legislative proposal. Abortion is not unique in this regard. The practical problems associated with nonincremental policy making can be seen in several cases where such policies have been considered in Congress in recent years. In addition to the health care proposals discussed in the previous section, consider the debates over the constitutional amendment that would require the federal budget to be balanced. The amendment was considered several times in the 1990s, but each time the vote came up short in the U.S. Senate. On several occasions, certain members of the Senate switched their vote from supporting the amendment to opposing the amendment, as the total number of votes in the chamber moved closer to the supermajority needed for passage. On several occasions, members modified the amendment to include new provisions in order to limit the impact of the amendment should it actually pass. These modifications became more prominent as the legislation moved closer to having supermajority support. Legislative proposals are often built on foundations of shifting political support. Support emerges, and then it disappears as passage looks more likely. New provisions to limit the impact of the proposed legislation sabotage the original intent of the nonincremental proposal. For nonincremental proposals, these shifting foundations of political support are particularly problematic. All-or-nothing claims on government do not lend themselves well to the institutional structure of congressional policy making or the behavioral foundations of strategic incrementalism.

INSTITUTIONAL VENUES FOR THE ABORTION
DEBATE: COURTS OR LEGISLATURES?

"*Roe v. Wade* is undoubtedly the best-known case the United States Supreme Court has ever decided: ... better known than *Marbury v. Madison* ... or *Dred Scott* ... or even *Brown v. Board of Education*" (Dworkin 1993, 102). Given the prominence of *Roe*, one might think that abortion policy is largely a legal affair to be decided by the courts. There are, of course, a wide range of scholars (e.g., Graber 1996) who feel that abortion policy is best left to the courts.[7] However one feels about the courts' role, the fact remains that the U.S. House of Representatives has spent considerable time addressing abortion policy.

Some abortion policy advocates created a false dichotomy, trying to separate courts and legislatures. On empirical grounds, the dichotomy is simply false. To ignore the House's role in abortion policy is akin to ignoring the obvious. Although there have been at least a dozen Supreme Court cases dealing with abortion since *Roe*, there are literally hundreds of legislative proposals in our dataset on abortion-related proposals in the U.S. House of Representatives. At the state level, both courts and legislatures remain very actively engaged in the abortion issue. Some people possess a healthy fear of the tyranny of the majority and think that courts must safeguard all individual rights. As noted in Chapter 4, determining which institution has best safeguarded rights is far from settled. At times, the Supreme Court appeared most interested in protecting a wide range of privacy rights but, at other times, the Court has recognized the state's right to regulate abortion-related decisions. By most measures, the Supreme Court has become much more conservative vis-à-vis

---

[7] One important scholar who disagrees strongly is the former federal judge Robert Bork. In *Slouching Toward Gomorrah* (1996), Bork notes: "no argument can be made that *Roe v. Wade* has any constitutional foundation whatever. The opinion by Justice Harry Blackmun does not trouble in just over 51-pages to make even the semblance of a legal argument ... The pro-abortion forces, largely centered in the intelligentsia, of course care nothing about constitutional disingenuity, much less the legitimacy of process; they want abortion and they do not care how they get it ... the constitution is indeed silent on the subject of abortion, being left, as most issues are, to the moral choice of the American people expressed in the laws of their various states ... The constitution has nothing to say on the subject [of abortion], but the states can address abortion."

abortion than the Warren Burger Court that heard *Roe*. Even on normative grounds, the presumed dichotomy between courts and legislatures is short-sighted. Although the *Roe* decision is considered a win for the pro-choice side, subsequent Supreme Court decisions have been much less supportive of unregulated access to abortion.

Similar to the Supreme Court, the U.S. House of Representatives has at times expanded and at other times restricted access to abortion. When compared to the courts, legislatures have a wider range of actions available to them as they address rights-related issues. "[W]e have ... a tendency to formulate important issues in terms of rights; a bent for stating rights claims in stark, simple, and absolute fashion; an image of the rights-bearer as radically free, self-determining, and self-sufficient" (Glendon 1991, 107). Appropriately or not, the courts' decisions are often accepted in an absolutist fashion. The intense focus on rights comes at a cost. Mary Ann Glendon's concern (1991) is that, after having conferred rights upon individuals, society may ignore the plights of those rights bearers. Legislatures have much more control of the varied issues tied to abortion. For instance, legislatures may promulgate limits on abortion and also provide support services for those affected by abortion decisions. Courts are not as well positioned for mandating or providing public services. To be certain, legislatures may fail to provide appropriate or sufficient services, but they are at least in a position to balance individual's rights and the responsibilities of a community to care for all who are in it. Courts cannot readily address the social costs tied to their decisions – their decisions stand alone. Legislators are able to consider an entire body of rights, responsibilities, and services – which means that legislatures can adjust the social costs of their abortion-related decisions.

In our view, legislatures have not unequivocally usurped citizens' rights or courts' responsibilities. Rather than addressing the rectitude of legislators' involvement, we examined what legislators have actually accomplished and assessed how such policy changes were accomplished. Lamentations about policy are rife in highly charged areas. Indeed, lamentations may crowd out careful social scientific analysis, which can highlight issues pertinent to abortion policy and abortion politics, as well as American politics and the policy process in general.

Some legal scholars and jurists have argued that technology will inevitably reaffirm the Court's role in abortion policy. Former Supreme Court Justice Sandra Day-O'Connor stated that *Roe* was "unworkable" and internally inconsistent (*Akron v. Akron Center for Reproductive Health, Inc.*). Simply stated, *Roe* was on a "collision course with itself" because technological advances would uncover the inherent difficulties of the trimester approach. Fetal viability, a key element of *Roe*, does not readily map onto trimesters, another key element of *Roe*. How far can the viability envelope be pushed? Increasingly, scholars are exploring technological advances related to ectogenesis – or fetal development outside of the mother (Zimmerman 2003). Pro-life Dr. Bernard Nathanson recognizes the possible links. Over forty states ban abortions after viability. If the fetus is "'viable from ten weeks on … you've destroyed *Roe v. Wade*. It collapses'" (Zimmerman 2003, 16). Technological advances will certainly affect *Roe* and the Supreme Court's decision making, but those advances will also affect members of the U.S. House. The judicial and legislative fronts will both remain prominent in abortion politics.[8]

UNDERSTANDING OUR POLITICAL INSTITUTIONS

Abortion politics and policy are worthy of focused study. However, our analysis of abortion politics is entwined with our understanding of key political institutions. Results from this book inform issues far removed from abortion. In this section, we assess how results in this book amend views of the design and functioning of the U.S. Congress, the behaviors of elected representatives, the mercurial aspects of public opinion, and the role of groups and elections in the policy process.

Models of Legislatures

For several decades, congressional literature has been dominated by a set of debates revolving around the nature and influence of committees and party systems. Consider the debates revolving around committees. Can congressional committees dominate the policy process or does the chamber median assert ultimate control? At times committees appear to dominate the policy process, but the floor does hold some trump cards. Committees have gatekeeping powers, but the floor can use discharge petitions to regain control of committee proposals (cf. Pearson and Schickler 2009). Although some legislation is protected by closed or modified rules, all rules guiding floor debates are adopted by majority vote on the floor.

---

[8] The executive branch also has an impact on abortion policy. The right of conscience regulations passed at the end of the George W. Bush administration allowed medical personnel to avoid working on particular procedures if they objected to them on moral grounds. Executive orders and signing statements may affect abortion policy, but those possibilities must be left for subsequent research.

The committee influence debates generally overlook the opportunities that legislators have to shop an issue around. The same basic issue (e.g., abortion) may be addressed in different committees and – as we noted in Chapter 4 – committee-floor relations vary by committee. In the committee constraint models (Gilligan and Krehbiel 1989; 1990), the willingness of the chamber median to yield influence to a committee depends on the uncertainty surrounding policy impact and the differences in committee and floor preferences. Evidence uncovered in our dataset suggests that pro-life advocates did not feel tightly tied to any particular committee. Furthermore, uncertainty surrounding abortion-related proposals varies widely, partly because the proposals themselves are so diverse in nature. Fluid committee jurisdictions and the tremendous variety in abortion-related proposals alter the committee dominance versus the chamber median debates.

Debates about party influence mirror aspects of the committee-floor debates. Scholars are interested in whether parties exert an influence *beyond* what the preferences of the party members might indicate: whether influence is based on partisanship or simply preferenceship.[9] There are now many, increasingly fine-tuned party influence arguments. Clearly, party has affected abortion politics but not always in clear, easy-to-understand ways. Gary Cox and Mathew McCubbins (2005) suggest that party influence stems from their control of the agenda. In their procedural cartel theory, any policy movement is biased by the majority party's control of the legislative agenda. The "block out zone" is predicated on the floor median defeating any status quo that is up for reconsideration, so control of the legislative calendars is key. Party influence over floor rules and amendments can be trumped by the floor median, whereas the control of the agenda is less vulnerable.[10]

A left-leaning majority party will prevent rightward moving proposals from ever being placed on the agenda. In contrast, leftward moving proposals will more readily find a friendly position on the agenda. In some ways, Cox and McCubbins's work presents a wholesale shift in the language of spatial models. Cox and McCubbins adopt the language of movement – leftward movement or rightward movement in policy. We may be parsing the Cox and McCubbins wording too finely but there is a difference between predicting movement and making an equilibrium

[9] "Preferenceship" was coined by Krehbiel (1993).
[10] Monroe and Robinson (2008) find that restrictive rules that limit amending opportunities often do enhance party agenda control.

point prediction. Like Cox and McCubbins, we envision movements in policy and we have not specified an equilibrium prediction.

Our work stands apart from Cox and McCubbins, however, in a specific sense and a general sense. In the specific sense, we explored a policy where the movement was in the direction opposite of what Cox and McCubbins would have predicted (2005, Chapter 9). If *Roe* defined a "leftish" status quo, Democratic majorities should have prevented any antiabortion measures from finding their way to the floor. The slow march of abortion policy has been rightward – whether under Democratic or Republican control of the agenda. One might argue that the Republicans moved it more but the Democrats did not shy away from making rightward adjustments. Of course, abortion is just one issue. Numerous other issues surely fit the procedural cartel theory better. Our work is also different from the procedural cartel model in that we explain the strategic rationale for making minor, incremental adjustments in policy.

All of these works highlight how legislators structure their chambers. As they structure their chambers, legislators' decisions may reflect many diverse concerns. Legislators may be motivated by reelection (Mayhew 1974), focused on other political bodies (Cameron 2000; Diermeier and Myerson 1999), focused on logrolls and policy gains for high demanders, focused on information processing (Ainsworth and Akins 1997; Krehbiel 1991), or concerned about resolving collective action problems within party structures (Aldrich 1995)? Our focus in this book is slightly different. We focus on how the policy itself is structured, which is to say that, after a committee system or a party system is structured, to serve whatever purposes, a closer look at the policy-making process suggests that another layer of strategic decision-making occurs. Spatial models are often used to illustrate aspects of the policy process, and spatial models remain the backbone of many congressional studies. Traditional spatial models, however, often pay only lip service to constituent pressures or interest group influence. In our model of strategic incrementalism, policy advocates consider countermobilizations.

Legislators' Decision Calculus

John Kingdon (1973, 267–271) envisions more and more constraints limiting legislators' choices. Elites, interest groups, public opinion, and party leaders all place constraints on legislators' actions. For Kingdon, legislators possess clarity in purpose but suffer from severe external constraints. "This conceptual framework is a model which emphasizes constraints on decision, rather than causes" of decisions (Kingdon 1973, 269). "The concept of successively narrowing boundaries emphasizes the limits [on decisions] ... But one interpretative question is whether the limits are important. Are they true limits on behavior, or are they so vague as to be meaningless" (Kingdon 1973, 271). Vagueness of limits creates uncertainty. Even in the face of considerable constraints, legislators found wiggle room and regularly engaged in abortion politics.

David Mayhew (1974) states that there may be constraints but those constraints are readily handled with simple position taking. After finding cover behind some readily staked out positions, legislators may pursue policy change in other areas. In regard to abortion policy, there are certainly legislators who stake out positions, offering proposals that they know will never be addressed on the floor. There are also a large number of legislators who pursue smaller policy gains with incremental proposals that sometimes pass. An improved chance of acceptance has a moderating influence on the proposal offered (see also Woon 2008).

The work presented in this book is, by some measures, noncanonical. We recognize that there are reasons to avoid noncanonical models. Models of adaptive decision making are typically less parsimonious than models of rational decision making. For some, stepping away from the hyper-rational assumptions is akin to stepping onto a slippery slope – you never know where you might settle. By most measures, however, our model of strategic incrementalism is canonical. We do not reject the spatial model nor do we reject utility maximization or suggest that poorly informed legislators settle for second best when they pursue incremental strategies. We simply suggest that there are hitherto overlooked reasons for legislators to resist the pull of the median legislator's ideal point as policy is structured. Vote maximization and concerns about sabotage promote strategic incrementalism and inhibit the pursuit of more sweeping policy proposals.

As scholars have debated the influence of committees and parties, the public's distrust of Congress (and sometimes outright anger toward Congress) has grown considerably. How do models of the U.S. Congress dovetail with the public's attitudes toward the institution and how does a little-liked institution handle such a volatile issue as abortion? The willingness of legislators to address abortion is puzzling, since in many instances members of Congress do everything they can to avoid difficult issues and rig policy shifts to hide or limit traceability (Arnold 1990;

Brady and Theriault 2001). Suppose, by a simple twist of fate, a congressional policy creates an utter catastrophe. Blame avoidance comes in many styles. Legislators might be able to limit traceability, but traceability is never fully eliminated. Legislators might be able to shift responsibility to the opposition party. Suppose, however, that the policy received broad legislative support. Vote maximization amplifies traceability but limits blame. Proposals that maximize legislative support insulate members of both parties from negative political fallout. As Benjamin Franklin was reported to have said, "We must all hang together or we will assuredly hang separately."

Is there consensual decision making in Congress? Some scholars argue that Congress has become more consensual, looking at the sizes of coalitions voting in favor of key legislation. Much of that literature ignores the fact that recorded votes occur on a small percentage of legislative proposals (e.g., Lynch and Madonna 2008; Smith 2007, 183). In addition, the probability of a recorded vote has changed dramatically over time (Lynch and Madonna 2008). None of these works develops a model or theory for consensual decision making. If legislative proposals are more and more incremental, then the size of supporting coalitions depends on the extremeness of the status quo in relation to the floor median. If votes are more likely to be recorded (Lynch and Madonna 2008), then legislators have an increased incentive to trade off the gains from policy with the gains from votes. What are the gains from votes? As we argued in Chapter 2, legislators have an easier time explaining their votes if there are numerous legislators in the enacting coalition. Risk-averse legislators may also be unaware of the impact of policy. Therefore, more votes are better than fewer votes. In sum, the recording of votes is not independent from the size of the coalition because the recording process avails a new set of rewards for legislators.

Joshua Clinton and John Lapinski (2008) note that salient bills are more likely to be recorded. Salience may or may not correspond with uncertainty of impact. If they correlate positively, then the recorded votes should be more consensual. If salience and uncertainty surrounding the impact of a policy are negatively correlated, then legislators might simply line up on opposite sides of the issue. That is, when Democrats and Republicans both find an issue salient and with little uncertainty of its impact, the division between yeas and nays should follow party lines. Vote maximization across party lines occurs in special circumstances: uncertainty about policy impact and uncertainty about political fallout.

Issue Ownership and Electoral Competition

Elected officials and candidates often fight for the control of issues and the issue agenda. Politicians like to play to their strengths. Some issues are considered Democratic territory and others are considered central to the Republican Party wheelhouse. John Petrocik (1989) developed the notion of issue ownership, whereby candidates avoid raising issues that remain a strong suit for their opposition. At some levels, there may be issue ownership (Damore 2004; Petrocik 1989; Pope and Woon 2008), but for abortion it is hardly a clear or fast line. For instance, Sunshine Hillygus and Todd Shields (2008) note that presidential campaigns regularly approach persuadable voters with divisive issues like abortion. The sense that abortion is a Republican issue belies a fundamental misunderstanding of abortion politics. As Jeremy Pope and Jonathan Woon (2008) show, party advantages are rarely permanent, and Hillygus and Shields (2008) note that inroads can be made in issue areas where partisans are cross-pressured by party and personal preferences.

The persuadable voter argument presumes that candidate platforms are generally fixed; however, over long political careers, positions on abortion often shift. Numerous presidential candidates altered their positions on abortion in the 1980s. Those candidates fine-tuning their positions included Democrats as well as Republicans. As candidates in Republican Party primaries, Ronald Reagan and George H. W. Bush became more pro-life and Jesse Jackson and Richard Gephardt became more pro-choice in their Democratic Party primaries. Shifts in position and talk of inoculation do not tell the whole story. There have always been prominent party members on both sides of the abortion issue. From the mid 1980s to the mid 1990s, Republicans in the Senate elected Alan Simpson (R-WY) as their chief whip. Throughout his public career, Simpson was pro-choice (as well as "pro-gun" and supportive of gay rights). Throughout most of the 1990s and the first two years of the twenty-first century, Democrats in the House of Representatives elected David Bonior (D-MI) as their whip even though, throughout his political career, Bonior was pro-life.

Personal roots (Burden 2007), inoculation (Sulkin 2005), and persuadable voters complicate issue ownership and abortion politics. For some legislators, abortion-related activity is tied to personal characteristics and concerns. For other legislators, a little abortion-related activity provides political protection for the next election. A standard claim is that abortion politics is used to "to gin up cultural conflict" and little else

(Oldmixon 2005, 178). We do not claim that abortion-related proposals created an easy legislative environment or pleasant electoral confrontations. But legislators themselves – from each party – pursued abortion-related proposals. Neither party was willing to cede the issue's ownership to the other.

Elections

Recent empirical work by Gregory Bovitz and Jamie Carson (2006) dovetails nicely with several arguments made earlier. Bovitz and Carson find that House roll call votes with greater consensus have limited electoral consequences for legislators. Although classic studies in the political science literature connect roll call voting behavior to electoral fates (e.g., Arnold 1990; Mayhew 1974; Miller and Stokes 1963), Bovitz and Carson show that legislators do not lose constituents' votes when those roll calls showed considerable consensus. Consensus in the U.S. Congress insulates legislators from electoral swings. Consensus can be manufactured by structuring proposals incremental shifts in policy.

Shifting Foundations for Public Opinion

David Brady and Sean Theriault (2001, 177) argue that members engage in "hyperbolic rhetoric" in which "consequences are overblown and exaggerated in hopes of demonizing ... proponents and killing ... proposals." The legislators "most influential in passing legislation are least likely to show up in newspapers and television talk shows" (Brady and Theriault 2001, 177). What one hears about on TV or reads about in the newspapers may not be reflected in actual legislative efforts. How does ambivalence survive in the face of such highly charged rhetoric?

To be certain, some individuals are not ambivalent at all about any aspect of abortion. But many others are less certain, and ambivalence often creeps in very quickly. Consider that many pro-choice advocates worry about women's rights. In their view, to limit abortion services is to limit rights. If women do not maintain absolute procreative autonomy, their rights are limited. Procreative autonomy empowers women by ensuring them domain over their own bodies and lives. The fact that abortion is now being used in the United States for sex selection purposes may or may not cause a pro-choice advocate to cringe just a bit. Sam Roberts (2009) has reported that Asian American birth statistics are consistent with a sex selection practice. Male fetuses are being favored over female fetuses. Choice maintains women's rights, but abortion can be used to perpetuate misogynist traditions. A little ambivalence about abortion is understandable, and the fact that many readers of this book are not ambivalent about abortion fails to undermine the general argument. Alas, most American voters will not read this book, and those who do are likely to have already strongly established views on abortion.

Finally, it should also be noted that over the last decade, both pro-choice and pro-life groups have worked diligently to reframe the abortion issue in ways that best suit them. Pro-choice forces successfully framed the clinic blocking efforts of some pro-life groups, such as Operation Rescue, in a way that lead to the passage of the Freedom of Access to Clinic Entrances Act of 1993. Similarly, pro-life groups used the partial-birth abortion issue as a way of reframing the abortion debate. Not surprisingly, for strong advocates, there is little variation in attitudes toward abortion even when primed with partial-birth abortion questions. For those respondents with less certainty in their attitudes, early questions about partial-birth procedures tend to make respondents less supportive of abortion access (Freedman 2003). Consider the role for viability and the trimester distinctions in *Roe*. Partial-birth abortion is only relevant for late term procedures. The words "partial-birth" imply the viability of a developed being. In 2003, the view by some was that "The more it is debated in Congress, the courts, and the presidential campaign, the more it helps turn the public opinion against abortion generally" (Freedman 2003). Although arguments related to abortion are regularly reframed, most abortion-related proposals remain incremental, and the impact of federal abortion policies on the rate and number of abortions remains incremental.

THE FULL PICTURE, THE FINAL STATEMENT

Numerous scholars have looked at general attitudes and public opinion related to abortion, organized groups and movements, court decisions related to abortion, religious and moral dimensions related to abortion, and the role of presidents and agency heads in the implementation of abortion policy. The U.S. House of Representatives, the people's chamber, has received much less attention. It is hard to develop a full picture of the policy-making environment, but, surely, the people's chamber is a crucial element. In this book, we explored the development of abortion policy, the manners in which legislators addressed the issue, and the impact of abortion on key political behaviors and political institutions.

When it comes to abortion politics in the House of Representatives, Representative Christopher Smith (R-NJ) has been a busy man. For several years, he was the head of the House Pro-Life Caucus and was chosen in 2001 by then President George H. W. Bush to read a statement by the president at the annual pro-life march on Washington to protest the anniversary of the *Roe v. Wade* decision. Of the seventy-eight abortion-related proposals offered in the House during the 106th Congress, Smith offered six. Where was all of this abortion-related activity aimed and how did the House handle it? Sharp divides over basic, fundamental rights continue to mark abortion politics, but Smith never sponsored a constitutional amendment related to abortion, even as chair of the Pro-Life Caucus or as a member of the Republican Party, which supports a human life constitutional amendment.[11] In fact, there were only two constitutional amendments introduced in the 106th Congress related to abortion, one of which was introduced by Representative James Oberstar (D-MN), who has introduced the same amendment since 1975. This book has systematically assessed how legislators like Oberstar and Smith have handled the abortion issue and how the issue has affected the legislative behaviors and institutional structures.

Many people feel that "moral issues" are somehow viewed differently by voters and legislators, making our application of standard political science models less appropriate.[12] The "otherness" claim, however, has limited usefulness. Are there any policies that fail the "otherness" claim? Gay marriage? Health care policy? Military policy? Bank or auto company bailouts? Legislators regularly craft policies that affect others more than they affect themselves or their own families. Indeed, if there were no "otherness" in a policy debate, one might question the ability of a legislator to act fairly. Mark Graber (1996) remains unconvinced, especially in light of the facts that most legislators developing abortion policy are relatively wealthy men, not women. Graber (1996, 160) forcefully states that "[n]o one who enjoys the status necessary to influence reproductive policy need fear that their procreative choices will depend on the next election or judicial decision ... Privileged pro-lifers believe they are committed to parenting every child they sire, knowing that they will have the

---

[11] Specifically, the 2000 Republican Party platform states "[w]e support a human life amendment to the Constitution and we endorse legislation to make clear that the Fourteenth Amendment's protections apply to unborn children." Accessed July 6, 2001, http://www.rnc.org/GOPInfo/Platform/2000platform4.

[12] There is evidence that the mobilization of abortion activists is readily studied with standard social science tools (Gross 1995).

power to change their minds should the unexpected pregnancy occur." We do not contend that Graber's statements are inaccurate or overblown – we simply note that those same concerns hold for virtually every policy. Laurence Tribe (1992, 240) contends, "a greater measure of humility seems in order" when considering abortion issues. Again, we agree – but when or for what policy would that not be the case? "*Voting and persuasion are all we have*" (Tribe 1992, 240, emphasis in the original).

"What is most fascinating about the abortion issue is the variety of reasons people bring to bear on their abortion attitudes" (Cook et al. 1992, 69). The range of issues tied to abortion attitudes may be fascinating for the scholar, but it can become problematic for the politician. How will voters interpret any particular abortion-related vote? Pat Robertson in his 1988 bid for the Republican presidential nomination linked his pro-life position to the strength of the Social Security system. For years, Social Security was considered the third rail of politics. Touching the third rail, the one carrying the electric current, is political suicide. Robertson not only touched Social Security, he connected it to another volatile issue – abortion. What Robertson intuited was that abortion had implications across a wide range of issues – including Social Security. It was not, in his view, a stand-alone issue that could be addressed without affecting other policies. Fewer children and smaller families will affect the maintenance of various programs that rely on cross-generational support.[13]

Some economists have linked abortion rates and crime rates. How is the causal link justified? Some scholars argue that increased access to abortion services reduces the number of unwanted children who would otherwise remain largely neglected by one or both parents.[14] There are also important geopolitical issues at play given that 90 percent of U.S. counties do not have abortion service providers (Becker 2003). Indeed, the array of issues tied to abortion has been virtually unlimited, and, as an issue, abortion will not be going away any time too soon. Every time we have a Supreme Court nominee, abortion again rears its head without regard to presidential control of the White House. Maybe under Obama, things will be different, but it is hard to imagine the abortion issue disappearing (Bazelon 2009).

---

[13] Japan and several western European nations have decreasing birth rates and aging populations. Economic revival is directly affected by such demographics.

[14] The number of works relating crime and abortion has grown steadily over the last decade. Donohue and Levitt (2001) remains one of the most influential works in this area, but the interested reader should also explore Gruber, Levine, and Staiger (1999) and Joyce (2003), as well as Donohue and Levitt (2004).

Abortion is not just a problem for the United States and its political institutions. Many countries are facing a similar set of questions surrounding abortion policy (see, e.g., Ferree et al. 2002; Stetson 2002). How political institutions in such diverse countries as China, Ireland, Mexico, and others handle abortion-related issues is a story yet to be told, but some of the issues raised here are being heard in other countries. "'It is a debate over absolutes,' said Armando Martinez, president of the College of Catholic Lawyers of Mexico. 'It is an issue that is not really subject to debate'" (Malkin and Cattan 2008). By some accounts over 85 percent of the licensed gynecologists in Mexico City are conscientious objectors to the provision of abortion-related services (Malkin and Cattan 2008). Some clinic and hospital violence has also occurred in Mexico.

Is our view of the policy-making process new or different? We see opportunity for legislators to tread where many would suggest no legislative efforts should occur. We see wiggle room where others see stark policy choices. Strategic incrementalism allows for credit claiming and demobilizes some potential opponents. Finally, Kingdon sees a wide range of constraints on policy makers. Kingdon speaks repeatedly of "successively narrowing boundaries" (e.g., 1973, 269, 271). Public opinion, committee jurisdictions, leadership concerns, and the House floor all constrain policy making. On the one hand, we agree with Kingdon, but abortion was able to permeate many committees, leaders from both parties sought to address abortion policies, and public opinion hardly seemed to constrain legislative activity. Sulkin (2005, passim, 71) finds that there are relatively few constraints on what she calls issue uptake. "[L]egislators enjoy considerable discretion in choosing their agendas" (Sulkin 2005, 71). Though we focus tightly on abortion policy, the legislative efforts related to abortion permeate much of the institution.

References

Abramowitz, Alan I. 1995. "It's Abortion Stupid: Policy Voting in the 1992 Presidential Election." *Journal of Politics* 57:176–186.

Abramowitz, Alan I. and Kyle L. Saunders. 2006. "Exploring the Bases of Partisanship in the American Electorate: Social Identity vs. Ideology." *Political Research Quarterly* 59:175–187.

Achen, Christopher. 2000. "Why Lagged Dependent Variables Can Suppress the Explanatory Power of Other Independent Variables." Presented at the Annual Meeting of the Political Methodology Section of the American Political Science Association, University of California, Los Angeles, July 20–22.

Adams, Greg D. 1997. "Abortion: Evidence of an Issue Evolution." *American Journal of Political Science* 41:718–737.

Adler, E. Scott. 2002. *Why Congressional Reforms Fail: Reelection and the House Committee System.* Chicago: University of Chicago Press.

Adler, E. Scott and John D. Wilkerson. 2008. "Intended Consequences: Jurisdictional Reform and Issue Control in the U.S. House of Representatives." *Legislative Studies Quarterly* 33:85–112.

2009. "The Evolution of Policy." Presented at the Annual Meeting of the Midwest Political Science Association, Chicago, April 2009.

Ainsworth, Scott H. 1993. "Regulating Lobbyists and Interest Group Influence." *Journal of Politics* 55:41–56.

2002. *Analyzing Interest Groups: Group Influence on People and Policies.* New York: W. W. Norton.

Ainsworth, Scott H. and Frances Akins. 1997. "The Informational Role of Caucuses in the U.S. Congress." *American Politics Quarterly* 25:407–430.

Ainsworth, Scott H. and Itai Sened. 1993. "Interest Group Entrepreneurs: Entrepreneurs with Two Audiences." *American Journal of Political Science* 37:834–866.

Albritton, Robert B. 1979. "Measuring Public Policy: Impacts of the Supplemental Security Income Program." *American Journal of Political Science* 23:559–578.

Aldrich, John. 1983. "A Downsian Spatial Model with Party Activism." *American Political Science Review* 77:974–990.

Aldrich, John H. 1995. *Why Parties? The Origin and Transformation of Political Parties in America*. Chicago: University of Chicago Press.

Aldrich, John H. and David W. Rohde. 2001. "The Logic of Conditional Party Government: Revisiting the Electoral Connection," *Congress Reconsidered*, 7th ed., eds. Lawrence C. Dodd and Bruce I. Oppenheimer. Washington, DC: CQ Press.

Alvarez, R. Michael and John Brehm. 1995. "American Ambivalence toward Abortion Policy." *American Journal of Political Science* 39:1055–1082.

  2002. *Hard Choices, Easy Answers: Values, Information, and American Public Opinion*. Princeton, NJ: Princeton University Press.

Anderson, William D., Janet M. Box-Steffensmeier and Valerie Sinclair Chapman. 2003. "The Keys to Legislative Success in the US House of Representatives." *Legislative Studies Quarterly* 28:357–386.

Arnold, R. Douglas. 1990. *The Logic of Congressional Action*. New Haven, CT: Yale University Press.

Austen-Smith, David and John R. Wright. 1994. "Counteractive Lobbying." *American Journal of Political Science* 38:25–44.

Bach, Stanley and Steven S. Smith. 1988. *Managing Uncertainty in the House of Representatives*. Washington, DC: Brookings.

Baker, George. 1992. "Incentive Contracts and Performance Measurement." *Journal of Political Economy* 100:598–614.

Banks, Jeffery S. 1990. "A Model of Electoral Competition with Incomplete Information." *Journal of Economic Theory* 50:309–325.

Bartels, Larry M. 2008. *Unequal Democracy: The Political Economy of the New Gilded Age*. Princeton, NJ: Princeton University Press.

Baumgartner, Frank R. and Bryan D. Jones. 1991. "Agenda Dynamics and Policy Subsystems." *Journal of Politics* 53:1044–1074.

  1993. *Agendas and Instability in American Politics*. Chicago: University of Chicago Press.

  2005. "A Model of Choice for Public Policy." *Journal of Public Administration Research and Theory* 15:325–351.

  2009. *Agendas and Instability in American Politics*, 2nd ed. Chicago: University of Chicago Press.

Baumgartner, Frank R. and Beth L. Leech. 1998. *Basic Interests: The Importance of Groups in Politics and in Political Science*. Princeton, NJ: Princeton University Press.

Bazelon, Emily. 2008. "Required Viewing: Oklahoma's Gallingly Paternalistic Ultrasound Law." *Slate* October 22. http://www.slate.com/id/2202765/.

  2009. "What Will Kill the Next Supreme Court Nominee? A) abortion, B) gay rights, or C) neither." *Slate* May 12. http://www.slate.com/id/2218169/.

Becker, Elizabeth. 2003. "Head of Group Backing Right to Abortion to Step Down." *New York Times* September 22.

Beisel, Nicola and Tamara Kay. 2004. "Abortion, Race and Gender in Nineteenth Century America." *American Sociological Review* 69:498–518.

Bendor, Jonathon. 1995. "A Model of Muddling Through." *American Political Science Review* 89:819–840.

Bentley, Arthur. 1908. *The Process of Government*, ed. Peter Odegard. Cambridge, MA: Harvard University Press, 1967.

Berinsky, Adam J. 2004. *Silent Voices: Public Opinion and Political Participation in America*. Princeton, NJ: Princeton University Press.

Berry, William D. 1990. "The Confusing Case of Budgetary Incrementalism: Too Many Meanings for a Single Concept." *Journal of Politics* 52:167–196.

Bianco, William T. 1994. *Trust: Representatives and Constituents*. Ann Arbor: University of Michigan Press.

Binder, Sarah A. 1999. "The Dynamics of Legislative Gridlock, 1947–96." *American Political Science Review* 93:519–533.

    2003. *Stalemate: Causes and Consequences of Legislative Gridlock*. Washington, DC: Brookings Institution Press.

Black, Duncan. 1958. *Theory of Committees and Elections*. Cambridge: Cambridge University Press.

Bork, Robert H. 1996. *Slouching towards Gomorrah: Modern Liberalism and American Decline*. New York: Regan Books.

Bovitz, Gregory L. and Jamie L. Carson. 2006. "Position-Taking and Electoral Accountability in the U.S. House of Representatives." *Political Research Quarterly* 59:297–312.

Brady, David W. and Sean M. Theriault. 2001. "A Reassessment of Who's to Blame: A Positive Case for the Public Evaluation of Congress," in *What Is It about Government that Americans Dislike*? eds. John R. Hibbing and Elizabeth Theiss-Morse. New York: Cambridge University Press.

Brady, David W. and Craig Volden. 1998. *Revolving Gridlock*. Boulder, CO: Westview Press.

Brazzell, Jan F. and Alan C. Acock. 1988. "Influence of Attitudes, Significant Others, and Aspirations on How Adolescents Intend to Resolve a Premarital Pregnancy." *Journal of Marriage and the Family* 50:413–425.

Brehm, John and Scott Gates. 1999. *Working, Shirking, and Sabotage: Bureaucratic Response to a Democratic Public*. Ann Arbor: University of Michigan Press.

Burden, Barry C. 2007. *Personal Roots or Representation*. Princeton, NJ: Princeton University Press.

Calvert, Randall. 1985. "Robustness of Multidimensional Voting Models." *American Journal of Political Science* 29:69–95.

Camerer, Colin F. 1997. "Progress in Behavioral Game Theory." *Journal of Economic Perspectives* 11:167–188.

Cameron, Charles M. 2000. *Veto Bargaining: Presidents and the Politics of Negative Power*. New York: Cambridge University Press.

Carmines, Edward G. and James Woods. 2002. "The Role of Party Activists in the Evolution of the Abortion Issue." *Political Behavior* 24:361–377.

Cassidy, Keith. 1996. "The Right to Life Movement: Sources, Development, and Strategies," in *The Politics of Abortion and Birth Control in Historical Perspective*, ed. Donald T. Critchlow. University Park, PA: Penn State University Press.

Chiou, Fang-Yi and Lawrence S. Rothenberg. 2003. "When Pivotal Politics Meets Partisan Politics." *American Journal of Political Science* 47:503–522.

    2006. "Preferences, Parties, and Legislative Productivity." *American Politics Research* 34:705–731.

Clinton, Joshua and John Lapinski. 2008. "Laws and Roll Calls in the U.S. Congress, 1891–1994." *Legislative Studies Quarterly* 33:511–541.

Cochran, John K., Mitchell B. Chamlin, Leonard Beeghley, Angela Harnden, and Brenda Sims Blackwell. 1996. "Religious Stability, Endogamy, and the Effects of Personal Religiosity on Attitudes toward Abortion." *Sociology of Religion* 57:291–309.

Collie, Melissa P. 1989. "Electoral Patterns and Voting Alignments in the U.S. House, 1886–1986." *Legislative Studies Quarterly* 14:107–127.

Combs, Michael W. and Susan Welch. 1982. "Blacks, Whites, and Attitudes toward Abortion." *Public Opinion Quarterly* 46:510–520.

Condit, Celeste Michelle. 1990. *Decoding Abortion Rhetoric: Communicating Social Change*. Urbana: University of Illinois Press.

Cook, Elizabeth Adell, Ted G. Jelen, and Clyde Wilcox. 1992. *Between Two Absolutes: Public Opinion and the Politics of Abortion*. Boulder, CO: Westview Press.

  1993a. "State Political Cultures and Public Opinion about Abortion." *Political Research Quarterly* 46:771–781.

  1993. "Generational Differences in Attitudes toward Abortion." *American Politics Quarterly* 21:31–53.

Cox, Gary W. and Mathew D. McCubbins. 1993. *Legislative Leviathan: Party Government in the House*. Berkeley: University of California Press.

  2005. *Setting the Agenda: Responsible Party Government in the U.S. House of Representatives*. New York: Cambridge University Press.

Craig, Barbara Hinkson. 1993. *Abortion and American Politics*. Chatham, NJ: Chatham House Publishers.

Craig, Stephen C., James G. Kane and Michael D. Martinez. 2002. "Sometimes You Feel Like a Nut, Sometimes You Don't: Citizens' Ambivalence About Abortion." *Political Psychology* 23:285–301.

Critchlow, Donald T. 2001. *Intended Consequences: Birth Control, Abortion, and the Federal Government in Modern America*. New York: Oxford University Press.

Damania, Richard. 2002. "Influence in Decline: Lobbying in Contracting Industries." *Economics and Politics* 14:209–223.

Damore, David F. 2004. "The Dynamics of Issue Ownership in Presidential Campaigns." *Political Research Quarterly* 57:391–397.

Davey, Monica. 2006. "Sizing Up the Opposing Armies in the Coming Abortion Battle." *New York Time* February 26.

Davidson, Roger H. 1983. "Procedures and Politics in Congress," in *The Abortion Dispute and the American System*, ed. Gilbert Yale Steiner. Washington, DC: Brookings Institution Press.

Davis, Otto A., M. A. H. Dempster, and Aaron Wildavsky. 1966. "A Theory of the Budgetary Process." *American Political Science Review* 60:529–547.

  1974. "Towards a Predictive Theory of Governmental Expenditure." *British Journal of Political Science* 4:419–452.

Deering, Christopher J. and Steven S. Smith. 1997. *Committees in Congress*. Washington, DC: CQ Press.

Denzau, Arthur, William H. Riker, and Kenneth A. Shepsle. 1985. "Farquharson and Fenno: Sophisticated Voting and Home Style." *American Political Science Review* 79:1117–1134.

Denzau, A. T. and R. J. Mackay. 1983. "The Gatekeeping and Monopoly Power of Committees." *American Journal of Political Science* 27:740–761.

Dewar, Helen. 2002. "Senate Votes to Lift Military Abortion Ban." *Washington Post* June 22, A5.

Diermeier, Daniel and Roger B. Myerson. 1999. "Bicameralism and Its Consequences for the Internal Organization of Legislatures." *American Economic Review* 89:1182–1196.

Dillon, Michele. 1993a. "Argumentative Complexity of Abortion Discourse." *Public Opinion Quarterly* 57:305–314.

1993b. "Cultural Differences in the Abortion Discourse of the Catholic Church: Evidence from Four Countries." *Sociology of Religion* 57:25–36.

Dilulio, John J., Jr. 2006. "The Catholic Voter: A Description with Recommendations." *Commonweal: A Review of Religion, Politics and Culture* 133:6.

Dion, Douglas and John D. Huber. 1996. "Procedural Choice and the House Committee on Rules." *Journal of Politics* 58:25–53.

1997. "Sense and Sensibility: The Role of Rules." *American Journal of Political Science* 41:945–957.

Donohue, John J., III and Steven D. Levitt. 2001. "Legalized Abortion and Crime." *Quarterly Journal of Economics* 116:379–420.

2004. "Further Evidence that Legalized Abortion Lowered Crime: A Reply to Joyce." *Journal of Human Resources* 39:29–49.

Downs, Anthony. 1957. *An Economic View of Democracy*. New York: Harper & Row.

Dror, Yehezkel. 1968. *Public Policymaking Reexamined*. Scranton, PA: Chandler Publishing Company.

Dworkin, Ronald. 1993. *Life's Dominion: An Argument about Abortion, Euthanasia, and Individual Freedom*. New York: Vintage Books.

Edelman, Murray. 1985. *The Symbolic Uses of Politics*. Chicago: University of Chicago Press.

Eggen, Dan and Rob Stein. 2009. "Health-Care Reform Efforts Marred by Abortion Dispute." *Washington Post* July 22.

Eilperin, Juliet. 2001. "House Health Bill Scuttled by Abortion Rider." *Washington Post* December 21, A07.

2002. "Abortion Issue Stalls U.N. Family Planning Funds." *Washington Post* May 16, A06.

2007. *Fight Club Politics: How Partisanship Is Poisoning the House of Representatives*. Lanham, MD: Rowman & Littlefield Publishers.

Ely, John Hart. 1980. *Democracy and Distrust: A Theory of Judicial Review*. Cambridge, MA: Harvard University Press.

Emerson, Michael O. 1996. "Through Tinted Glasses: Religion, Worldviews, and Abortion Attitudes." *Journal for the Scientific Study of Religion* 35:41–55.

Epstein, Gil S. and Shmuel Nitzan. 2004. "Strategic Restraint in Contests." *European Economic Review* 48:201–210.

Eskridge, William N. and John Ferejohn. 2001. "Super-Statutes." *Duke Law Journal* 50:1215–1276.

Esterling, Kevin M. 2004. *The Political Economy of Expertise.* Ann Arbor: University of Michigan Press.

Evans, C. Lawrence. 1999. "Legislative Structure: Rules, Precedents, and Jurisdictions." *Legislative Studies Quarterly* 24:605–642.

    2001. "Committees, Leaders, and Message Politics," in *Congress Reconsidered*, 7th ed., eds. Lawrence C. Dodd and Bruce I. Oppenheimer. Washington, DC: CQ Press.

Evans, J. H. 2002. "Polarization of Abortion Attitudes in U.S. Religious Traditions, 1972–1998." *Sociological Forum* 17:397–422.

Fenno, Richard. 1973. *Congressmen in Committees.* Boston: Little Brown.

    1978. *Home Style: House Members in Their Districts.* Boston: Little Brown.

Ferree, Myra Marx, William Anthony Gamson, Jürgen Gerhards, and Dieter Rucht. 2002. *Shaping Abortion Discourse: Democracy and the Public Sphere in Germany and the United States.* Cambridge: Cambridge University Press.

Finocchiaro, Charles J. and David W. Rohde. 2008. "War on the Floor: Partisan Theory and Agenda Control in the U.S. House of Representatives." *Legislative Studies Quarterly* 33:35–61.

Fiorina, Morris P. 1973. "Electoral Margins, Constituency Influence, and Policy Moderation: A Critical Assessment." *American Politics Quarterly* 1:479–498.

Fiorina, Morris P. with Samuel J. Abrams and Jeremy C. Pope. 2005. *Culture War? The Myth of a Polarized America.* New York: Pearson/Longman.

Frank, Thomas. 2005. *What's the Matter with Kansas?: How Conservatives Won the Heart of America.* New York: Henry Holt.

Franklin, Charles H. and Liane C. Kosaki. 1989. "Republican Schoolmaster: The U.S. Supreme Court, Public Opinion, and Abortion." *American Political Science Review* 83:751–771.

Freedman, Paul. 2003. Partial Victory: The Power of an Unenforced Abortion Ban." *Slate* December 9. http://www.slate.com/id/2092192/.

Fried, Amy. 1988. "Abortion Politics as Symbolic Politics." *Social Science Quarterly* 69:137–154.

Fried, Amy and Douglas B. Harris. 2001. "On Red Capes and Charging Bulls: How and Why Conservative Politicians and Interest Groups Promoted Public Anger," in *What Is It about Government that Americans Dislike?* eds. John R. Hibbing and Elizabeth Theiss-Morse. New York: Cambridge University Press.

Friedman, Milton. 1962. *Capitalism and Freedom.* Chicago: University of Chicago Press.

Gelman, Andrew, Nate Silver, and Daniel Lee. 2009. "The Senate's Health Care Calculations." *New York Times* November 18.

Gerson, Michael. 2009. "Justice Ginsburg in Context." *Washington Post* July 17.

Gibbons, Robert. 1998. "Incentives in Organizations." *Journal of Economic Perspectives* 12:115–132.

Gilens, Martin. 2009. "Preference Gaps and Inequality in Representation." *PS: Political Science and Politics* 42:335–341.

Gilligan, Thomas W. and Keith Krehbiel. 1989. "Asymmetric Information and Legislative Rules with a Heterogeneous Committee." *American Journal of Political Science* 33:459–490.

1990. "Organization of Informative Committees by a Rational Legislature." *American Journal of Political Science* 34:531–564.

Gist, John R. 1977. "'Increment' and 'Base' in the Congressional Appropriations Process." *American Journal of Political Science* 21:341–352.

1982. "'Stability' and 'Competition' in Budgetary Theory." *American Political Science Review* 76:859–872.

Glendon, Mary Ann. 1991. *Rights Talk: The Impoverishment of Political Discourse*. New York: The Free Press.

Glosser, Asaph, John Wilkerson, and E. Scott Adler. 2009. "Does Accomplishment Matter? Congressional Policymaking and Its Impact on Public Approval." Presented at the Annual Meeting of the Midwest Political Science Association, Chicago, April 2–5.

Godwin, R. Kenneth. 1988. *One Billion Dollars of Influence*. Chatham, NJ: Chatham House.

Graber, Mark A. 1996. *Rethinking Abortion: Equal Choice, the Constitution, and Reproductive Politics*. Princeton, NJ: Princeton University Press.

Granberg, Donald and James Burlison. 1983. "The Abortion Issue in the 1980 Elections." *Family Planning Perspectives* 15:231–238.

Gray, Virginia and David Lowery. 1995. "Interest Representation and Democratic Gridlock." *Legislative Studies Quarterly* 20:531–552.

Gross, Michael L. 1995. "Moral Judgment, Organizational Incentives and Collective Action: Participation in Abortion Politics." *Political Research Quarterly* 48:507–534.

Gruber, Jonathan, Phillip Levine, and Douglas Staiger. 1999. "Abortion Legalization and Child Living Circumstances: Who is the Marginal Child?" *Quarterly Journal of Economics* 114:263–291.

Hall, Elaine J. and Myra Marx Ferree. 1986. "Race Differences in Abortion Attitudes." *Public Opinion Quarterly* 50:193–207.

Hall, Thad. 2004. *Authorizing Policy*. Columbus: Ohio State University Press.

Halva-Neubauer, Glen. 1990. "Abortion Policy in the Post-Webster Age." *Publius* 20:27–44.

Hammond, Thomas H. and Gary J. Miller. 1987. "The Core of the Constitution." *American Political Science Review* 81:1155–1174.

Hansen, John Mark. 1985. "The Political Economy of Group Membership." *American Political Science Review* 79:79–96.

Hardin, John W. 1998. "Advocacy versus Certainty: The Dynamics of Committee Jurisdiction Concentration." *Journal of Politics* 60:374–397.

Hayes, Michael T. 1987. "Incrementalism as Dramaturgy: The Case of the Nuclear Freeze." *Polity* 19(3): 443–463.

Hibbing, John R and Elizabeth Theiss-Morse. 2001. *What Is It about Government that Americans Dislike?* eds. John R. Hibbing and Elizabeth Theiss-Morse. New York: Cambridge University Press.

Hillygus, D. Sunshine and Todd G. Shields. 2008. *The Persuadable Voter: Wedge Issues in Presidential Campaigns.* Princeton, NJ: Princeton University Press.

Holmstrom, Bengt and Paul Milgrom. 1994. "The Firm as an Incentive System." *American Economic Review* 84:972–991.

Howell, Susan E. and Robert T. Sims. 1993. "Abortion Attitudes and the Louisiana Governor's Election," in *Understanding the New Politics of Abortion*, ed. Malcom L. Goggin. Newbury Park, CA: Sage Publications.

Howell, William, Scott Adler, Charles Cameron, and Charles Riemann. 2000. "Divided Government and the Legislative Productivity of Congress, 1945–94." *Legislative Studies Quarterly* 25:285–312.

Huckfeldt, Robert and John Sprague. 2000. "Political Consequences of Inconsistency: The Accessibility and Stability of Abortion Attitudes." *Political Psychology* 21:57–79.

Hunter, James Davison. 1991. *Cultural Wars: The Struggle to Define America.* New York: Basic Books.

Jelen, Ted G. 1984. "Respect for Life, Sexual Morality, and Opposition to Abortion." *Review of Religious Research* 25:220–231.

Jelen, Ted G. and Clyde Wilcox. 2003. "Causes and Consequences of Public Attitudes toward Abortion: A Review and Research Agenda." *Political Research Quarterly* 56:489–500.

Jeong, Gyung-Ho, Gary J. Miller, and Itai Sened. 2009. "Closing the Deal: Negotiating Civil Rights Legislation." *American Political Science Review* 103:588–606.

Johnson, Timothy R. and Andrew D. Martin. 1998. "The Public's Conditional Response to Supreme Court Decisions." *American Political Science Review* 92:299–327.

Jones, Bryan D. and Frank R. Baumgartner. 2005. "A Model of Choice for Public Policy." *Journal of Public Administration Research and Theory* 15:325–351.

Jones, Bryan D., Heather Larsen, and Tracy Sulkin. 2003. "Policy Punctuations in American Political Institutions." *American Political Science Review* 97:151–169.

Jones, Bryan D., James L. True, and Frank R. Baumgartner. 1998. "Policy Punctuations: U.S. Budget Authority, 1947–1995." *Journal of Politics* 60:1–33.

Joyce, Theodore. 2003. "Did Legalized Abortion Lower Crime?" *Journal of Human Resources* 38:1–37.

Kahane, Leo H. 2000. "Anti-Abortion Activities and the Market for Abortion Services: Protest as a Disincentive." *American Journal of Economics and Sociology* 59:463–485.

Kahneman, Daniel and Amos Tversky. 1979. "Prospect Theory: An Analysis of Decisions under Risk." *Econometrica* 47:263–291.

Kessler, Daniel and Keith Krehbiel. 1996. "Dynamics of Cosponsorship." *American Political Science Review* 90:1–12.

King, David C. 1997. *Turf Wars: How Congressional Committees Claim Jurisdiction.* Chicago: University of Chicago Press.

King, David C. and Richard J. Zeckhauser. 2003. "Congressional Vote Options." *Legislative Studies Quarterly* 28:387–412.

Kingdon, John W. 1973. *Congressmen's Voting Decisions*. Ann Arbor: University of Michigan Press.

Kloppenberg, Lisa A. 2001. *Playing It Safe: How the Supreme Court Sidesteps Hard Cases and Stunts the Development of the Law*. New York: NYU Press.

Knight, Jack. 1992. *Institutions and Social Conflict*. New York: Cambridge University Press.

Knott, Jack H. and Gary J. Miller. 1987. *Reforming Bureaucracy: The Politics of Institutional Choice*. Englewood Cliffs, NJ: Prentice-Hall.

Kollman, Ken. 1998. *Outside Lobbying: Public Opinion and Interest Group Strategies*. Princeton, NJ: Princeton University Press.

Krehbiel, Keith. 1985. "Obstruction and Representativeness in Legislatures." *American Journal of Political Science* 29:643–659.

1991. *Information and Legislative Organization*. Ann Arbor: University of Michigan Press.

1993. "Where's the Party?" *British Journal of Political Science* 23: 235–266.

1997a. "Restrictive Rules Reconsidered." *American Journal of Political Science* 41:919–944.

1997b. "Rejoinder to 'Sense and Sensibility.'" *American Journal of Political Science* 41:958–964.

1998. *Pivotal Politics*. Chicago: University of Chicago Press.

Krehbiel, Keith and Douglas Rivers. 1990. "Sophisticated Voting in Congress: A Reconsideration." *Journal of Politics* 52:548–578.

Krutz, Glen. 2005. "Issues and Institutions: Winnowing in the U.S. Congress." *American Journal of Political Science* 49:313–326.

Krutz, Glen S. 2001. *Hitching a Ride: Omnibus Legislating in the U.S. Congress*. Columbus: Ohio State University Press.

Ladwein, Peter M. 2008. "Discerning The Meaning of *Gonzales v. Carhart*: The End of the Physician Veto and the Resulting Change in Abortion Jurisprudence." *Notre Dame Law Review* 84:1847–1887.

Lapinski, John S. 2008. "Policy Substance and Performance in American Lawmaking, 1877–1994." *American Journal of Political Science* 52: 235–251.

Lasch, Christopher. 1991. *The True and Only Heaven: Progress and Its Critics*. New York: W. W. Norton.

Lazear, Edward P. 1989. "Pay Equality and Industrial Politics." *Journal of Political Economy* 97:561–580.

Legge, Jerome S., Jr. 1983. "The Determinants of Attitudes toward Abortion in the American Electorate." *Political Research Quarterly* 36:479–490.

1987. "Abortion as a Policy Issue." *Women & Politics* 7:63–82.

Legge, Jerome S., Jr. and Zhirong Zhao. 2002. "Morality Policy and Unintended Consequences: China's One Child Policy." Presented at the annual Southern Political Science Association Meeting, November 7–9, Savannah, GA.

Leighley, Jan E. 2001. *Strength in Numbers? The Political Mobilization of Racial and Ethnic Minorities*. Princeton, NJ: Princeton University Press.

Lindblom, Charles E. 1959. "The Science of 'Muddling Through.'" *Public Administration Review* 19:79–88.

Long, J. Scott. 1997. *Regression Models for Categorical and Limited Dependent Variables*. Thousand Oaks, CA: Sage Publications.

Lowi, Theodore J. 1969. *The End of Liberalism*. New York: W. W. Norton.

Luker, Kristin. 1984. *Abortion and the Politics of Motherhood*. Berkeley: University of California Press.

Lynch, Michael S. and Anthony Madonna. 2008. "Viva Voce: Implications from the Disappearing Voice Vote, 1807–1990." Paper presented at the annual meeting of the Midwest American Political Science Association, April 3–6, Chicago.

Malkin, Elisabeth and Nacha Cattan. 2008. "Mexico City Struggles with Law on Abortion." *New York Times* August 25, http://www.nytimes.com/2008/08/25/world/americas/25mexico.html?fta=y.

Maltzman, Forrest. 1995. "Meeting Competing Demands: Committee Performance in the Postreform House." *American Journal of Political Science* 39:653–682.

1998. "Maintaining Congressional Committees: Sources of Member Support." *Legislative Studies Quarterly* 23:197–218.

Maltzman, Forrest and Charles Shipan. 2008. "Continuity and Change: The Evolution of the Law." *American Journal of Political Science* 52:252–267.

Mann, Thomas E. and Norman J. Ornstein. 2008. *The Broken Branch: How Congress Is Failing America and How to Get It Back on Track*. New York: Oxford University Press.

March, James G. and Herbert A. Simon. 1993. *Organizations*. Cambridge, MA: Blackwell.

Mathews, Anna Wilde. 2010. "States Reignite Abortion Debate." *Wall Street Journal* April 8, A1, A6.

Maxwell, Carol J. C. 1995. "Beyond Polemics and Toward Healing," in *Perspectives on the Politics of Abortion*, ed. Ted G. Jelen. Westport, CT: Praeger.

2002. *Pro-Life Activists in America*. New York: Cambridge University Press.

Mayhew, David R. 1974. *Congress: The Electoral Connection*. New Haven, CT: Yale University Press.

1991. *Divided We Govern*. New Haven, CT: Yale University Press.

2005. *Divided We Govern*, 2nd ed. New Haven, CT: Yale University Press.

McCarty, Nolan, Keith T. Poole, and Howard Rosenthal. 2006. *Polarized America: The Dance of Ideology and Unequal Riches*. Cambridge, MA: The MIT Press.

McFarlane, Deborah R. and Kenneth J. Meier. 2001. *The Politics of Fertility Control: Family Planning and Abortion Policies in the American States*. New York: Chatham House.

Meckler, Laura. 2008. "Bush Era Abortion Rules Face Possible Reversal." *Wall Street Journal* December 17, A5.

Meernik, James and Joseph Ignagni. 1997. "Judicial Review and Coordinate Construction of the Constitution." *American Journal of Political Science* 41:447–467.

Meier, Kenneth J., Donald P. Haider-Markel, Anthony J. Stanislawski, and Deborah R. McFarlane. 1996. "The Impact of State-Level Restrictions on Abortion." *Demography* 33:307–312.

Merriam, Charles E. 1921. "The Present State of the Study of Politics." *American Political Science Review* 15:173–185.

Milbrath, Lester W. 1963. *The Washington Lobbyists*. Chicago: Rand McNally.

Miller, Warren E. and Donald E. Stokes. 1963. "Constituency Influence in Congress." *American Political Science Review* 57:45–56.

Monroe, Nathan W. and Gregory Robinson. 2008. "Do Restrictive Rules Produce Nonmedian Outcomes? A Theory with Evidence from the 101st–108th Congresses." *Journal of Politics* 70:217–231.

Montesano, Aldo. 1994. "Non-Additive Probabilities and the Measure of Uncertainty and Risk Aversion: A Proposal," in *Models and Experiments in Risk and Rationality*, eds. Bertrand Munier and Mark J. Machina. Norwell, MA: Kluwer.

Mooney, Christopher Z. and Mei-Hsien Lee. 1995. "Legislating Morality in the American States." *American Journal of Political Science* 39:599–627.

____ 2000. "The Influence of Values on Consensus and the Contentious Morality Policy: U.S. Death Penalty Reform, 1956–1982." *Journal of Politics* 62:223–239.

Mulligan, Kenneth. 2006. "Pope John Paul II and Catholic Opinion Toward the Death Penalty and Abortion." *Social Science Quarterly* 87:739–753.

Munson, Ziad W. 2009. The Making of Pro-Life Activists: How Social Movement Mobilization Works. Chicago: University of Chicago Press.

Nice, David C. 1987. "Incremental and Nonincremental Policy Response: The States and the Railroads." *Polity* 20:145–156.

Nokken, Timothy P. 2003. "The Ideological Ends against the Middle: House Roll Call Votes on Normal Trade Relation Status for China, 1990–2000." *Congress and the Presidency* 30:153–170.

Nossiff, Rosemary. 1995. "Pennsylvania: The Impact of Party Organization and Religious Lobbying," in *Abortion Politics in American States*, eds. Mary C. Segers and Timothy A. Byrnes. Armonk, NY: M. E. Sharpe.

O' Connor, Karen. 1996. *No Neutral Ground? Abortion Politics in an Age of Absolutes*. Boulder, CO: Westview Press.

Oldmixon, Elizabeth Anne. 2005. *Uncompromising Positions: God, Sex, and the U.S. House of Representatives*. Washington, DC: Georgetown University Press.

Padgett, John F. 1980. "Bounded Rationality in Budgetary Research." *American Political Science Review* 74:354–372.

Palfrey, Thomas R. 1984. "Spatial Equilibrium with Entry." *Review of Economic Studies* 51:139–156.

Palfrey, Thomas R. and Howard Rosenthal. 1985. "Voter Participation and Strategic Uncertainty." *American Political Science Review* 79:62–78.

Penn, Elizabeth Maggie. 2009. "A Model of Farsighted Voting." *American Journal of Political Science* 53: 36–54.

Perry, Michael J. 1982. *The Constitution, the Courts, and Human Rights: An Inquiry into the Legitimacy of Constitutional Policymaking by the Judiciary*. New Haven, CT: Yale University Press.

Peterson, Larry R. 2001. "Religion, Plausibility Structures, and Education Effects on Attitudes toward Elective Abortion." *Journal for the Scientific Study of Religion* 40:187–203.

Petrocik, John. 1989. "Issue Ownership in Presidential Elections, with a 1980 Case Study." *American Journal of Political Science* 40:825–850.

Pianin, Eric and Don Phillips. 1988. "Abortion Deadlock Stalls D.C. Funding." *Washington Post* September 30, C1.

Polsby, Nelson W. 1968. "The Institutionalization of the U.S. House of Representatives." *American Political Science Review* 62:144–168.

Poole, Keith T. and Howard Rosenthal. 1997. *A Political-Economic History of Roll-Call Voting.* New York: Oxford University Press.

Pope, Jeremy and Jonathan Woon. 2008. "Measuring Changes in American Party Reputations, 1939–2004." *Political Research Quarterly* 62:653–661.

Press, Andrea L. and Elizabeth R. Cole. 1999. *Speaking of Abortion: Television and Authority in the Lives of Women.* Chicago: University of Chicago Press.

Price, David E. 1978. "Policy Making in Congressional Committees: The Impact of 'Environmental' Factors." *American Political Science Review* 72: 548–574.

Reiter, Jerry. 2000. *Live From the Gates of Hell: An Insider's Look at the Anti-Abortion Movement.* Amherst, NY: Prometheus Books.

Riker William H. 1980. "Implications from the Disequilibrium of Majority Rule for the Study of Institutions." *The American Political Science Review* 74:432–446.

1986. *The Art of Political Manipulation.* New Haven, CT: Yale University Press.

Risen, James and Judy L. Thomas. 1998. *Wrath of Angels: The American Abortion War.* New York: Basic Books.

Roberts, Sam. 2009. "U.S. Births Hint at Bias for Boys in Some Asians." *New York Times* June 16. http://www.nytimes.com/2009/06/15/nyregion/15babies.html.

Rohde, David W. 1991. *Parties and Leaders in the Post Reform House.* Chicago: University of Chicago Press.

Rose, Melody. 2006. *Safe, Legal, and Unavailable: Abortion Politics in the United States.* Washington, DC: CQ Press.

Rosenberg, Gerald N. 1991. *The Hollow Hope: Can Courts Bring about Social Change?* Chicago: University of Chicago Press.

Rubin, Eva R. 1987. *Abortion, Politics, and the Courts.* Westport, CT: Greenwood Press.

Rubinstein, Ariel. 1982. "Perfect Equilibrium in a Bargaining Model." *Econometrica* 50:97–109.

1985. "A Bargaining Model with Incomplete Information About Time Preferences." *Econometrica* 53:1151–1172.

Sabatier, Paul A. and Hank C. Jenkins-Smith, eds. 1993. *Policy Change and Learning: An Advocacy Coalition Framework.* Boulder, CO: Westview Press.

Saletan, William. 1998. "Frame Game: *Roe v. Wade.*" *Slate* January 24. http://www.slate.com/id/2698/.

2004. *Bearing Right: How Conservatives Won the Abortion War.* Berkeley: University of California Press.

2009. "Culture of Death: The Right-Wing Assault on Abortion Reduction." *Slate* July 27. http://www.slate.com/id/2223661/.

Salisbury, Robert H. 1990. "The Paradox of Interest Groups in Washington – More Groups, Less Clout," in *The New American Political System*, 2nd ed., ed. Anthony King. Washington, DC: AEI Press.

2002. "The Dependent Variable." Mimeo, Washington University in St. Louis.

Sawyer, Darwin O. 1982. "Public Attitudes toward Life and Death." *Public Opinion Quarterly* 46:521–533.

Schiller, Wendy J. 1995. "Senators as Political Entrepreneurs: Using Bill Sponsorship to Shape Legislative Agendas." *American Journal of Political Science* 39:186–203.

Schonhardt-Bailey, Cheryl. 2008. "The Congressional Debate on Partial Birth Abortion: Constitutional Gravitas and Moral Passion." *British Journal of Political Science* 38:383–410.

Schulman Paul R. 1975. "Nonincremental Policy Making: Notes Toward an Alternative Paradigm." *American Political Science Review* 69:1354–1370.

Scott, Jacqueline and Howard Schuman. 1988. "Attitude Strength and Social Action in the Abortion Dispute." *American Sociological Review* 53: 785–793.

Segers, Mary C. 1995. "The Catholic Church as a Political Actor," in *Perspectives on the Politics of Abortion*, ed. Ted G. Jelen. Westport, CT: Praeger.

Segers, Mary C. and Timothy A. Byrnes. 1995. *Abortion Politics in American States*. Armonk, NY: M. E. Sharpe.

Seib, Gerald F. 2009. "Abortion Upends Health-Bill Alliance." *Wall Street Journal* November 13.

Sezer, L. Kent. 1995. "The Constitutional Underpinnings of the Abortion Debate," in *Perspectives on the Politics of Abortion*, ed. Ted G. Jelen. Westport, CT: Praeger.

Sharkansky, Ira. 1967. "Economic and Political Correlates of State Government Expenditures." *Midwest Journal of Political Science* 11:173–192.

1968. "Agency Requests, Gubernatorial Support and Budget Success in State Legislatures." *American Political Science Review* 62:1220–1231.

Sheingate, Adam D. 2006. "Structure and Opportunity: Committee Jurisdiction and Issue Attention in Congress." *American Journal of Political Science* 50:844–859.

Shenon, Philip. 2002. "Bankruptcy Bill, Caught in Abortion Dispute, Dies in Congress." *New York Times* November 16.

Shepsle, Kenneth A. 1978. *The Giant Jigsaw Puzzle: Democratic Committee Assignments in the Modern House*. Chicago: University of Chicago Press.

1979. "Institutional Arrangements and Equilibrium in Multidimensional Voting Models." *American Journal of Political Science* 23:27–59.

Shepsle, Kenneth A. and Barry R. Weingast. 1984. "Uncovered Sets and Sophisticated Voting Outcomes with Implications for Agenda Institutions." *American Journal of Political Science* 28:49–74.

1994. "Positive Theories of Congressional Institutions." *Legislative Studies Quarterly* 19:149–179.

1987. "The Institutional Foundations of Committee Power." *American Political Science Review* 81:85–104.

Shin, Youseop. 2004. "Constituency Opinion and PAC Contributions: A Case of the National Abortion and Reproductive Rights Action League." *Public Choice* 118:133–149.

Shipan, Charles R. 1992. "Individual Incentives and Institutional Imperatives: Committee Jurisdiction and Long Term Health Care." *American Journal of Political Science* 36:877–895.

Silverstein, Helena. 2007. *Girls on the Stand: How Courts Fail Pregnant Minors.* New York: New York University Press.

Simon, Herbert A. 1957. *Administrative Behavior,* 2nd ed. New York: Macmillan.

    1957. *Models of Man.* New York: John Wiley & Sons.

Simon, Stephanie. 2009. "Limited Effect Seen in Abortion Clause." *Wall Street Journal* November 17, A-4.

Sinclair, Barbara. 2000. *Unorthodox Lawmaking: New Legislative Processes in the U.S. Congress.* Washington, DC: CQ Press.

Smith, Gregory Allen. 2008. *Politics in the Parish: The Political Influence of Catholic Priests.* Washington, DC: Georgetown University Press.

Smith, Page and Charles Daniel. 2000. *The Chicken Book.* Athens: University of Georgia Press.

Smith, Steven S. 2007. *Party Influence in Congress.* New York: Cambridge University Press.

Sniderman, Paul M. and Sean M. Theriault. 2004. "The Dynamics of Political Argument and The Logic of Issue Framing," in *Studies in Public Opinion: Gauging Attitudes, Nonattitudes, Measurement Error and Change,* eds. Willem E. Saris and Paul M. Sniderman. Princeton, NJ: Princeton University Press.

Staggenborg, Suzanne. 1991. *The Pro-Choice Movement: Organization and Activism in the Abortion Conflict.* New York: Oxford University Press.

    1996. "The Survival of the Pro-Choice Movement," in *The Politics of Abortion and Birth Control in Historical Perspective,* ed. Donald T. Critchlow. University Park: Penn State University Press.

Stein, Rob. 2008. "Study Finds Major Shift in Abortion Demographics." *Washington Post* September 23, A-03.

Stetson, Dorothy McBride. 2002. *Abortion Politics, Women's Movements, and the Democratic State,* ed. Dorothy McBride Stetson. Oxford: Oxford University Press.

Stolberg, Sheryl Gay. 2003a. "Politics of Abortion Delays $15 Billion to Fight Global AIDS." *New York Times* March 6.

    2003b. "Abortion Vote Leaves Many in the Senate Conflicted." *Washington Post* October 22.

Stone, Deborah. 2001. *Policy Paradoxes and Political Reason.* Glenview, IL: Scott Foresman.

Sulkin, Tracy. 2005. *Issue Politics in Congress.* New York: Cambridge University Press.

Sunstein, Cass. 2005. *Radicals in Robes: Why Extreme Right-Wing Courts are Wrong for America.* New York: Basic Books.

Tatalovich, Raymond and David Schier. 1993. "The Persistence of Ideological Cleavage in Voting on Abortion Legislation in the House of Representatives, 1973–1988," in *Understanding the New Politics of Abortion*, ed. Malcolm L. Goggin. Newbury Park, CA: Sage Publications.

Toner, Robin. 2003. "At a Distance, Bush Joins Abortion Protest." *New York Times* January 23.

2004. "Abortion's Opponents Claim the Middle Ground." *New York Times* April 25.

2007. "Abortion Foes See Validation for New Tactic." *New York Times* May 22, A-1.

Trent, Katherine and Eve Powell-Griner. 1991. "Differences in Race, Marital Status, and Education among Women Obtaining Abortions." *Social Forces* 69:1121–1141.

Tribe, Laurence H. 1992. *Abortion: The Clash of Absolutes*. New York: W. W. Norton.

Truman, David B. 1971. *The Governmental Process*. New York: Alfred A. Knopf.

Uslaner, Eric M. 1993. *The Decline of Comity in Congress*. Ann Arbor: University of Michigan Press.

Volden, Craig and Alan E. Wiseman. 2008. "Legislative Effectiveness in Congress." Paper presented at the annual meeting of the Southern Political Science Association, January 10–12, New Orleans.

Wanat, John. 1974. "Bases of Budgetary Incrementalism." *American Political Science Review* 68:1221–1228.

Wawro, Gregory. 2000. *Legislative Entrepreneurship in the U.S. House of Representatives*. Ann Arbor: University of Michigan Press.

Weaver, R. Kent. 1988. *Automatic Government: The Politics of Indexation*. Washington, DC: The Brookings Institution Press.

Wetstein, Matthew E. and Robert B. Albritton. 1995. "Effects of Public Opinion on Abortion Policies and Use in the American States." *Publius* 25:91–105.

Wilcox, Clyde. 1995. "The Sources and Consequences of Public Attitudes toward Abortion," in *Perspectives on the Politics of Abortion*, ed. Ted G. Jelen. Westport, CT: Praeger.

Wildavsky, Aaron. 1992. *The New Politics of the Budgetary Process*. Boston: Little Brown.

1964. *The Politics of the Budgetary Process*. Boston: Little Brown.

Wilkerson, John D. 1990. "Reelection and Representation in Conflict: The Case of Agenda Manipulation." *Legislative Studies Quarterly* 15:263–282.

1999. "'Killer' Amendments in Congress." *American Political Science Review* 93:535–552.

Williams, Dorie Giles. 1982. "Religion, Beliefs about Human Life, and the Abortion Decision." *Review of Religious Research* 24:40–48.

Wlezien, Christopher B. and Malcolm L. Goggin. 1993. "The Courts, Interest Groups, and Public Opinion about Abortion." *Political Behavior* 15:381–405.

Wolbretch, Christina. 2000. *The Politics of Women's Rights*. Princeton, NJ: Princeton University Press.

Woodrum, E. and B. L. Davison. 1992. "Reexamination of Religious Influences on Abortion Attitudes." *Review of Religious Research* 33:229–243.

Woon, Jonathon. 2008. "Bill Sponsorship in Congress: The Moderating Effect of Agenda Positions on Legislative Proposals." *Journal of Politics* 70:201–216.

Zaller, John R. 1992. *The Nature and Origins of Mass Opinion*. New York: Cambridge University Press.

Zernike, Kate. 2003. "30 Years after *Roe v. Wade*, New Trends but the Old Debate." *New York Times* January 20.

Zimmerman, Sacha. 2003. "The Real Threat to *Roe v. Wade*: Fetal Position." *The New Republic* August 18 & 25, 14–17.

Index